ABOUT THE EDITORS

DAVID M. FETTERMAN, a member of Stanford University's administration, conducts qualitative formative evaluations and audits of the management process in university departments, the hospital, and the linear accelerator center. He is also Assistant Professor in the School of Education. Formerly Senior Associate and Project Director at RMC Research Corporation, he conducted national and state-level ethnographic evaluations. Fetterman is Chairperson of the Council on Anthropology and Education's Ethnographic Approaches to Evaluation in Education committee. In addition, he also served the Council as the first Contributing Editor for the *Anthropology Newsletter.* Fetterman has published significant works in both educational and anthropological journals and was recently awarded the Praxis Publication Award from the Washington Association of Professional Anthropologists and the President's Award from the Evaluation Research Society for his work in ethnographic educational evaluation. Fetterman is the editor of *Ethnography in Educational Evaluation* (Sage, 1984).

MARY ANNE PITMAN is Assistant Professor in the Department of Foundations of Education at Youngstown State University. Her research addresses issues of cultural learning and her current field site is a rural community of home schoolers in the northeastern United States. Pitman has served as Program Chair for the Minnesota Association of Professional Anthropologists and currently serves as Co-Chair of the Council on Anthropology and Education's Ethnographic Approaches to Evaluation in Education committee. She has published articles on multidisciplinary team and contract research and on cultural learning theory.

EDUCATIONAL EVALUATION

ethnography in theory, practice, and politics

EDUCATIONAL EVALUATION
ethnography in theory, practice, and politics

Edited by

David M. Fetterman
Mary Anne Pitman

SAGE PUBLICATIONS
The Publishers of Professional Social Science
Beverly Hills Newbury Park London New Delhi

For information address:

SAGE Publications, Inc.
275 South Beverly Drive
Beverly Hills, California 90212

SAGE Publications Inc.
2111 West Hillcrest Drive
Newbury Park
California 91320

SAGE Publications Ltd.
28 Banner Street
London EC1Y 8QE
England

SAGE PUBLICATIONS India Pvt. Ltd.
M-32 Market
Greater Kailash I
New Delhi 110 048 India

Printed in the United States of America

Library of Congress Cataloging-in-Publication Data

Main entry under title:

Includes bibliographies and indexes.
    1. Educational anthropology—Addresses, essays,
lectures. 2. Education—Research—Evaluation—
Addresses, essays, lectures. 3. Ethnology—Methodology—
Evaluation—Addresses, essays, lectures. 4. Evaluation
research (Social action programs)—Addresses, essays,
lectures. 5. Educational accountability—Addresses,
essays, lectures. I. Fetterman, David, M. II. Pitman,
Mary Anne.
LB45.E838   1986   370'7.8'4   85-25025
ISBN 0-8039-2571-9

Contents

To our families
and to pioneers and cultural brokers
in every field

Acknowledgments

I am indebted to Courtney Cazden, Fred Erickson, Harry Wolcott, and many others for their valuable comments on the first drafts of these chapters. In addition, I would like to thank my coeditor for her diligent efforts. Her conscientiousness and pragmatic style were greatly appreciated. I also found Deborah Waxman's assistance invaluable in the preparation of this collection.

I am also grateful to Elizabeth Eddy for her insightful comments concerning my chapter "The Ethnographic Evaluator."

Thanks are also extended to librarians, who make modern-day scholarship possible.

—*David M. Fetterman*

PART I

Overview

1

Beyond the Status Quo in Ethnographic Educational Evaluation

DAVID M. FETTERMAN

Ethnographic education evaluation is a form of ethnographic research that has gone beyond the status quo. Cazden (1983:35) has called for greater participation in the design for change. This specialized discipline within educational anthropology responds to her concern. Ethnography in educational evaluation does not simply provide "anthropological explanations of school failure."[1] Ethnographic evaluators have adopted Mills's (1959: 177) position that we have the capability and responsibility to shape the destiny of our work. They have made a conscious decision to participate in the social and political arena. Ethnographic evaluators are integrally involved in describing, designing, and participating in the processes of change[2] (see Fetterman 1984a, 1984c, 1984d; Firestone and Herriott 1984; Goldberg 1984; Hemwall 1984; LeCompte and Goetz 1984; Messerschmidt 1984; Smith and Robbins 1984; Wolcott 1984). Ethnographic evaluators conduct their research holistically, nonjudgmentally, and contextually. Based on the results of this research they judge, assess, and evaluate educational systems. Their assessments identify discrete elements or variables as levers of change within a complex network of interrelationships. Policy recommendations weigh the effects of manipulating these variables against the knowledge of how change can alter sociocultural systems.[3] In essence, ethnographic educational evaluation provides an emically oriented description of events and an etically sculptured set of explanations of adaptive and maladaptive behavior. It then presents policy and programmatic recommendations for policy makers and practitioners. Ethnographic educational evaluation addresses McDermott and Hood's (1982:236) concerns about how schooling is organized and sheds light on how it might be better organized.

This collection builds on *Ethnography in Educational Evaluation* (Fetterman 1984b), which laid the foundation for the field. The purpose of this collection is to present the latest stage in the emerging field

of ethnographic educational evaluation. The most significant developments to surface in the field have been in three areas: theory, practice,
and politics. The studies in this collection include international, national, and locally based ethnographic evaluations. They explore
educational innovations in high schools, youth employment and training programs, day care centers, and hospitals. Topics include school
management and decision making, teacher training, student attrition
rates, physician peer review, bilingual curriculum models, desegregation, gifted education, and in-school truancy. These contributors produce ethnographically informed reports and report summaries as compared with full-blown ethnographies. As ethnographic evaluators,
they function in a multidisciplinary, typically government sponsored,
social research context. They all make policy and programmatic
recommendations.

Ethnographic evaluators, if they are to survive in this environment,
learn to be practical and effective. Out in the field few can afford the
luxury of preaching or practicing an orthodox version of any discipline. Typically, ethnographic evaluators recognize that no single approach or theory is sufficient to solve the plethora of educational
problems that we face nationally and internationally. First and foremost, however, they are guided by their own disciplinary training. In
this cosmopolitan context, they are strangers in a strange land. Ethnographers function with an environment dominated by a positivistic
world view. Their environment shapes the method and tone of their
research. These studies display various degrees of assimilation, acculturation, and deacculturation—or "the change of the minority's
culture away from that of the 'host' or core society" (Sharot 1974:
330)—to the dominant context of evaluation. The theory section evi-
dences a quasi-defensive structuring[4] response to this stage of culture
contact. The emphasis on the explicit use of anthropological theory is
a call to return to key elements of the native anthropological culture.
The practice and politics sections focus on adaptation and are
therefore more varied. Some chapters may sound more sociological
than others, some more positivistic than phenomenological. Despite
their differences, each of the contributors produces an ethnographer's
account of fieldwork in a foreign culture at home and abroad. These
studies also represent a step beyond the methodological status quo.
The practice section of this collection demonstrates how to integrate
qualitative and quantitative data within a single study. Part IV focuses
on the politics of conducting an ethnographic evaluation. In essence,

these studies represent new developments and new directions in ethnographic educational evaluation. Ethnographers are expanding their participation in the design for change in education.

Understanding ethnographic evaluation's contribution to education requires an understanding of what ethnographers do in practice (Fetterman 1984a). Moreover, the ethnographic evaluator's contribution can be understood more fully by examining the nature and character of this change agent's role in the pursuit of his or her mission. I provide an insight into the field of ethnographic evaluation by depicting the ethnographic evaluator as a cultural broker in the second chapter. I discuss the bicultural and hybrid nature of this scholar who communicates cultural knowledge across disciplinary boundaries. In essence, the ethnographic evaluator must be able to speak and think in two different languages and articulate the conceptual concerns of contrasting cultures. I use an assimilation-acculturation (culture contact) model to discuss the ethnographic evaluator's adaptation to an environment consisting of conflicting world views and work settings. This environment with its accompanying incentives and constraints shapes the ethnographic evaluator's work. I provide additional depth and breadth to our understanding of the ethnographic evaluator's role by tracing the life cycle of this academic entrepreneur. This chapter constructs a contextual framework within which this collection takes shape.

Simon begins the second section by calling to our attention the next stage in the development of ethnographic evaluation—the role of theory. She argues for a transition from the current use of a general meta-theory to the selection of explicit anthropological theories that guide our research. This transition will help researchers focus and bound their inquiry. Simon demonstrates how the use of cognitive and decision-making theories made her own ethnographic evaluation and policy research more compatible with the focused research designs of traditional evaluation.

Pitman and Dobbert reinforce and build upon Simon's position regarding the paramount significance of theory in ethnographic evaluation. Pitman and Dobbert demonstrate how the use of explicit theories can also be used in mini-studies. They present a 10-week evaluation of the training program in a day care center to illustrate the process of matching theory and method in the pursuit of research. They also discuss the team approach to documentation and analysis and the iterative nature of theory selection. Like Simon's discussion,

Pitman and Dobbert believe that the use of theory will help demystify the ethnographic process for sponsors and educational evaluators.

Studstill's work endorses the belief that ethnography must be founded upon an adequate theoretical base. He is, however, primarily concerned with the larger socioeconomic picture in the study of education. He believes it is time to return to a systems theory approach using the culture concept as our guide. He warns of the danger of overly descriptive microethnographic approaches. Studstill fears microethnographic approaches alone may divert our attention from the broader policy issues and concerns. Studstill challenges the work of mainstream cultural transmission and acquisition theorists and concludes his discussion by calling for proposals aimed at large-scale social transformation.

In Part III, we move from theory to practice. Maxwell, Bashook, and Sandlow are also interested in bridging the gap between ethnographers and educational evaluators. They attempt to demystify further the ethnographic process by breaking methodological ground in ethnographic evaluation. They represent the handful of researchers who have successfully combined contrasting paradigms in their research. Maxwell, Bashook, and Sandlow use ethnographic methods *within* an experimental framework to study the educational effects of physicians' participation in peer review committees. Much like Reichardt and Cook (1979), they discuss the presuppositions of both approaches to demonstrate why they are not incompatible. Moreover, they discuss the mutually reinforcing nature of the two approaches when combined in a single study.

Chesterfield is another ethnographic evaluator who chooses to combine qualitative and quantitative methods in his research. Chesterfield explains how the combination of two approaches strengthens the reliability and validity of the study findings. He demonstrates how naturalistic observation techniques are used to expand the experimental pre- and posttest design of a national evaluation of bilingual curriculum models. Quality control, data reduction and analysis, among other concerns, are addressed. Chesterfield describes how naturalistic techniques are used to match specific types of models with specific types of students. He also discusses the importance of matching specific models with appropriate communities, thus providing program developers with the type of contextual knowledge required to make constructive choices among a plethora of alternatives.

Ferrell and Compton also combine in part four quantitative and qualitative methods in their study. They represent, however, a shift in focus from practice to politics—in this case to the politics of desegregation. In contrast to Studstill, they focus on the way society shapes the evaluation design, rather than with the way ethnographic evaluations might shape society. Their study of a gifted program is as much a study of the political process of evaluation as it is a study of a district program. Ferrell and Compton provide the local social and political context of their evaluation—on school and community levels. In Ferrell and Compton's study, political forces restricted their use of ethnographic methods and explorations. As a result the tone of their discussion is sociological. Nevertheless, they are successful in generating ethnographic insights. In addition, they demonstrate how findings, recommendations, and responses to recommendations are negotiated settlements. Their description of program operations allows policy makers to identify levers of change in the system.

Marotto concludes this section of the collection by describing a school also undergoing court-ordered desegregation. His discussion is presented from the dual perspective of an ethnographic evaluator and local school board member. Marotto's purpose is to sensitize educators to the politics of everyday life. He points to the social and structural elements of a school that produce in-school truancy. Marotto presents the insider's view of how and why the competing rule systems of school and ghetto street corner result in disproportionate minority suspension. Marotto's findings are aimed at solving real problems resulting from cultural miscommunication. His application of a "games playing" perspective to the in-school truancy problem enables teachers to understand school disciplinary problems and respond appropriately. Moreover, Marotto presents the teachers' and students' roles in turning the problem around.

This chapter also has another purpose. It demonstrates the telling nature of the language we use to tell our story. Geertz more than any other living anthropologist has sensitized us to the way we write and how our language shapes the way we describe what we have observed. Marotto's code-switching language conveys a sense of the transitional process an ethnographer goes through as he or she emerges from the immersion experience required of good ethnography. In addition, ethnographic evaluators must speak to a number of audiences in the course of a study. Marotto writes to influence educators on the school level. He illustrates another social arena in which the ethnographic evaluator operates. His presentation portrays another (often political) dimension of the ethnographic evaluator's skills and responsibilities.

This work represents a second wave of ethnographic educational evaluation. In some cases, junior and senior scholars have been combined. Some of the studies in this collection are more assimilated and acculturated than earlier works. Some are deacculturated in tone. Part V reflects on the evolution of the discipline as it is presented in this collection. The work of these contributors demonstrates a continuing concern with the health of our educational programs and institutions. Individually and collectively, these studies move beyond explanations of school failure to offer specific designs for change. They take us beyond the status quo in the theory, practice, and politics of ethnographic educational evaluation.

NOTES

1. I think Cazden delivers an important message to anthropologists, however unfavorably received. The identification of inhibiting social and structural conditions within the educational domain is only the first step. Identifying elements of the system that facilitate equal educational opportunity is the second and more important step if we are to be of assistance in the educational arena. For details regarding the debate on whether ethnographic research can go beyond the status quo of simply explaining school failure see Cazden (1983:33-41; 1984:184-187), Kleinfeld (1983:282-287; 1984:180-184), Bishop (1984:167-168), Amsbury (1984:168-169), Harrison (1984: 169-170), Greenbaum and Greenbaum (1984:171-173), Stearns (1984:174-176), Chandler (1984:176-178), Grubis (1984:178-179), and Barnhardt (1984:179-189).

2. Formative evaluation and technical assistance represent instrumental means for designing and implementing change in the educational system.

3. See Sharp (1952) for a classic example of unintended social consequences of social intervention.

4. See Siegel (1970) for a detailed discussion of defensive structuring.

REFERENCES CITED

Amsbury, C.
  1984 The Problem of Simplicity. Anthropology and Education Quarterly 15(2): 168-169.
Barnhardt, R.
  1984 Anthropology Needs No Apology. Anthropology and Education Quarterly 15(2):179-180.

Bishop, R. J.
 1984 Educational Failure and the Status Quo. Anthropology and Education Quarterly 15(2):167-168.
Cazden, C. B.
 1983 Can Ethnographic Research Go Beyond the Status Quo? Anthropology and Education Quarterly 14(1):33-41.
 1984 Response. Anthropology and Education Quarterly 15(2):184-187.
Chandler, J. M.
 1984 Education Equals Change. Anthropology and Education Quarterly 15(2): 176-178.
Fetterman, D. M.
 1984a Doing Ethnographic Educational Evaluation. *In* Ethnography in Educational Evaluation. D. M. Fetterman, ed. pp. 13-19. Beverly Hills, CA: Sage.
 1984b Ethnography in Educational Evaluation. Beverly Hills, CA: Sage.
 1984c Ethnography in Educational Research: The Dynamics of Diffusion. *In* Ethnography in Educational Evaluation. D. M. Fetterman, ed. pp. 21-36. Beverly Hills, CA: Sage.
 1984d Guilty Knowledge, Dirty Hands, and Other Ethical Dilemmas: The Hazards of Contract Research. *In* Ethnography in Educational Evaluation. D. M. Fetterman, ed. pp. 211-236. Beverly Hills, CA: Sage.
Firestone, W. A., and R. E. Herriott
 1984 Multisite Qualitative Policy Research: Some Design and Implementation Issues. *In* Ethnography in Educational Evaluation. D. M. Fetterman, ed. pp. 63-88. Beverly Hills, CA: Sage.
Goldberg, H. E.
 1984 Evaluation, Ethnography, and the Concept of Culture: Disadvantaged Youth in an Israeli Town. *In* Ethnography in Educational Evaluation. D. M. Fetterman, ed. pp. 153-173. Beverly Hills, CA: Sage.
Greenbaum, S. D., and P. E. Greenbaum
 1984 Integrating Ethnographic and Quantitative Research: A Reply to Kleinfeld and Implications for American Indian Self-Determination. Anthropology and Education Quarterly 15(2):171-173.
Grubis, S.
 1984 A Teacher Perspective. Anthropology and Education Quarterly 15(2):178-179.
Harrison, B.
 1984 Training for Cross-Cultural Teaching. Anthropology and Education Quarterly 15(2):169-170.
Hemwall, M. K.
 1984 Ethnography as Evaluation: Hearing Impaired Students in the Mainstream. *In* Ethnography in Educational Evaluation. D. M. Fetterman, ed. pp. 113-152. Beverly Hills, CA: Sage.
Kleinfeld, J.
 1983 First Do No Harm: A Reply to Courtney Cazden. Anthropology and Education Quarterly 14(4):282-287.
 1984 Some of My Best Friends Are Anthropologists. Anthropology and Education Quarterly 15(2):180-184.
LeCompte, M. D., and J. P. Goetz
 1984 Ethnographic Data Collection in Evaluation Research. *In* Ethnography in

Educational Evaluation. D. M. Fetterman, ed. pp. 37-59. Beverly Hills, CA: Sage.

McDermott, R. P. and L. Hood
    1982 Institutionalized Psychology and the Ethnography of Schooling. *In* Children In and Out of School: Ethnography and Education. P. Gilmore and A. A. Glatthorn, eds. pp. 232-249. Washington, DC: Center for Applied Linguistics.

Messerschmidt, D. A.
    1984 Federal Bucks for Local Change: On the Ethnography of Experimental Schools. *In* Ethnography in Educational Evaluation. D. M. Fetterman, ed. pp. 89-114. Beverly Hills, CA: Sage.

Mills, C.
    1959 The Sociological Imagination. New York: Oxford University Press.

Reichardt, C., and T. Cook
    1979 Beyond Qualitative Versus Quantitative Methods. *In* Qualitative and Quantitative Methods in Evaluation Research. T. Cook and C. Reichardt, eds. pp. 7-32. Beverly Hills, CA: Sage.

Sharot, S.
    1974 Minority Situation and Religious Acculturation: A Comparative Analysis of Jewish Communities. Comparative Studies in Society and History 16: 329-354.

Sharp, L.
    1952 Steel Axes for Stone-Age Australians. Human Organization 11(2): 17-22.

Siegel, B.
    1970 Defensive Structuring and Environmental Stress. American Journal of Sociology 76:11-32.

Smith, A. G., and A. E. Robbins
    1984 Multimethod Policy Research: A Case Study of Structure and Flexibility. *In* Ethnography in Educational Evaluation. D. M. Fetterman, ed. pp. 115-132. Beverly Hills, CA: Sage.

Stearns, R.
    1984 Beyond an Emic View of Anthropologists and Anthropology: An Alaskan Perspective. Anthropology and Education Quarterly 15(2):174-176.

Wolcott, H. F.
    1984 Ethnographers sans Ethnography: The Evaluation Compromise. *In* Ethnography in Educational Evaluation. D. M. Fetterman, ed. pp. 177-210. Beverly Hills, CA: Sage.

2

The Ethnographic Evaluator

DAVID M. FETTERMAN

Anthropologists have planted deep roots in the soil of educational evaluation. They have been able to generate useful insights and effective solutions to contemporary social problems. This contribution has gained them a measure of acceptance and popularity in educational evaluation. They have offered evaluators a new paradigm, a new way of looking at educational innovations, and new methods of data collection and analysis. Moreover, they have diffused a cultural interpretation of behaviors and events in educational research.

Ethnographic educational evaluators have contributed to theory, theory testing, and practice in the course of their studies. They are characterized by their ability to step analytically beyond description to judgment. These judgments are made within the highly politicized environment of education. Ethnographic evaluators must adapt to this niche if they are to be effective. Finally, the work of ethnographic evaluators is reflexive. They contribute to practice, specifically to the development of design, data collection, and analysis in ethnography. They contribute to both anthropology and education; revitalizing one and expanding the horizons of the other.

AUTHOR'S NOTE: I am indebted to many other risk takers who helped to shape my own role as an ethnographic evaluator. I thank Pertti J. Pelto for grounding me firmly in anthropological theory and the ethnographic method. I am grateful for the guidance of my mentor, George D. Spindler. His intelligence and friendship made my scholarly rites of passage challenging and enlightening. I also appreciate his encouragement to work in this brave new world. Lee J. Cronbach's critical eye sharpened my focus and helped me to hit my target squarely in addressing national and state-level policy matters. NIE sponsorship of ethnographically informed work contributed to an educational research environment conducive to the application of ethnographic concepts and techniques. G. Kasten Tallmadge was one of the early risk takers in hiring an ethnographic evaluator. I also appreciate the supportive attitude and assistance of Elizabeth M. Eddy and Deborah S. Waxman toward this new venture.

CULTURAL BROKER

The ethnographic evaluator is a cultural broker. He or she communicates cultural knowledge across disciplinary boundaries. The ethnographic evaluator's contribution can be understood more fully by examining the nature and character of this change agent's role in practice. The cultural broker is bicultural and must be a hybrid to be effective. In essence, evaluator's must be able to speak and think in two different languages and to articulate the conceptual concerns of contrasting cultures; they are interdisciplinary ground breakers.

During culture contact, assimilation and acculturation occur. The new environment consists of conflicting world views and work settings, and ethnographic evaluators adapt to it in a variety of ways. This context, with its accompanying incentives and constraints, shapes the ethnographic work. The ethnographic evaluator is also a human being. Tracing the life cycle of this academic entrepreneur gives depth as well as breadth to our understanding of the role of this cultural risk taker.

BICULTURAL

As noted above, the educational ethnographic evaluator is an educational anthropologist and as such is bicultural, like most applied anthropologists. Educational anthropologists work within the two very different worlds of education and anthropology. Luminaries in the field such as Mead, Spindler, Kimball, and Eddy, among others, have worked effectively with educators and established the foundation upon which the ethnographic evaluator works. Nevertheless, the cultural chasm between anthropology and education periodically erupts in conflict. Evaluation is one of the areas in which conflict still exists.

Educational evaluators and anthropologists experienced severe cognitive dissonance in the early days of their union. In the late 1960s and 1970s educational anthropologists and educational evaluators were concerned with different topics. Educational evaluators focused typically on such professional topics as teaching, curriculum, and administration, whereas educational anthropologists were preoccupied with such topics as culture, religion, social structure, and human organization. Moreover, as these differences in topic preferences suggest, these two fields represented different ways of thinking about the world.

Conflict, misunderstanding, and miscommunication resulted from poorly communicated expectations of each other's performance. A rapprochement between educational evaluators and anthropologists has grown as their respective cultural values are being made more explicit and as an interest has developed in pursuing more topics of mutual concern. Anthropologists increasingly are focusing on new topics of interest to educational evaluators. They study these new topics, however, from their unique cultural perspective. The classroom is viewed as part of a larger sociocultural system. This perspective focuses attention on the processes of schooling, teaching, learning, cultural transmission, and social change. To function within these two worlds, educational anthropologists must learn the rules dictated by each. These rules govern speech, dress, and both public and private behavior. They must be able to translate what they see into a format useful to educators, and yet communicate with academic anthropologists in their own language as well. This often requires linguistic competence as code switchers when working with mixed groups.

HYBRID

The ethnographic educational evaluator is not only bicultural, he or she is also a hybrid. The label *ethnographic evaluator* suggests a contradiction in terms to some scholars. How can an anthropologist be nonjudgmental and judgmental at the same time? The question provides a handle by means of which we can clarify the role of the ethnographic evaluator.

First, it is a myth that anthropologists are completely nonjudgmental. The selection of a topic itself reflects built-in biases. The process of collecting data requires discrimination and judgment. Analysis and the manner in which findings are skillfully crafted and communicated reveal explicit and implicit biases. The aim, however, is to assume a nonjudgmental orientation toward different cultural practices. Ideally, value judgments are not made about marriage practices such as polygamy, gender-favored inheritance patterns, the lifestyle of a merchant or beggar, or personal hygiene practices. Both traditional ethnographers and ethnographic evaluators attempt to adopt this posture throughout a study and to make explicit their more conscious and obvious biases. A nonjudgmental orientation and an evaluative approach are not mutually exclusive. Evaluation simply represents another level of analysis. The evaluator can assess the functions and adaptations of a system, program, or policy without making a value judgment about the cultural practice per se.

The major difference between the traditional ethnographer and the ethnographic evaluator is that the traditional ethnographer *concludes* the study with a description of the culture, whereas an ethnographic evaluator *begins* the evaluative segment of the study with a description of the culture. The ethnographic evaluator describes what it going on and then makes a qualitative leap beyond description to the explicit appraisal and assessment of the cultural system in terms of its own cultural norms. As an ethnographer and an ethnographic evaluator, I have found explicit assessment to be a more honest and useful approach to the study of human beings.

Ethnographers, in practice, are continually making assessments regarding the nature of the people and the system under study. Ethnographic evaluators simply bring this subconscious, and often subliminal, process to the surface of conscious expression. Moreover, participants and clients in educational research have learned to expect feedback as part of their daily lives. Holding back one's assessments upsets a delicate balance of reciprocity and mutual expectations. Educators perceive evaluation in a positive manner. They understand the role and recognize the evaluator's work as a useful contribution to the group. The typical ethnographic endeavor by comparison seems less relevant and inadequately reciprocal, almost exploitive, in nature.

ASSIMILATION AND ACCULTURATION

Basically, the key to understanding the label *ethnographic evaluator* can be found in a simple grammatical analysis of the term. The word *ethnographic* is an adjective, characterizing an anthropological type of evaluator. Whether this means an anthropologist is walking around in an evaluator's moccasins or an evaluator is walking around wearing an anthropological lens is simply a function of who is doing the study. Each individual finds what Aristotle called a "natural resting spot" from which to see the world. The ethnographic evaluator's selection of a resting spot determines how he or she will conduct the study. The traditional ethnographer will not survive in an interdisciplinary environment requiring flexibility, adaptation, and innovation. The poorly trained ethnographer will not be able to differentiate between adaptation, mutation, and mutilation. The well-trained ethnographic evaluator is able to apply anthropological theory, concepts, and methods to new areas in new ways without compromising the integrity of the endeavor.

In addition, a competent ethnographic evaluator, like a seasoned researcher, recognizes his or her limitations. We cannot be experts in all matters. The secure ethnographic evaluator recognizes it is as important to know when one does not know the answer or even the right questions as it is to know whom to ask for assistance. The insecure ethnographer who enters educational evaluation is likely to overcompensate by applying rigid standards to a situation requiring a novel approach. On the other end of the spectrum, there are some insecure ethnographers who become elite acculturationists. They may deny or disparage their own methodological heritage and assume a highly stylized version of the dominant evaluation culture. Finally, there are a number of individuals who begin as ethnographic evaluators and, if they remain in the profession at all, are fully assimilated into the dominant culture. They either identify themselves simply as evaluators or fade into the woodwork.

CONTRASTING WORLD VIEWS AND WORK SETTINGS

We are all products of our environment, and it is necessary to analyze our environment to identify how we have come to select our own way of looking at the world, our own natural resting spot. Ethnographic evaluators function within three conflicting world views: academe, the research corporation, and the federal bureaucracy. The manner in which ethnographic evaluators identify with and cope with these competing versions of reality determines the nature of the home or prison they construct for themselves. A particular source of difficulty for many lies in the transition process from academe to the world of contract research. A brief discussion of these world views will serve to identify the variables that shape the character of the ethnographic evaluator and, in turn, the quality of his or her work.

ACADEME

The university environment has traditionally represented "home base" for most anthropologists. Anthropologists and other social scientists operating within the academic sphere are socialized to place a high value on autonomy and independence in their research endeavors (Clinton 1976). Universities provide a supportive context for the pursuit of these aims, preventing the more obvious vested interests and biases of external agencies from contaminating research. Academe is able to pursue this course because the economic support system for research is based primarily on grants. Most grants provide academics with a relatively small fiscal budget and a lengthy period of time for investigation in contrast to contracts, which usually provide larger budgets and less time. In addition, academics typically specify the problem and formulate the study design.

Sponsors of grants within academe are more flexible than the contract monitors or sponsors of research in the corporation. They are typically more generous in their consideration of research design and implementation modifications than are contract sponsors. This is a function of the sponsors' differing environments, a topic that will be discussed below. Anthropologists in academe conduct exploratory, traditionally long-term studies and are provided considerable flexibility in terms of time and focus. An academic orientation collides head on with the demands of work in the "outside world" of contract research. It is a contradiction or "culture shock" that all applied anthropologists must face eventually.

The academic orientation is enhanced by additional scholastic trappings. The university environment fosters the development of the lone scholar. The promotion and tenure of an individual in this setting is dependent on a personal publication record, as well as other economic and political factors in the academic department. The hackneyed formula "publish or perish" still applies to modern university-based scholarship. In the humanities and social sciences, including anthropology, interdisciplinary research is praised but atypical; it is considered a marginal contribution to one's professional development. In addition, coauthored works or works with multiple authorship are viewed less favorably than publications representing the efforts of one person. Graduate students are socialized to accept these fundamental tenets of the academic world view. Unfortunately, many elements of this world view clash with the values guiding the worlds of educational evaluation and the federal bureaucracy. The ethnographic evaluator is most likely to confront these new worlds for the first time within an office in a research corporation.

THE RESEARCH CORPORATION

The ethnographic evaluator entering the research corporation is confronted immediately with a different set of values and research paradigms. Traditional educational researchers dominate evaluation research corporations. They have been socialized by graduate training to accept the educational research establishment's orthodox credo.

This view is characterized by the experimental, quantitative approach to research. Campbell and Stanley (1963) and Riecken et al. (1974) are among the most widely recognized proponents of this approach. Campbell and Stanley (1963:2) have traditionally viewed the experiment as follows:

> the only means for settling disputes regarding educational practice, as the only way of verifying educational improvements, and as the only way of establishing a cumulative tradition in which improvements can be introduced without the danger of a faddish discard of old wisdom in favor of inferior novelties.

Educational researchers employing alternative methods or perspectives have been, until recently, regarded as operating outside the mainstream of "acceptable" educational research. An overemphasis on the importance of the design has led to a situation in which the methodological tail wags the proverbial research dog. Researchers have often allowed specific tools to dictate the way research is conducted, rather than first identifying the research questions and then selecting the appropriate methods to respond to them. This is partially a function of federal dictates.

Fundamentally, the confrontation between the ethnographic evaluator and the traditional research corporation employee is paradigmatic in nature. My own first days in a research corporation were marked by loud arguments with the president of the company. I would argue about the low validity of his approach and he would argue about the low reliability of mine. The ritual hazing was rooted in our paradigmatic differences, in phenomenology and logical positivism. In time, this phase passed. Once the tribal chief was convinced of the utility of the ethnographic approach, others in the office followed, albeit cautiously and reluctantly. In some cases, ethnographic evaluators are too quick to follow the path of least resistance and accept without question assertions and untested assumptions. In such cases, both parties are denied an opportunity to learn from each other on basic paradigmatic levels—questioning basic assumptions about how we view the world.

The research corporation has another significant difference from home base. The evaluation corporation is fundamentally a business that is primarily concerned with producing a reputable research product, advancing the state of the art, and making a profit. (In nonprofit organizations the profit is referred to as the "margin.") It stays in business by bidding for proposals in which the problem, and often the research design, has been defined in advance. "Independently the agencies push out tentacles, brandishing separate RFP's [requests for proposals]. Firms on the other side of the chasm send out tentacles in response and, as on the Sistine ceiling, a spark leaps across" (Cronbach et al. 1980a:463). The contracting process itself shapes the evaluation as Keith Baker has discussed:

> Many applied research administrators push for such a detailed specification of the problem and research design that the only important question left for the contractor is how much it will cost to carry out the agency's plan. The agency, knowing what it wants done and how it wants it done, is looking for a skilled staff to carry out its needs, not somebody else's desires....
>
> The agency's desire to maximize control over the research, to make sure its problems get addressed the way the agency thinks [they] should be addressed, is precisely the reason why it uses contracts rather than grants. The important feature of a contract is that it maximizes the agency's control (1975:210).
>
> The RFP is very important in the research process. It fixes the outline and many of the details of the study's methodology as well as specifying the problem to be studied. The RFP will generally define the population to be studied, sample sizes, and whether the study will be experimental, post-hoc interviews, or pre- and post-field observations. The RFP may even specify the instruments to be used and the type of statistical analysis to be employed. In general, the two areas where the RFP leaves greatest discretion to the proposer is in the instrument content (the specific items) and data analysis. Note again that the RFP is prepared by the agency. The people who ultimately do the work have no involvement in many of the basic decisions of the research process (1975:213-214).

There is room for negotiation, but the above pattern encourages the adoption of research proposals and designs without sufficient scrutiny. The day-to-day operations of the research corporation described by Cronbach et al., in which there are plenty of "mouths to feed," provides an insight into the research corporation's behavior in this regard:

> Life in the contracting firm is dominated by the scramble for contracts. At every turn new money must be won to keep a staff in place. However, only large and experienced organizations can successfully solicit and manage large evaluations. A stack of blue chips is required merely to enter the bidding. The competitor must have a sophisticated business office for preparing proposals and keeping track of expenses. A public-relations staff stands by, ready to protect the flanks of a

politically sensitive study. Computer facilities have to be extensive and up-to-date. Professional managers are needed to keep activities on schedule. And behind the scenes the firm's Washington representative keeps in touch with those who will be commissioning evaluations. Abert (quoted in Biderman & Sharp, 1972, p. 49) commented cynically that good research directors are far less necessary to a firm's success than are intelligence agents able to pick up early word on bidding opportunities. But the firm does what it can to maintain a staff of professionals qualified to plan, collect, and interpret data.

Some firms offer services of many kinds, in many program areas. Once well established, a diversified firm can take the ups and downs of fortune more easily than a specialized firm. But even the largest firm shivers during a budget freeze, and it goes into a spasm of readjustment when it wins an unusually large contract. A narrow specialty makes an organization highly sensitive to the funding priorities of agencies. Over and over the same tale is told. A firm waxes as federal interest in its specialty grows. It welds together a team with complementary skills. The team accumulates special knowledge of the social problem. Then support disappears, the team splits up, and a capable organization is lost (Abt 1979, p. 50) [Cronbach et al. 1980b:329].

Excessive protests regarding the study's design jeopardize the corporation's chances of winning a contract. This business orientation promotes compromises that may contribute to the overall pattern of misused designs. In addition, corporation researchers look at present sponsors as potential future sponsors, and are therefore more likely to adopt research proposals and designs without sufficient scrutiny. Most successful proposals are characterized by the quantitative designs that reflect the dominant culture of the educational research establishment, the research corporation, and the federal bureaucracy.

THE FEDERAL BUREAUCRACY

A brief examination of the federal agencies' real world constraints and views provides a rationale for the research corporation's perspective and behavior.[1] One of the primary responsibilities of the federal sponsor is to produce the most credible and socially relevant research (Holcomb 1974) dictated by congressional mandate. Policy research, in contrast to basic research, represents another significant facet of the federal bureaucratic perspective.

[Policy research in juxtaposition to basic research] is much less abstract, much more closely tied to particular actions to be undertaken or avoided. While basic [research] aims chiefly to uncover truth, policy research seeks to aid in the solution of fundamental problems and in the advancement of major programs (Etzioni 1971).

Policy research seeks immediate action in response to a troubled situation such as unemployment, a high dropout rate, and so on. It attacks a discrete facet of the situation to "avoid turf problems." Decisions are made in a context of accommodation rather than command (von Neuman and Morganstern 1953). Policy is more a process of drifting toward a decision than a Platonic pattern of a single commander handing down decisions affecting the entire social sphere (see March and Olsen 1976). There is, according to Mulhauser (1975:311) "no search for a comprehensive understanding of the problem's nature or origin." Glennan (1972) pointed out that significant go/no-go decisions are rare in policy. Cronbach et al. (1980b:287) add to the picture the fact that "Policy makers do weigh alternatives that have incommensurable outcomes—reduced-crime versus community-harmony, say, or children's shoes-versus-Army boots." The ever present time pressure requires immediate identification of politically viable "levers of action." Often, Mulhauser (1975:311) points out, "the action taken is a minor variation on what was done the last time something like this came up."

Federal agencies are also constrained by the responsibility for providing timely input for policymakers. As Coward (1976:14) points out, "Evaluation data presented after a policy decision has been made can have little impact on the decision." The role of evaluation itself is limited in the policy arena. It is used, according to Rich (in Weiss 1977:200), in "groups and clusters" as one piece of evidence or data in the larger fundamentally political equation (Acland 1979). Cronbach et al. (1980b:294) point out that "What impresses a research expert obsessed with method may not impress someone who sees the larger picture." Elisburg (1977:67-68) similarly places the congressional role of evaluation into perspective:

> It cannot be stressed too strenuously that scientific program evaluation is itself evaluated by the Congress in terms of its utility to promote the effectiveness and precision of legislative judgments in a political milieu.

Furthermore, according to Cronbach et al. (1980b:251),

> Knowing this week's score does not tell the coach how to prepare for next week's game. The information that an intervention had satisfactory

or unsatisfactory outcomes is of little use by itself; users of the study need to know what led to success or failure. Only with that information can the conditions that worked be replicated, or modified sufficiently in the next trial to get better results.

In addition, federal agencies must maximize their returns in efforts with limited fiscal resources. Combining scarce resources with pressures of accountability produces a climate of interagency rivalry over those resources and thus the need to employ the maximization model (McClelland and Winter 1969). The maximization model suggests "that human beings everywhere tend to choose the personal action that they feel will gain them the greatest benefit (or avoid the greatest loss) with the smallest expenditure of resources" (Bee 1974:198; see also Bailey 1960; Barth, 1963, 1966, 1967; Erasmus, 1961; Kunkel, 1970).

These fundamental constraints shape the agencies' perspective and enable them to adapt successfully to the federal environment. The federal agencies' survival literally depends on an adequate understanding of, adherence to, and manipulation of these norms. The fluidity of funding from year to year, political fluctuations and alliances, career-building concerns, and the acquisition-maintenance of power games all contribute to the political instability of the bureaucratic hierarchy and federal perspective. "The political process has a lifestyle and morality of its own—a lifestyle and morality that evaluators have to respect if they are to be of use" (Lindblom and Cohen 1979, as paraphrased by Cronbach et al. 1980b: 349).

The demands for data, according to strict guidelines and time tables, are generated from this environment. Knowledge is power, and information is required at prespecified periods to assist in the federal decision-making process, which entails the assessment of the relative merits of competing programs. Coward (1976:14) warns, "Agencies place themselves in highly vulnerable positions if they sponsor a research effort that is unable to provide data under constraints imposed by policy deadlines." The inability to address these concerns in this fashion may leave an agency "out in the cold," with little or no future funding. These constraints and the socialization of federal bureaucrats according to the the canons of the traditional educational establishment have guided the federal government into the pattern of traditionally associating the most credible and timely research with the experimental design, regardless of the task at hand. The federal climate of inflexible deadlines, interagency rivalry, and scarce resources shapes the behavior of its primary client—the research corporation. Research corporations respond to their sponsors with a watchful eye toward future funding. Overspending and ignoring deadlines does not sit well with sponsors whose very survival is dependent upon the delivery of information to policymakers at a fixed time. Ethnographers who enter this environment very quickly sink or swim,.

These three conflicting world views are logical expressions of their respective environments. Unfortunately, graduate training rarely prepares anthropologists for this culture shock. A conversion process is required when moving from one environment to the next. In fact, academic training compounds the difficulties encountered in this transition. Ethnographers trained in the academic sphere must learn to readjust many ingrained patterns of behavior as they enter a new field; these include accepting rather than generating a problem to be researched (although they select the RFP of interest) and working in multidisciplinary teams. These alternatives should be regarded as real but superficial concerns in the adaptation process.

The way an ethnographic evaluator functions is shaped by the influences and pressures discussed above. In combination with the individual personality and training of the ethnographer, these pressures determine whether a traditionalist, a moderate, or a completely coopted posture will be adopted. The tensions produced by the reinforcing world views of the educational research establishment, the research corporation, and the federal bureaucracy have been reduced in recent years by more open discussion of these problems (Fetterman 1982, 1984b). In addition, at least on the paradigmatic level, some of the leading proponents of the educational research establishment have expressed a change of heart in their attitudes toward qualitative research. Campbell, for example, has written in "an extreme oscillation away from [his] earlier dogmatic disparagement of case studies" as follows:

> We should recognize that participants and observers have been evaluating program innovations for centuries without the benefit of quantification or scientific method. This is the common-sense knowing which our scientific evidence should build upon and go beyond, not replace. But it is usually neglected in quantitative evaluations, unless a few supporting anecdotes haphazardly collected are included. Under the epistemology I advocate, one should attempt to systematically tap all the qualitative common sense program critiques and evaluations that have been generated among the program staff, program clients and their families, and community observers. While quantitative procedures such

as questionnaires and rating scales will often be introduced at this stage for reasons of convenience in collecting and summarizing, non-quantitative methods of collection and compiling should also be considered, such as hierarchically organized discussion groups. Where such evaluations are contrary to the quantitative results, the quantitative results should be regarded as suspect until the reasons for the discrepancy are well understood. Neither is infallable, of course. But for many of us, what needs to be emphasized is that the quantitative results may be as mistaken as the qualitative (1979:52-53).

This position is symbolic of a much larger change taking place in the field of educational evaluation. It is a silent scientific revolution.

Increasingly, evaluators are turning away from quantitative designs and toward the acceptance and use of qualitative concepts and techniques in educational evaluation. *Qualitative and Quantitative Methods in Evaluation Research* (Cook and Reichardt 1979) opened a new door on the discussion of qualitative methods in evaluation. *Ethnography in Educational Evaluation* (Fetterman, 1984a) focused the discussion on ethnography, specifically the role of ethnographic techniques and a cultural interpretation in educational evaluation. This collection contributed to this shift in professional allegiances by presenting a series of systematically rigorous ethnographic studies that have worked. The change is reflected also in graduate school curricula throughout the country. Qualitative course sequences are becoming common features of graduate training for educators. This shift in professional allegiances has been somewhat turbulent, but the change has served to raise the methodological consciousness of evaluators and to ease the tensions endemic to this enterprise.

THE LIFE CYCLE OF THE ETHNOGRAPHIC EVALUATOR

The above cultural and paradigmatic backdrop of the ethnographic evaluator is important, but a more revealing picture can be seen by tracing the development of an ethnographic evaluator. This development is closely tied to the cyclical process of contract research, a pattern that characterizes the inception and growth not only of a particular project, but of the researcher's career as well.

CONCEPTION

The life cycle of both researcher and project begins with conception, writing a proposal for funding. This lays the foundation and sets the tone of the study. Experienced ethnographic evaluators have learned to take charge during this critical phase of the life cycle. This is the period in which to establish the budget: to provide for field workers, equipment, and time to think, analyze the data, and write up the findings. The time devoted to planning and designing the ethnographic component of the evaluation is well spent. The proposal reflects the creativity of the ethnographic evaluator or the degree of assimilation to the mainstream of evaluation design.

BIRTH

The next stage is birth, receiving a contract to begin the study. This is an occasion for celebration—champagne, Brie, chocolate cake, and popcorn. Jokes are told and moments of desperation are remembered, such as the time a photocopying machine broke down hours before a deadline. Moments of high tension are relived, as when one corporation learns that a competitor has found a "ringer" or has supplied misinformation. The formal celebration usually lasts for only an hour or less (in proportion to the size of the contract) but the atmosphere remains highly charged for weeks. The president or project directors are quick to remind researchers of the tasks remaining on ongoing work and everyone settles back into work. By the same token, when a large contract has been lost to a competitor, there is a subtle form of mourning that shrouds the atmosphere. Eventually, this somber mood is eased by some form of comic relief or work on another proposal or current project.

Immediately following the receipt of a contract, it is necessary to receive routine check-ups. Meetings are scheduled immediately with the sponsor to reaffirm what was promised and agreed to in the proposal. Most surprises are mitigated if caught early. Periodically, however, gross misunderstandings occur between contractors and their sponsors even in the early stages. In one case, I won a contract that was explicitly ethnographic in design. One week after the award, the sponsors demanded a change to a closed questionnaire approach with both the questions and the choice of interview subjects under their control. They wanted us to provide compliance information about each of the programs during the course of the study and to increase the number of sites visited without altering the funding. As an ethnographic evaluator and project director, I found it necessary to take a firm stance against this mutilation of methodology, ethics, and fiscal administration. In this instance, we convinced the sponsors of the untenable ethical and fiscal problems their alterations imposed.

Unfortunately, we were unable to come to a satisfactory solution to the radical methodological alterations imposed on the study after the fact. The proposed ethnographic methods and concepts were selected by the sponsors over those of such major competitors as ETS (Educational Testing Service). Their subsequent flip-flop in orientation appears, in retrospect, to have been in part a power play to establish their control over the study. This case has entered litigation and was successfully argued on methodological-contractual grounds.

CHILDHOOD

Assuming a healthy birth, the ethnographic evaluator enters his or her formative years. This period involves identifying key actors and informants in the project and making detailed schedules, appointments, and other plans. Letters and phone calls are used to arrange for entrance into the field. During this period, first impressions dominate interactions. The more common errors that may cause irreparable damage to a working relationship involve the formalities of contract research. It is critical, for example, to recognize and respect protocol. Educational settings are governed by hierarchical relations. Permission from the superintendent must be granted before permission from a principal is proposed. The impact of protocol on one's ability to gain access to documents and people should not be underestimated. Respecting protocol can create a halo effect; ignoring protocol can place obstacles in the ethnographer's path throughout the entire study.

ADOLESCENCE

Conducting field work is much like entering and reentering adolescence. The field worker must learn a new language, new rituals, and a wealth of new cultural information. This period is marked by tremendous excitement, frustration, and confusion. The ethnographic evaluator exposes him- or herself to personal and professional turmoil as a part of the experience. One of my first site visits for a research corporation that had never heard of an ethnographer prior to my hiring is highly illustrative. I had convinced them of the utility of the approach and had made successful agruments for doubling the budget of the ethnographic evaluation section of the study to accommodate field work and equipment. I was therefore under considerable pressure either to show them a few interesting insights provided by using ethnographic evaluation or at least to come back with some basic information in hand.

I collected a mountain of material during the first two weeks, from interviews, observation, and documents. I sketched a few informal networks and felt that I had accomplished a great deal for a very short time. On what was to have been the last day of the site visit, a student befriended me. He was tall and weighed over two hundred pounds. After a few hours of conversation about his life and the neighborhood, he decided to show me around. He introduced me to a number of the characters who ran the street life. It was getting hot and he knew that I was from California so he brought me to a health food store for a cold drink and a snack. We went in and my new friend winked at the owner of the store and told him to give me a granola bar with some natural soda. I said thanks and reached out my hand for the granola bar and felt something else under the bar. It was a nickel bag of marijuana.

I looked at the owner, then I looked at my friend. I didn't want to show any form of disapproval or ingratitude, but this was not exactly what I had had in mind when I agreed to play the role of guest, visitor, and friend. A moment later, I heard steps in perfect stride. I looked over to the front window and I saw two policemen walking by, looking right in the window. My hand was still in the air with the mixed contents for all to see. My heart dropped to the floor.

My first thought was "I'm going to get busted. How am I going to explain this to my colleagues at the research corporation?" They were already skeptical about ethnography. How was I going to explain to them why I was studying the community outside the school program? Fortunately, the police disappeared as quickly as they had appeared. I asked my friend what had just transpired. He explained to me that they were paid off regularly and would bother you only if they needed money or if an owner had not made his or her contribution. After picking myself up emotionally and finishing the tour of the neighborhood, I went back to my hotel room and furiously wrote up the event. I later used it in one of my governmental reports to describe the neighborhood context of these students. This provided a context for assessing the relative success of an educational program that had tremendous competition for the students' attention. The incident was useful also in showing me that my informant was both proud of his cultural knowledge ("knowing where to cop dope") and capable of experimenting with a conventional lifestyle by entering the educational program under study. This experience reveals some of the benefits of living and working in a natural setting, as well as the role of serendipity in field work (see Fetterman 1984c).

During this period the ethnographic evaluator begins to gather the strands of information that will form the fabric of his or her understanding of the culture. The ability to gather this information relies on an early recognition of the formal and informal power brokers within a community and school. Establishing contacts with clergymen, politicians, local business people, police, and gang leaders opened door to me throughout my national study of dropouts, potential dropouts, and push outs. The ethnographic evaluator must keep one foot on either side of the ethnographic-evaluation line. As an ethnographer, he or she must remain nonjudgmental and maintain confidentiality. Identifying with one side or the other will close important lines of communication and allow access to only half the story. On the other hand, one must remind informants that, as an evaluator, one is assessing the functional or dysfunctional qualities of the program or situation. On an administrative level, this role is generally understood; however, sometimes things go wrong. Generally, a constructive orientation can be conveyed by playing the role of management consultant informing administration of positive and negative elements of the system with the aim of improving the system's operation. On a student level, all that is necessary is to be honest about the two halves of one's role: part student trying to understand how the system works and part professional evaluator trying to come up with recommendations to improve the school program. Adolescent students possess a psychological "radar" that tells them if someone is being honest. If they sense dishonesty or insincerity, they can undermine the value of any study.

One of the dangers of this period is miscalculation about the appropriate degree of reciprocity required. Ethnographic evaluators can become easy targets for informants who feed them the information they think the evaluators want to hear and then collect the rewards for that information. Another problem that can emerge is field work paralysis. Ethnographic evaluators, like conventional ethnographers, attempt to remain as unobtrusive as possible. Unfortunately, this can be carried to an extreme. I have observed cases in which my own staff felt unable to collect any information for fear of disrupting the system. They overdramatized the sensitivities of their prospective informants and withdrew from any data collection. After I convinced one of them to break the ice with a few nonthreatening questions, he realized that he had projected his own concerns on the informant and that the system was not quite as delicate as he had assumed. In a second case, the individual had to be replaced.

A similar danger occurs when a field worker goes native. In one case, a staff member felt so strongly affiliated with the group under study that he decided to join them and leave his data collection responsibilities behind. In such a situation, the cost to the study and the sponsors and to the credibility of co-workers can be devastating. Ethnography is a personal science, and individuals must make personal decisions about how they are going to live their lives, even in the middle of a study. Careful consideration should go into the decision to enter any role that may have competing obligations and responsibilities. Ethnographic evaluators should err on the side of professionalism and responsibility; a large number of individuals rely on their data, ranging from the sponsors to the students in the programs being evaluated.

ADULTHOOD

The ethnographic evaluator reaches adulthood when he or she has gained acceptance into the community or school under study. Acceptance improves the quality of data by opening up new levels of previously undisclosed symbols and cultural knowledge. Within the research corporation, adulthood for the ethnographic evaluator is knowing when to wear an ethnographer's cap and when to wear an evaluator's suit. This may sound simple, but in fact it is not time-bound or purely situationally directed. An ethnographic evaluator is always collecting information throughout the study; in the streets and in plush conference rooms in Washington, D.C. Similarly, the ethnographic evaluator continually appraises how well the system works, whether it is the system of administering funds for the program or of classroom instruction. The key to being an adult ethnographic evaluator is, first, knowing when to allow one approach to dominate one's mode of operation, and, second, knowing how to present oneself for the right audiences.

There is a delicate balance between collecting enough information and making an assessment. Additional information will always be informative. There is, however, a law of diminishing returns in any endeavor. There are also many time pressures, such as sponsor deadlines and proposal writing for the next project. Judgments must be made to allow the next stage of the study to begin. The ethnographic evaluator must constantly guard against making assessments prematurely. At the same time, he or she must be able to get at the heart of an issue and often make best guesses about the fate of a school.

I encountered a difficult decision of this nature several years ago, involving the fate of one of the educational programs for dropouts (discussed earlier). The sponsors were unhappy with the progress of a particular program and did not want to wait for the results of the study, which was only one-third complete at the time. They informed us that they were ready to make a go or no-go decision regarding continued funding of the program. They asked for our assessment of the program before all the data were collected, analyzed, synthesized, and reported. We objected to being put in this position, and informed them that we would not be a part of such a travesty. The sponsors explained to us that based on their perception of the program's progress it did not warrant additional funding. The phone call ended with this ultimatum: either we provide insights into the program or, if we maintained our ethical stance, they would act on the information they had (or didn't have) in hand. They gave us two and a half hours to think about it before calling us back.

We sat there stunned, irritated, and unsure. We discussed the matter for about fifteen minutes. We went over the reasons for not disclosing any information about the program. Then a few pragmatic arguments were made for providing our opinions to the sponsors. Reluctantly, we decided that some input would be better than no input, given the present circumstances. Unfortunately, we didn't have many data to go on. The traditional evaluators had only some of the pretests. The scores were terrible, which was expected because they were received prior to treatment in the program. I went through my precoded, preanalyzed field notes and found a few points that could be interpreted in favor of the program and a few against. In sum, we pooled our information together and took our best guess. We believed that the program merited further funding and further consideration.

The ethnographic data were useful on two levels. First, they documented when the sponsors had collected their information and what they collected. Thus, I was able to explain that the reason they didn't see any students around during their visit was because it was during the middle of the summer and it was at 4:30 p.m. (after regular school hours). Second, the attendance data did look bad. The average attendance level was less than 60%. I simply offered the observation that it depends on one's perspective. The sponsors were comparing this program's attendance figure with local school attendance reports of 70% to 75% average daily attendance. I explained that, given this comparison, the program did not look good; however, this was comparing apples with oranges. The students in this program were not the same as the average student in the regular school; in fact, they were systematically different from the average student. These were students who dropped out of the neighborhood schools, they were the regular nonattendees. In addition, assessments of this nature are determined according to some baseline. Once again, the assumed baseline for comparison was the local high school. I provided a sense of proportion and context to the discussion by explaining that in this case the local school baseline was not appropriate. The accurate baseline to use was 0% attendance because these students were dropouts. This made 55% attendance look surprisingly good. These arguments, in conjunction with additional anecdotes, saved the program.

In a more pristine ethnographic endeavor, it is unlikely that these pressures would have surfaced. External pressures are a routine part of applied anthropology, particularly ethnographic educational evaluation. In this case, it was crucial that the ethnographic data be used as appropriately as possible; but the information had to be presented in the form of an evaluator's appraisal of program progress. An ethnographic evaluator should have enough experience with the educational and evaluation subcultures to know how to act or how to get around conforming to educational and evaluation norms in an appropriate (nondisruptive and nonobtrusive) manner. An inability to adapt in these situations manifests a mind set that may have deleterious effects as the study unfolds.

Similarly, at advisory panel or professional association meetings or in the classroom it is important to know when to argue as an evaluator and when it is imperative that you be a participant-observer. In advisory panel meetings, a ritual common to evaluations in which experts sit in judgment of the progress of the study, an ethnographic evaluator must be prepared to be a player in the politics of emergent vested interests. This role requires an adept evaluator or politician to maintain the integrity of the study, defend its progress, and mold it in the right direction. During the same meeting, as ethnographer, he or she presents descriptions, patterns, and preliminary findings for discussion. This is easy to do at separate association meetings, where the audience is more homogeneous. Periodically, however, the presentation draws a mixed crowd, as with the advisory panel, and it is incumbant upon the ethnographic evaluator to becomne a cognitive code switcher. This requires the ability to think in two conceptual frameworks simultaneously—addressing concerns of reliability and validity (from a logical positivist's perspective), and at the same time ensuring a phenomenologically based study.

MARRIAGE

Marriage is an interlocking of fates and a commitment to meet mutual emotional, social, and fiscal responsibilities. For the ethnographic evaluator, this involves making a long-term commitment to working in an interdisciplinary team in a policy research context. The benefits of this union are rewarding. Financially, the field can be extremely lucrative. The opportunities to travel are plentiful and the opportunity to conduct policy research at the cutting edge is enviable. In addition, the experience of sharing your interests and insights with scholars with a different, if not conflicting, world view is profound. This commitment, however, should not be entered into lightly.

Team members come to depend on the stability of this relationship in writing proposals, conducting research, and writing reports. A creative and financial interdependency evolves in an interdisciplinary team setting. Leaving the team or dismantling it, like a divorce, can be costly for everyone. Staff no longer have the financial and emotional security that is taken for granted. Peers lose the synergistic effect of working together and learning from one another. Superiors have a hole in the organization that may have legal as well as social and emotional overtones. The ripple effect runs all the way from the sponsor to staff to the students involved in the study.

FAMILY

The ethnographic evaluator's family includes not only the interdisciplinary team, but the network of colleagues in the field as well. They serve as a quality control to maintain methodological rigor. Experiments and innovations are required when working as an ethnographic evaluator. Working at the cutting edge of research is an exhilarating but unsettling experience. There is no situation with a greater need for judiciously imposed quality controls. Effective ethnographic evaluators use members of the team to test their ideas. They solicit opinions from scholars from different disciplines to determine if a specific adaptation will address methodological concerns across disciplines. This is particularly important when attempting to combine ethnographic, survey, and experimental or quasi-experimental designs in the same evaluation study.

Similarly, a network of ethnographic evaluation colleagues can be used to test the appropriateness of novel methodological innovations (e.g., projective techniques, short-term, multisite field work schedules). This network is established and maintained by telephone, correspondence, professional meetings, scholarly literature, and computer communications. The Bitnet (Because It's Time), EARN (European Academic Research Network), and ARPANET (Advanced Research Projects Agency) systems facilitate communication. These systems link more than 1,400 computer nodes together, connecting universities and research facilities throughout the world, ranging from the City University of New York to Stanford University in California and from the Ecole Centrale de Paris to Hebrew University in Israel. Brief messages, letters, and manuscripts are shared through an electronic mail system. This type of network provides feedback that can be measured in nanoseconds (Fetterman 1985b).

RETIREMENT

The ethnographic evaluator lives a relatively fast-paced life on a project. When projects end, the ethnographic evaluator must be able to wrap up his or her work and move on. Ethnographic evaluators immerse themselves in the field like conventional ethnographers. This long-term personal involvement can make it difficult to recognize when participant-observation has ended. The ethnographic evaluator has a responsibility to his or her team, the network of coresearchers, to disengage from his or her segment of the study at the appropriate time. This often involves beginning the disengagement process before all the findings have been reported and the money is spent.

The ethnographic evaluator's talents may be needed elsewhere in the corporation. New proposals need to be written all the time, ideally before the team runs out of money, if continuity and quality are to be maintained. In addition, coresearchers often need the ethnographic information to help them interpret their own segments of the study. They cannot wait for a self-indulgent ethnographer to dawdle with the delivery of his or her findings. In some cases, retirement for the ethnographic evaluator may involve recognizing when it is time to enter a new phase of his or her career. A career change or advancement, such as making the transition from ethnographic evaluator to administrator, is a form of retirement.

LAST RITES

There is a final stage for some ethnographic educational evaluators, and that is recognizing when to leave the profession entirely. Methodological sloppiness, job burnout, and a significant shift in disciplinary interests mark the point at which it is time to shift gears and leave ethnographic pursuits to the next generation. A lack of commitment to this enterprise has devastating effects on the quality of the profession and, in turn, on how it is perceived by the outside world. In addition, ethnographic educational evaluation is a highly demanding profession personally. Conducting ethnographic evaluations places the ethnographic evaluator in a schedule in which he or she is on the road and away from home for months. The insecurity of federal funding, the pressures of proposal competition to support staff members, arguments with sponsors regarding deadlines and methodological designs, and arguments with colleagues in the process of creating a new field can take their toll. Not knowing when to completely disengage can be lethal, mentally and physically.

CONCLUSION

The promise of this new branch within anthropology and education has come to fruition in evaluation and policy settings. Ethnographic educational evaluation has addressed the needs of children ranging from the disenfranchised dropout (Fetterman 1981b) to the envied and neglected gifted child (Fetterman 1984a, in press c). Topics range from improving parental involvement (Smith and Robbins 1984) to mainstreaming the hearing impaired (Hemwall 1984). Ethnographic educational evaluation is what ethnographers do in the process of adapting ethnography to educational evaluation. Ethnographic evaluators have increased our understanding of educational issues and the processes of cultural transmission. They have broken down myths and misperceptions about anthropology—demythologizing the qualitative-quantitative dichotomy. They have offered a contextualized, nonjudgmental, holistic perspective to educational problems.

Moreover, they have been able to generate policy and programmatic recommendations for change and improvement. In the process of contributing to evaluation and policy research, ethnographic educational evaluation has been reflexive. This new hybrid has made contributions back to anthropology and education in the areas of ethics (Fetterman in press a, 1984c, 1981a), theory (Fetterman in press b; Goetz and LeCompte 1984; Pitman and Dobbert this volume; Simon this volume; Studstill this volume), methodology (Chesterfield this volume; Fetterman 1984b, 1985a; LeCompte and Goetz 1984; Maxwell et al. this volume; Messerschmidt 1984; Firestone and Herriott 1984; Goldberg 1984; Wolcott 1984), and politics (Ferrell and Compton this volume; Marotto this volume). In the process of coping and adapting to the strange new land of ethnographic educational evaluation, the ethnographic evaluator has become a part of the intellectual landscape of educational evaluation and educational anthropology, and indeed of anthropology as a whole.

NOTE

1. The perspective of federal government policymakers is clearly presented in the literature by Mulhauser (1975), Coward (1976), Holcomb (1974), Etzioni (1971), von Neuman and Morganstern (1953), March and Olsen (1976), Acland (1979), Cronbach et al. (1980b), Rich (in Weiss 1977), Elisburg (1977), Lindblom and Cohen (1979), and Baker (1975).

REFERENCES CITED

Abt, C.C.
    1979 Government Constraints on Evaluation Quality. *In* Improving Education.
        L. E. Datta and R. Perloff, eds. pp. 43-52. Beverly Hills, CA: Sage.
Acland, H.
    1979 Are Randomized Experiments the Cadillacs of Design? Policy Analysis 5:
        223-241.
Bailey, F.
    1960 Tribe, Caste, and Nation. Manchester: Manchester University Press.
Baker, K.
    1975 A New Grantsmanship. American Sociologist 10:206-219.
Barth, F.
    1963 The Role of the Entrepreneur in Social Change. Bergen: Scandinavian University Books.
    1966 Models of Social Organization. Royal Anthropological Institute of Great Britain and Ireland. Occasional Paper 23.
    1967 On the Study of Social Change. American Anthropologist 69(6):661-669.
Bee, R. L.
    1974 Patterns and Processes: An Introduction to Anthropological Strategies for the Study of Sociocultural Change. New York: Free Press.

Biderman, A. D., and L. M. Sharp
  1972 The Competitive Evaluation Research Industry. Washington, DC: Bureau of Social Science Research.
Campbell, D. T.
  1979 "Degrees of Freedom" and the Case Study. *In* Qualitative and Quantitative Methods in Evaluation Research. T. D. Cook and C. S. Reichardt, eds. Beverly Hills, CA: Sage.
Campbell, D. T., and J. C. Stanley
  1963 Experimental and Quasi-Experimental Designs for Research. Chicago: Rand McNally.
Clinton, C. A.
  1976 On Bargaining with the Devil: Contract Ethnography and Accountability in Fieldwork. Anthropology and Education Quarterly 8:25-29.
Cook, T. D., and C. S. Reichardt, eds.
  1979 Qualitative and Quantitative Methods in Evaluation Research. Beverly Hills, CA: Sage.
Coward, R.
  1976 The Involvement of Anthropologists in Contract Evaluation: The Federal Perspective. Anthropology and Education Quarterly 7:12-16.
Cronbach, L. J. et al.
  1980a Toward Reform of Program Evaluation: Aims, Methods, and Institutional Arrangements. Prepublished manuscript.
  1980b Toward Reform of Program Evaluation: Aims, Methods, and Institutional Arrangements. San Francisco: Jossey-Bass.
Elisburg, D. A.
  1977 Congressional View of Program Evaluation. *In* A Symposium on the Use of Evaluation by Federal Agencies, Vol. 1. E. Chelimsky, ed. pp. 67-70. McLean, VA: Mitre Corporation.
Erasmus, C.
  1961 Man Takes Control. Indianapolis: Bobbs-Merrill.
Etzioni, A.
  1971 Policy Research. American Sociologist 6:8-12.
Fetterman, D. M.
  1981a New Perils for the Contract Ethnographer. Anthropology and Education Quarterly 12(1):71-80.
  1981b Study of the Career Intern Program: Final Report—Task C: Program Dynamics: Structure, Function, and Interrelationships. Mountain View, CA: RMC Research Corporation.
  1982 Ibsen's Baths: Reactivity and Insensitivity (A Misapplication of the Treatment-Control Design in a National Evaluation). Educational Evaluation and Policy Analysis 4(3):261-279.
  1984a Ethnography in Educational Evaluation. Beverly Hills, CA: Sage.
  1984b Ethnography in Education Research: The Dynamics of Diffusion. *In* Ethnography in Educational Evaluation. D. M. Fetterman, ed. pp. 21-35. Beverly Hills, CA: Sage.
  1984c Guilty Knowledge, Dirty Hands, and Other Ethical Dilemmas: The Hazards of Contract Research. *In* Ethnography in Educational Evaluation. D. M. Fetterman, ed. pp. 211-236. Beverly Hills, CA: Sage.

1985a Focusing on a Cross-Cultural Lens in Evaluation. Evaluation Research Society Newsletter 9(2):1-5.

1985b The CAE Newtwork. Anthropology Newsletter 26(1):8.

in press a Conceptual Crossroads: Methods and Ethics in Ethnographic Evaluation. *In* Conflicts and Possible Solutions in the Practice of Naturalistic Evaluation. D. D. Williams, ed. San Francisco: Jossey-Bass.

in press b Ethnographic Educational Evaluation. *In* Educational Anthropology Now. G. D. Spindler, ed. New York: Academic Press.

in press c A Beacon of Excellence: Reevaluating Gifted and Talented Education Programs. Stanford, CA: Hoover Institution Press and Pergamon Press.

Firestone, W. A., and R. E. Herriott

1984 Multisite Qualitative Policy Research: Some Design and Implementation Issues. *In* Ethnography in Educational Evaluation. D. M. Fetterman, ed. pp. 63-88. Beverly Hills, CA: Sage.

Glennan, T. K.

1972 Evaluating Federal Manpower Programs: Notes and Observations. *In* Evaluating Social Programs: Theory, Practice, and Politics. P. H. Rossi and W. Williams, eds. pp. 187-220. New York: Seminar Press.

Goetz, J. P., and M. D. LeCompte

1984 Ethnography and Qualitative Design in Educational Research. New York: Academic Press.

Goldberg, H. E.

1984 Evaluation, Ethnography, and the Concept of Culture: Disadvantaged Youth in an Israeli Town. *In* Ethnography in Educational Evaluation. D. M. Fetterman, ed. pp. 153-173. Beverly Hills, CA: Sage.

Hemwall, M. K.

1984 Ethnography as Evaluation: Hearing-Impaired Students in the Mainstream. *In* Ethnography in Educational Evaluation. D. M. Fetterman, ed. pp. 133-152. Beverly Hills, CA: Sage.

Holcomb, H.

1974 Tell Congress Results of Research. Education Daily 7(4):313.

Kunkel, J.

1970 Society and Economic Growth. New York: Oxford University Press.

LeCompte, M. D., and J. P. Goetz

1984 Ethnographic Data Collection in Evaluation Research. *In* Ethnography in Educational Evaluation. D. M. Fetterman, ed. pp. 37-59. Beverly Hills, CA: Sage.

Lindblom, C. E., and D. K. Cohen

1979 Usable Knowledge. New Haven, CT: Yale University Press.

March, J. G., and J. P. Olsen

1976 Ambiguity and Choice in Organizations. Bergen: Harold Lyche.

McClelland, D., and D. Winter

1969 Motivating Economic Achievement. New York: Free Press.

Messerschmidt, D. A.

1984 Federal Bucks for Local Change: On the Ethnography of Experimental Schools. *In* Ethnography in Educational Evaluation. D. M. Fetterman, ed. pp. 89-113. Beverly Hills, CA: Sage.

Mulhauser, F.
   1975 Ethnography and Policymaking: The Case of Education. Human Organization 34:311.
Reicken, W. R. et al.
   1974 Social Experimentation: A Method for Planning and Evaluating Social Intervention. New York: Academic Press.
Smith, A. G., and A. E. Robbins
   1984 Multimethod Policy Research: A Case Study of Structure and Flexibility. *In* Ethnography in Educational Evaluation. D. M. Fetterman, ed. pp. 115-132. Beverly Hills, CA: Sage.
von Neuman, J., and O. Morganstern
   1953 The Theory of Games and Economic Behavior. 3rd. ed. Princeton, NJ: Princeton University Press.
Weiss, C. H., ed.
   1977 Using Social Research in Public Policy Making. Lexington, MA: Lexington Books.
Wolcott, H. F.
   1984 Ethnographers sans Ethnography: The Evaluation Compromise. *In* Ethnography in Educational Evaluation. D. M. Fetterman, ed. pp. 177-210. Beverly Hills, CA: Sage.

PART II

Theory

3

Theory in Education Evaluation
Or, What's Wrong with
Generic-Brand Anthropology

ELAINE L. SIMON

T he purpose of this discussion is to suggest a framework for understanding the role of theory in ethnographic evaluation and to show how making theory explicit contributes to the quality of ethnography as a tool in educational evaluation and policy research.

For the most part, the role of theory and the diverse theoretical approaches that guide ethnographic research have been minimized in representing ethnography to educational researchers. In order to introduce or explicate ethnography, its proponents have distilled the anthropological research endeavor into basic and essential features. The result has been the creation of a kind of generic definition of ethnography. This distillation was motivated by the need to define ethnography to an unfamiliar audience, and to defend it from faddism or abuse, which could endanger its future as a research approach in education (Fetterman 1982; Wolcott 1975). The generic definition I refer to here has been built up over the past decade through a number of articles that set forth minimum criteria for ethnography (Erickson 1973, 1977; Fetterman 1982; McDermott et al. 1977; Wolcott 1975).

Developing and using the generic definition has had two contradictory results. On the one hand, it has functioned as a tactic for boundary maintenance, in Barth's (1969) sense of the term. That is, members use techniques of exclusion and incorporation to maintain group identity. For example, the generic definition can be invoked when group members want to define membership requirements, such as the requirement that ethnographers have familiarity with a wide range of anthropological literature or that they have worked outside of their own culture.

As another example of boundary maintenance behavior, representatives of both research traditions have expressed pessimism about the possibility of long-lasting collaboration, pointing out ways in which traditional educational research and ethnography are simply incompatible (Everhart 1971; Herriot 1977; Mulhauser 1975; Wolcott 1975).

On the other hand, the abstractness of the generic definition has made ethnography seem like everyman's nonquantitative approach, fueling debate over whether some nonquantitative work in educational research ought to be considered ethnography. In response, a third category of research has been created, neither ethnography nor traditional educational research, but "the use of ethnographic techniques in educational research" (Fetterman 1982; Ianni 1971; Wolcott 1975). Others recognize a multidimensional continuum of ethnographicness that permits classification of an effort as more or less ethnographic (Agar 1980). Fetterman (1982), who warns that a "too liberal stance" may limit ethnography to a fad also cautions that a "strict constructionist view" may stifle the development of innovative approaches to research in education (Fetterman 1982:22). Overall, however, the generic definition is the standard.

Although advocates who have developed the generic definition in the interest of explaining ethnography to others acknowledge the importance of theory, they have downplayed theoretical divisions or incorporated their own theoretical approaches into the definition. For example, since many cognitive anthropologists have turned their attention to education, the generic definition tends to reflect a cognitive bias. Unfortunately, by glossing over the theoretical diversity, ethnographers unintentionally may have limited their influence on educational research in at least two ways. Despite the logic of the generic definition, when explicit theoretical premises are not required or revealed consistently, ethnographic work can be dismissed as irrelevant or subjective with no basis for argument. Explicit theoretical premises that guide research are the critical standards by which the validity of the work can be judged. Second, the generic definition calls for open-endedness, which contrasts with the requirements of traditional evaluation research and has earned it a prima donna image. This requirement may be overemphasized. The use of explicit theory within the ethnographic endeavor in fact can enhance the compatibility of the ethnographic approach with this aspect of the traditional educational research approach by focusing the research design. These points are discussed later in greater detail.

The discussion thus far has pointed out that, in their boundary maintenance role, ethnography's representatives have developed a definition of ethnography that does not address adequately the role of theory, and has left the approach vulnerable to abuse and attack. Furthermore, the differences between the ethnographic and traditional educational research approach have been described as incompatibilities or special considerations are seen to be necessary. I argue here that being specific about theoretical orientation can enhance the compatibility and long-term efficacy of ethnographic approaches in educational research.

THEORY IN ETHNOGRAPHIC RESEARCH

The emergent nature of problem definition in ethnographic research is one feature of ethnography that authors have included in the generic definition and used as grounds for its incompatibility with other approaches. This stands in contrast to the traditional educational research approach of hypothesis testing requiring pre-definition of problems (Agar 1980; Rist 1977; Wolcott 1975). Agar (p. 70) echoes many other field research instructors when he states,

> You can't specify the questions you're going to ask when you move into the community; you don't know how to ask questions yet. You can't define a sample; you don't know what the range of social types is and which ones are relevant to the topics you're interested in.

Agar's words reflect an ideal in anthropology based on the assumption that understanding the internal coherence of a culture setting is the aim of ethnography. In the interest of generating exhaustive and detailed ethnographies to assure such understanding, the researcher aspires to a kind of naiveté that prevents imposing frameworks that could limit the data or structure the findings. Based on this ideal, Wolcott (1975) recommends as a requirement for ethnographic research in education that funding agents give the ethnographer sufficient leeway and time to define the problems once in the field. Yet the opportunity for such open-endedness is rare in evaluation and policy research. Even though ethnographic components may be included in evaluations for their perceived descriptive advantage, there are certain questions that gave rise to the research effort in the first place and that funding agents expect to be addressed. This requirement for open-endedness, although an ideal to which ethnographers may aspire, rarely is achievable even in traditional anthropological fieldwork where funding agents or host organizations, for example, require a specified agenda.

Furthermore, it generally is accepted that the ethnographer starts with interests and questions, and that these affect what topics are pursued. For example, Kluckhohn (1952) bemoaned the lack of comparability across ethnographies, citing a study that analyzed the relative amount of space accorded different topics in community studies and found that "the proportion of space given to various topics reflects, of course, theoretical orientation and personal interests" (Kluckhohn 1952:307). Kluckhohn's recommendation was to define "universal categories of culture" that would not be ethnocentric and would "beg no needless questions" (Kluckhohn 1952:308). More recently, however, this variability across researchers has become integrated into definitions of ethnography. Drawing on the large body of knowledge and ethnological theorizing currently accessible, ethnographers consciously assume a theoretical stance and anthropology has moved into an era of reflexivity and incorporation of the ethnographer's interpretative role. Methodologists, including those who contributed to the generic definition, generally acknowledge that the ethnographer has a shaping effect on the direction of research and the questions that are asked (Agar 1980; Erickson 1973; Ianni 1971; Wolcott 1975). The notion of ethnographer-as-instrument reflects this recognition (Herriot 1977; Wolcott 1975).

It is more than the general anthropological world view that guides the ethnographer in data collection. A host of idiosyncratic factors influences the research process from start to finish—how problems are defined, what data gets collected, how data are analyzed, and what is reported. One of these factors, as Kluckhohn noted, is the ethnographer's particular theoretical orientation within anthropology or sociology. This recognition of the ethnographer-as-instrument and ethnography as a point of view informed by theory qualifies the extent to which the ethnographer can demand open-endedness. In fact, both focus and open-endedness co-exist in ethnography, with the general ethnographic world view giving rise to open-endedness while the idiosyncrasies of the setting, including the researcher's theoretical perspective, channel attention and screen information. Awareness of how explicit theoretical perspectives focus research makes it possible to specify beforehand what one is likely to explore, and what questions (in the general sense) are going to occupy the researcher in the course of fieldwork.

In insisting that ethnographers have the freedom to define problems after they get into the field, ethnography's representatives inadvertently may do more to keep ethnography out of policy research than to keep pretenders out of doing ethnography. In addition there are instances when well-meaning researchers using ethnographic approaches find themselves groping for meaning in a morass of data, their products reflecting poorly on the potential of the approach to contribute to understanding a particular issue. The generic definition is too abstract, too removed from the things ethnographers actually do and what they have said about what they do, to guide practice. Assurance that one can choose a focus in advance actually can be comforting. This is not to suggest that the generic definition is not a correct characterization of ethnography. Furthermore, its specification has been a necessary step in establishing ethnography as an approach to educational research, which has contributed to a current interest in clarifying ethnography within the broad discipline of anthropology itself.[1] The point is, the evaluation and policy research demand for focus does not necessarily contradict ethnographic method, as elements of the generic definition would suggest. The specification of a particular theoretical perspective can accommodate this demand. Furthermore, the specification of a theoretical perspective can enhance ethnography's image in the evaluation and policy research arena by demystifying the processes of data collection, analysis, and reporting.

In the remainder of this chapter, I would like to sketch a framework for the role of explicit social science theory in ethnographic research and to present as illustrations two examples from my work in evaluation and policy research.

LEVELS OF THEORY

As a basis for this discussion of theory in ethnography, I would like to establish a way of talking about the term. It generally is assumed that the theory in anthropology is the province of ethnology, the analysis of cross-cultural data. In fact, traditional ethnography was atheoretical, since it was considered to be the basis for ethnological theory building. As I have pointed out, this is an ideal, but unreachable.

For my purposes, Pelto's (1970) treatment of theory in anthropology as multileveled is useful. Pointing out that atheoretical description is not logically possible, Pelto (1970: 17) notes,

Anthropologists (and other researchers) vary a great deal in the extent to which they organize research in terms of explicit theoretical systems.

In Pelto's view, however, such research, at a minimum, is structured in terms of "a very generalized 'meta-theory' of anthropology" (Pelto 1970:18). In addition to meta-theory, Pelto describes two other levels of theory that are dependent for their specification on the identity of the ethnographer and the details of the research setting. A second level is the ethnographer's "personal theory," bias, or point of view. The third level is that of "explicit special anthropological theory." This level refers to sets of assumptions characterizing recognized theoretical systems.[2] Putting the three levels together, Pelto (1970:18) says,

All anthropological researchers structure their research in terms of the general meta-theory, plus liberal amounts of (usually unanalyzed) "personal theory," plus varying amounts of explicit special anthropological theory.

As I use it here, the term *meta-theory* refers to those aspects of the definition of ethnography that can be said to be common in the perspective and approach of ethnographers and corresponds to the generic definition that has evolved in educational ethnography.

Pelto also depicts the problems anthropologists have in communicating among themselves and with nonanthropologists in terms of these levels of theory and explains the pressure for a generic definition in an alien research territory. He points out that when anthropologists talk to each other, they argue over explicit special theory or personal theory, accepting without challenge the principles of the meta-theory. When anthropologists talk to those outside the membership, they are "often more concerned about the meta-theory of anthropology, especially those portions affecting standards of representativeness, reliability and validity of observations" (Pelto 1970: 19). Hence, the primary emphasis on meta-theory or a generic definition to outsiders.

This multilevel view of theory is useful for interpreting the methodological injunctions of ethnography's generic definition. Turning to this definition, let me identify the meta-theory represented.

META-THEORY IN EDUCATIONAL ETHNOGRAPHY

As explained above, the generic definition of ethnography for educational research corresponds to the level of meta-theory in Pelto's scheme. In order to characterize the meta-theory of educational ethnography, I have drawn from the several characterizations of ethnography in this literature. The meta-theory, specifying minimum requirements or the lowest common denominator for classifying research as ethnographic, covers three areas of concern: what an ethnography should look like, what is entailed in doing ethnography, and guiding principles.

What an Ethnography Should Look Like. Most authors agree on these points: Ethnographies should describe cultural forms and patterns, and the regularities of social behavior (Erickson 1973; Fetterman 1982; Wolcott 1975). Such regularities must be described as they naturally occur in contexts (McDermott, Gospodinoff, and Aron 1977). A good ethnography should be comprehensive and detailed, providing a rich descriptive account. These accounts should present a theory of culture, that is, the content of the ethnography should represent the researcher's theory of what culture is and how it is expressed by individuals in a social network (Erickson 1973; Frake 1969). Ethnographers may be concerned to describe aspects of human behavior, such as social organization, belief systems, ritual, and the like, although agreement does not exist as to the particular set of topics which should be included. Many would insist that ethnography should provide the reader with the viewpoint of the insider, and should make sense of a system of knowledge by that insider's view. Current thinking, expressed by Wolcott (1975), among others, is that a single ethnography is never complete, but forms part of a collection of ethnographies about the setting that will approach completeness. Agar (1982) echoes this view although with slightly different implications when he says that an ethnography is never definitive.

The Process of Doing Ethnography. Authors agree on these points: In order to get adequate contextualized detail, the ethnographer him or herself usually spends time *on the scene* over a relatively long period of time (Agar 1980; Cassell 1978; Wolcott 1975). This period can be as long as two years, although educational ethnographers have adapted to the practical requirements of contract research and have demonstrated that much shorter periods of time can be sufficient[3] (Fetterman 1982). The fieldworker acts as his or her own instrument, that is, data are collected by the ethnographer in direct interaction with informants rather than through other media such as survey forms

or standardized tests (although these can and have been used to aug-
ment or cross-check data).

The process of doing ethnography often characterized as a process
of learning to become a member of the group under study (Agar 1980;
Frake 1969). The ethnographer's role is characterized as that of a student, child, or apprentice. For this reason, ethnographers are warned
not to limit their data collection strategy to testing a limited set of
preestablished hypotheses. Rather, he or she is supposed to enter the
field setting with a guiding set of questions and be open to lines of inquiry that arise in the course of fieldwork. In so doing, the
ethnographer may be nudged in a particular direction when he or she
identifies contrasts or paradoxes in behavior and explanations, or
becomes "angry" in a personal reaction to phenomena being observed
(Agar 1982; Erickson 1973; Wolcott 1975). According to Erickson,
the ethnographer's "rage" can be important because it points to an
item of "high salience," something to be explained as sensible within
the system being studied. But even if the researcher does not run across
something that stirs anger, the job is to describe what the participants
in that setting take for granted, or, as Erickson says can be useful in
doing ethnography in one's own culture, to "make the familiar
strange" (Erickson 1973:16). In doing this, the ethnographer is applying a "cultural interpretation" based on his or her theory of culture
(Agar 1982; Fetterman 1982).

Guiding Principles for Ethnography. In order for the ethnographic
enterprise to work, there is a set of values that guide researchers and
warnings for the ethnographic researcher to heed. Without exception,
ethnographic research is to aim for holism; again, unlike the
hypothesis testing approach, the ethnographer seeks to understand
what he or she is observing from as many points of view as possible,
and takes into consideration all conceivable influences on a situation.
Ethnographers are not supposed to be concerned with predicting
behavior, but rather with understanding it in its own context.
Ethnographers should also take into consideration what is known
about human behavior in other settings. The final product should
reflect the data, so that there is a balance of explanation and data,
allowing the data to speak for themselves as much as possible.[4] The
ethnographer is advised to make his or her point of view explicit not
only in the finished ethnographic report but also in the course of doing
the fieldwork. This caution is given so that the anthropologist

understands how his or her point of view is affecting the course of fieldwork and so that he or she can make decisions about the process of inquiry (Erickson 1977).

EXPLICIT THEORY

This generic definition of educational ethnography, or its meta-theory, drawn from the work of its major representatives, underlies all ethnographic research, but, in itself, is not sufficient to guide a research effort. The reports that ethnographers produce inevitably will differ in many ways other than in terms of subject matter. In fact, this is considered one of ethnography's unique, and sometimes problematic, features (Agar 1982). As Agar points out, no two ethnographies come out alike because of various influences on the ethnographer. The divergence occurs at the levels of personal and explicit special anthropological theory.

Pelto characterizes personal theory as the researcher's implicit set of assumptions that forms his or her biases, determines the sort of data most likely to be attended to, and so on. For Pelto, personal theory usually goes "unanalyzed" (Pelto 1970:18). In Agar's (1980) scheme, personal theory would be a function of one's past experiences, one's own culture, and the like. Since it is tacit, or implicit, it is difficult for the ethnographer to have access to it, its influence may not reveal itself until fieldwork and analysis has begun, but understanding is possible when assumptions are questioned or pointed out. Presumably, part of ethnographers' training is to understand something about *how* they know what they know, so that personal biases can be brought to conscious awareness. Although it is an interesting discussion, I do not concern myself with personal theory here.

The third level of theory, Pelto's explicit special anthropological theory, is the level of theory exemplified by such systems of thought as cognitive, interactionist, evolutionist, materialist, symbolic or structural anthropology. In 1970, Pelto listed nine separate theoretical viewpoints. The number of identifiable specific theoretical perspectives has certainly expanded or changed since then as new versions and combinations of old theoretical viewpoints have arisen from the cross-fertilization of philosophical and practical traditions within anthropology and sociology. The choice of explicit special theory further defines what the ethnography will look like, and focuses the researcher's inquiry beyond the degree possible based on meta-theory alone. Pelto's view is that researchers use varying amounts of explicit special theory; many authors argue it is impossible or ill-advised to do ethnography without such theory (Berreman 1968; Erickson 1977; Frake 1969; Ianni 1971). One's particular choice of explicit special anthropological theory is influenced by a variety of factors, including one's training, the nature of the audience to be addressed, and the particular problem introduced by the group under study.[5]

By focusing on meta-theory, the development of educational ethnography probably has been of service to anthropology as a whole. As Pelto pointed out ten years ago, anthropologists usually left meta-theory unacknowledged, fueling theoretical debate. In ethnographic evaluation and policy research, however, specification of explicit theory has been notably absent despite its recognized importance in focusing inquiry. Explicit theory determines the problems fieldworkers address and how, as well as contributing to what the ethnography will look like in the end. Although the ethnographic enterprise values open-endedness, an ethnographer's choice of explicit theory influences significantly the research process. Rather than muddle the identity of ethnography in educational research, specification of theory and the use of theory can make the approach more responsive to the demands for a focused research design, and, at the same time, supply the basis for verification of findings. Erickson calls this furnishing "guidelines for the falsification of data" (Erickson 1973:14). In a more positive vein, a central theme of Birdwhistell's (1977) methodological advice is that the data and how you got it must be retrievable and documentable or you are not doing science.

Next I want to explain *how* explicit special theory influences the research process in ethnography, and to do this I draw on a framework developed by Agar (1982) in an article in which he sought to establish an ethnographic language.

THEORY AS A FOCUSING MECHANISM

In a recent article, Agar (1982) reconciles open-endedness and focus in ethnography. He introduces a set of terms for talking about the experience of ethnographic research and at the same time explores the mechanism by which one's theoretical orientation affects the course of research. Agar uses the term "tradition" to subsume all three levels of theory, although any one level can be separated out for consideration. Essentially, Agar sees ethnography as the encounter of two traditions, that of the group being studied and that of the ethnographer. In the encounter, the differences that exist between the two traditions appear when something does not make sense and a "breakdown" occurs. Agar characterizes the ethnographic endeavor as a process by which these breakdowns are resolved, and a coherence is achieved. That is, the ethnographer accounts for what had been perceived as a breakdown, making sense of it such that the expectations available in the ethnographer's tradition accommodate it. Agar (1982:787) characterizes this process in the following manner,

> Ethnographic coherence, in short, occurs when an initial breakdown is resolved by changing the knowledge in our tradition so that the breakdown is newly seen as an expression of some part of a plan (where a plan refers to the combination of interests/goals and knowledge structures characteristic of the group members being observed). [Words in parentheses are mine.]

As an example of a breakdown, Agar uses an incident from his own fieldwork experience in South India. In a lunch prepared for him to eat on a trip to visit another village, the cook placed a small lump of charcoal before wrapping the package. Agar was unable to understand why the charcoal was there. Later, he learned that the charcoal had to do with repelling spirits on a trip during a time when spirits were believed to be particularly active. As he points out, he could not make sense of the act within his own tradition. He notes that had he been attuned to the importance of the spirit world, he may have been better prepared for the encounter.

The process of resolution, for Agar, involves application of the knowledge in one's own tradition, or one's *schema,* to the phenomenon being observed, which Agar calls a *strip.* He defines a strip as, "any bounded phenomenon against which ethnographers test their understanding of the group" (Agar 1982:789). The observer's schema is modified and reapplied to the strip until the breakdown is resolved and coherence is achieved. In the example Agar gives and cited above, the role of the spirit world in this setting is applied and resolves the breakdown.

The notion of a breakdown, as Agar expands it, is useful in discussing the role of theory in ethnography and will help to illustrate how theory affected the research design in the examples from my work I give below. Agar distinguishes kinds of breakdowns on two bases. The first basis is intentionality. Some breakdowns are occasioned, that is, they come up unexpectedly in the course of fieldwork. Others are mandated breakdowns, and are those which, in Agar's terms, "one sets out to create" (Agar 1982:787). A major determinant of what the ethnographer will expect or mandate as a breakdown is a function of explicit special anthropological theory. Agar, trained as a cognitive anthropologist, explains that he enters a field situation expecting to focus on meaning and knowledge structures. This will affect what he does and the questions he asks. In addition, he will experience occasioned breakdowns in the course of inquiry like the charcoal incident. In these cases, explicit theory, or the researcher's current explanation of the setting derived from the application of explicit theory, may be applied to resolve these breakdowns.

The role of explicit theory in ethnography, then, is to provide the researcher with a basis for mandating breakdowns, or determining, given a particular set of questions and propositions, what is important to question as well as to aid in resolving occasioned breakdowns. In Agar's terms "mandated breakdowns allow for a stance that encourages questioning one's understanding of situations as a general principle" (Agar 1982:788). Of particular relevance for evaluation research is the statement that follows, "Such a stance is particularly important when working in one's own culture" (Agar 1982:788).

The second way he distinguishes among kinds of breakdowns is on the basis of their importance to the ethnographer's work. Importance is determined in various ways, including time limitations, interest, and the comprehensiveness of the study. Core breakdowns become the focus of an ethnographer's work. Less important breakdowns are called derivative, and these may be mentioned in passing or omitted from consideration completely.

Agar's distinctions give the ethnographer a way of talking about what he or she has done in fieldwork, as well as a framework for focusing before fieldwork begins, as it goes on, and afterward during analysis and write up. The ethnographer still remains true to the principles of ethnography and the emergent nature of the process, while justifiably focusing attention, at least initially, in specific ways. What Agar describes as the process of ethnography is not so much a recommendation for how to do ethnography, as it is a detailed articulation of what ethnographers really do. By Agar's scheme, a fairly explicit and defensible research design can be set out at the beginning of the research process. Taking into consideration the problem to be addressed, and the audience of the report, the ethnographer selects an appropriate theoretical perspective. The theoretical perspective guides the ethnographer in specifying what phenomena will be considered the basis of mandated, core breakdowns. At the same time, the agreed upon emergent nature of ethnographic research can hold and be explained. In Agar's (1982:788) terms,

> It is one of the special strengths of ethnography that a breakdown that was originally mandated disappears or becomes derivative, while something that came up serendipitously as an occasioned breakdown moves to center and becomes core.

Below I offer two examples from my own work in ethnographic evaluation and policy research which illustrates these notions. The first is a study of the process of implementing an educational innovation. The second is a study designed to suggest to career education and training program planners how to get graduates jobs in private sector settings.

IMPLEMENTATION OF A SCHOOL INNOVATION

The first example demonstrating the role of theory in policy research is a study of the implementation of a school innovation project. The Junior High School Network Project was to introduce a new system of school management and decision making in which principals would share authority as teachers participated in planning for the school as a whole. The approach was an adaptation for schools of "management by objectives," a system of accountability and incentive developed originally for use in business. A teacher center in a large urban school district was funded to carry out the project in three schools. In the three-year funding period, the project had its failures, but when formal funding ended, school personnel were generally positive about their participation. Evidence from the ethnographic study suggested, however, that the planning system had not become institutionalized in the schools and probably would not be fully in use the following year.

This project was one of nine funded by the National Institute of Education (NIE) to serve as the basis of a study of the innovation process in schools.[6] The study design called for site researchers to conduct field research at each site and prepare case studies that would explain how innovation and problem solving occurs in schools. The series of case studies would form the basis for recommendations for effective technical assistance strategies.

The experience of NIE and the research group funded to oversee the study demonstrates the inadequacy of meta-theory alone to guide ethnographic research. NIE and the study's directors forwarded the meta-theory of ethnography, but they encountered serious problems in obtaining satisfactory ethnographic case studies from many of the nine site researchers. Research supervisors stressed one aspect of the generic definition in particular, Glaser and Strauss' guidlines in *The Discovery of Grounded Theory* (1967) that everything is data and it is important not to focus data collection too quickly. The Director of Research exhorted site researchers to collect as much information about as many different aspects of their projects as possible. When researchers' field notes reported about the project implementers, supervisors encouraged them to switch gears and get into the schools or attend city political events with the rationale that these data might offer crucial insights. While the supervisors' interpretation of Glaser and Strauss fits the meta-theory of anthropology, site researchers found it difficult to structure the data for later analysis and write up without explicit theory as a guide to define the boundaries of what to look at and to focus on particular avenues of investigation. Many of the case study drafts lacked focus and few presented analysis.

Aside from idiosyncracies of site and researcher, from my perspective as a consultant called in to complete research and write a case study for one site, the problem stemmed from the fact that the meta-theory alone, communicated to nonanthropologically trained researchers, resulted in too diffuse a data collection strategy and a concommitant lack of a basis for analysis. Essentially, many of the site researchers lacked the means to determine what ought to be mandated breakdowns, and the criteria to classify breakdowns as core or derivative. By avoiding focus, they ended up with more data than they could handle and no analytic framework. Most of the case study drafts were lengthy chronological accounts of events. Although exhaustive in chronicling events, these drafts did not provide the reader a clear idea of what the project actually was about or an explanation for what happened.

The original site researcher for the Junior High School Network Project was unable even to produce an early draft of the case study, and I was hired in the hope of salvaging the site and fulfilling contractual obligations to produce a case study. I had access to the data collected by the first site researcher, and I was supposed to incorporate the latest events and write an acceptable case study.

In my view, the case study needed to describe the project, offer a framework for seeing the events, and suggest an explanation for what happened. The challenge was to determine what would constitute an ethnography in the face of several constraints. First, the case study had to address NIE's interest in the innovation process in schools, and, specifically, the question of what constituted a capacity for problem solving. Second, the Junior High School Network Project was a developing project. Project implementers were refining it and school staff were learning about it as the research went on. Finally, the project structure was diffuse. There was one project staff member, employed by the teacher center, who worked with staff in three school sites in a variety of settings and for a variety of purposes. Life in the schools went on around the project. These characteristics of the setting required that the researcher select some criteria to structure the research process.

Such a task differed from ethnography conducted within a bounded social group and capturing the "ethnographic present." For one thing, a project does not constitute an unambiguously defined social group, but rather requires that the researcher select criteria on which to base boundaries.[7] Second, because the study was to examine innovation, it demanded a framework that would accommodate ideas in process and learning.

In order to draw final boundaries for this particular case, I turned to explicit special theory in cognitive and interactional anthropology. Theory in cognitive anthropology suggests that what an ethnographer needs to describe is the knowledge participants would have to have in order to act appropriately as members of the group (Frake 1969; Goodenough 1964). In this case, to characterize the project ethnographically, I would have to describe the knowledge teacher center and school staff would have to act appropriately as project participants. Consequently, I defined the immediate boundaries as including all participants in activities prompted by the existence of the project. Although I considered the influence of external factors and players, they did not contribute to the ongoing "culture" of the innovation project the participants knew. By my approach, the culture of the innovation is defined as the understanding members came to have and act in terms of when participating in project activities.[8] I did not *expect* these same school staff to display the innovation project's cultural expectations in the larger context of the school culture. In fact, whether they did so was one of my mandated breakdowns, as I will discuss below.

In describing *how* project participants come to have the knowledge the ethnographer can describe, I had to address the problem of observing and accounting for processes of change. I wanted to see *how* members came to acquire their knowledge, and I also wanted to see what effect their new knowledge had on their ongoing behavior in the school setting. For this aspect of the research, I turned to several interrelated theoretical perspectives in anthropology, sociology, and psychology. I drew from recent work in cognitive anthropology which focuses on the interaction of cognitive and situational features; ethnomethodology and theories growing out of interpretive philosophies, including interaction analysis, discourse analysis, and communication theories; and some views on social learning (Bateson 1972; Cicourel n.d.; Corsaro 1981; Howard 1982; McDermott and Roth 1978). Taken together, these theoretical perspectives lead one to see how members in social groups work together to construct the social reality of the setting through their interaction. In interaction, members apply interpretive procedures in their observations of expressive acts (language and postural and nonverbal communication). They select an appropriate response, which itself forms part of the information others have to process by the same procedures. In this way, it is possible to see social reality as constantly up for grabs, constantly being recreated. These theorists closely examine human interaction in order to see the patterns and communicative mechanisms that give rise to cultural knowledge (Erickson and Mohatt 1982; McDermott and Roth 1978). In this view, culture consists of kinds of interaction settings or situations within which certain behaviors and the knowledge that generates them are appropriate (Howard 1982). Culture change would involve a change in the frequency of kinds of situations.

Applying this framework to a school change project, where the change agent seeks to bring participants to know the innovative idea and to act in terms of it, a change strategy can be seen as the assemblage of interaction settings the change agent provides for participants. By this theoretical perspective, then, the strips on which I chose to focus were interaction settings that included project participants. Members' expectations of each other (the knowledge they needed) and the details of how they communicate this knowledge to each other were mandated as breakdowns. I applied this scheme to making sense and sorting the data already collected and to my own collection and analysis of data.

Using the framework sketched above, I identified 95 interaction settings in the data, which consisted of a variety of meetings distinguished by purpose and by who participated.[9] (Simon 1983). These were the strips I analyzed. Through the analysis of these settings and the verbal exchanges of participants, I was able to describe the innovative idea or ideal culture of the innovation as it actually was implemented rather than as intended (the official project).

The intention of the Junior High School Network Project was to change traditional school social organization. Depicted in both the anthropology and education literature, traditional school social organization can be described in terms of the roles of teachers and principals. In their traditional roles, teachers cling to classroom walls as the boundaries of their power. Principals, while they fulfill required planning duties, such as filling out budget forms, actually operate regarding major school issues on a crisis basis. They maintain their images as final authorities and ultimate decision makers by limiting information flow and by keeping constituents away from each other (Gittell 1967; Sarason, 1971; Smith and Keith 1971; Spindler 1963; Wolcott 1977). Full participation in Junior High School Network activities would constitute a radically different social organization. Teachers would act as managers outside as well as inside their classrooms, assuming responsibility for schoolwide issues. Principals would act as planners and decision sharers.

I described the change agent's strategy as a process of change that occurred through her structuring of interaction settings to communicate the idea of the innovation. I identified two ways in which the strategy of implementation worked to communicate the innovative idea: through language use and through participation structures. Under the category of language use, participants communicated about the innovative idea in three ways: telling about roles, holding each other accountable for appropriate behavior, and staging demonstrations of their understanding. Through "participation structures" (Philips 1972) new role expectations implicit in the structure of interaction settings provided by the change strategy communicated the innovative idea.

Regarding the issue of the project's ultimate success, this framework helped to explain why, even though the change agent succeeded in conveying the idea of the project to interested participants, roles reverted back to the traditional pattern when funding ended and the change agent was no longer on the scene. Putting the project in the larger context of ongoing school life, one must consider the total array of interaction settings in which school staff participate. Those requiring them to act in the innovative roles the project required were only a small proportion of the total. Further, although the project was funded for three years, it was only fully operational for about one year. As a result, the role lessons the project offered over one year barely could counter the social role knowledge teachers and principals had acquired over many previous years as well as the reinforcement of traditional roles they experienced daily.

Viewing a change strategy as a collection of interaction settings structuring behavior was useful for making suggestions about effective change in schools that go beyond jargon (i.e., mutual adaptation, starting where the participants are) to behavioral operationalization of such notions.

YOUTH EMPLOYMENT

The second example of the use of theory to focus ethnographic research method and analysis was a study to examine how youth employment and training programs might address employers' biases in hiring and the usefulness of existing public incentives in overcoming barriers at the hiring gate. This study was conducted under the auspices of the Philadelphia Private Industry Council, a public agency set up to encourage the involvement of the private sector in public employment and training programs, and funded by Public Private Ventures, a nonprofit research and demonstration organization interested in issues related to youth employment. Both the funding agency and the Private Industry Council had extensive ties to business and it was expected that these relationships would be called upon to enlist participants for the project and to maximize sensitivity to a business point of view. A business association agreed to serve as advisors and to enlist its membership as interviewees for the study phase of the project.

This study was called for because of evidence that youth unemployment persisted even for those youth who participated in programs that gave them job training and work experience. The intention was to examine factors that might account for youth unemployment on the business side: the structure of the work force, access to entry-level jobs, the hiring requirements of certain industries and occupations, employers' awareness and attitudes toward public incentives, and employers' perceptions of youth as employees.

The only existing studies of youth unemployment that attended to business factors were surveys that asked employers to report their attitudes and preferences in hiring, including attitudes toward youth.

There were no investigations of how business factors worked to affect the hiring of youth that sought to understand the details of the hiring process, the criteria employers used and how these criteria were applied in real hiring situations.

We proposed to focus on employer decision making in hiring, and our proposal reflected an invocation of the meta-theory of anthropology. That is, we suggested using an interview guide and open-ended questions that would allow us to be exploratory in our approach, to understand the insider's point of view, to describe cultural and social forms and patterns, and to locate these activities in their contexts. (We would have done these things regardless of the specific issue involved.) We also were influenced by an explicit special theory in anthropology with which we were familiar and which we saw as useful in this situation. The study of decision making in anthropology has been undertaken by a number of theorists working also in the more general areas of cognitive anthropology, characterized by Quinn (1971) as "an approach to ethnographic description in terms of native cognition" (Quinn 1971:5). Decision making is one aspect of cognition that has been studied extensively as a means to explore cultural value systems, to explain patterns of behavior, and to understand cultural processes. Decision-making modelers adopt a view of human behavior as responsive to a complex set of meanings and values that form the basis of decision rules invoked according to situational considerations (Geoghegan n.d.; Gladwin and Gladwin n.d.; Stepick 1974). The order or pattern in society is seen as an outcome of the individual decisions societal members make, within a range of probable decisions, rather than obedience to formal rules or norms and rather than in reaction to external forces, although both of these may be influences. Decision-making theorists see behavior as highly context bound, so that choices are determined situationally and must be understood in the context of their occurrence. Using decision-making theory, it is possible to construct a model of the value system that would describe alternatives perceived, considerations affecting choice, and rewards and costs associated with various considerations.

The decision-making model seemed congenial to the study for several reasons. We argued against assuming employers considered only literal costs and benefits when making a hiring decision, especially in light of the survey research on employer attitudes which suggested employers use subjective rather than objective information in hiring decisions (National Manpower Institute 1973; National Urban League 1980). If we were to recommend to career education and training program administrators how they could convince employers to hire a youthful worker, we argued in our proposal it was first necessary to establish what subjective criteria employers used in evaluating applicants who were youth and what factors they weighed in deciding among youthful applicants and between young and older applicants. Specifically, we questioned the assumption that age itself was a consistently negative factor and wondered if other factors might outweigh youthfulness in some cases. We also were interested in employers' evaluation of public "incentives," such as tax credits, training, wage subsidies, and so on.

Much of the speculation surrounding the reasons that unemployment is so high among Black youths has to do with hypotheses about discrimination, and education and experience deficits. Without a close look at how employers evaluate candidates and what factors or situations influence their decisions, it is difficult to verify these hypotheses. Furthermore, studies of the gate-keeping function counselors perform in education led us to believe that a decision-making approach that considered features of the interaction of employers and job seekers could uncover some of the subtle and important ways in which individuals are sorted, having social consequences later identified as discrimination, stereotyping, and social class boundary maintenance. Notably, Erickson's study of gate-keeping encounters between counselors and students in high school seemed relevant for the study of employers and the hiring process (Erickson 1975; 1976).

The theoretical position suggested the general outlines of a research focus and techniques. That is, the choice of explicit special anthropological theory suggested the strips and the mandated breakdowns. We observed in as close to natural a setting as possible, actual hiring decisions, focusing on the details of the setting and the criteria employers used to judge applicants at each step in hiring. Essentially, then, we chose to "question our understanding" of the hiring process as a set of events, and how employers evaluate candidates in light of what they considered to be relevant information.

Unable directly to observe hiring as it was occurring, we used a retrospective interview approach to collecting data that, as much as possible, would simulate or have employers reconstruct actual hiring decisions. The interview guide was developed with the help of an advisory panel of employers and youth employment experts, consultants familiar with personnel practices in small business settings, and business persons with whom we field tested the questions and approach.

The interview guide followed the time-flow sequence of hiring from the point an employer first identifies an opening to the point at which they decide whether the newly hired employee will be successful on the job or not. The guide reviewed each of the procedural points in the hiring process—opening, recruitment, initial screening, hiring decision, initial training, and job performance. Employers were asked to describe what they did at each stage of the sequence, their considerations in sorting applicants and narrowing the field to the successful candidate, and how they evaluated the individual on the job. The theoretical perspective alerted us to possible contradictions between what informants say they do and what they actually do, so the guide required employers to discuss two actual examples of jobs that they recently had filled, and to refer to these actual decisions, one at a time, in the interview. In our questioning, we focused on the indices employers used to predict whether someone would be a good worker, and elicited criteria and situational constraints that affected their decisions at each point in the hiring process. We were warned that employers would be reluctant to talk about hiring decisions because of the legal implications and their desire to appear fair and objective, but employers gave us detailed information about hiring, and as they were challenged to explain real decisions, cited reasons I believe they would not have been likely to reveal in writing on a survey form regardless of the promise of anonymity. The interviews typically lasted for two to three hours.

We recruited 35 small business employers in the Philadelphia metropolitan area who represented a range of business types and sizes. These employers discussed with us a total of 61 entry-level positions in several areas reflecting the range of industry types.

Overall, we established that the hiring process is designed as an information gathering/risk reducing strategy, varying less as a function of the industry or occupational area than as a function of location in the city or suburbs. Suburban employers were more likely to recruit using ads while the urban employers used word of mouth. Second, we found employers used factors related to social identity rather than skill or other job-pertinent factors in their decision making, allowing social factors to override others in many cases. Fitting in socially with the rest of the work force or with others in a particular occupational category was a major concern of employers (Simon and Curtis 1981a, 1981b).

Our recommendations to the funding agency were based on information we obtained not only from the focus on mandated breakdowns, but also from a series of what could be considered occasioned breakdowns encountered in the course of research. For example, from the advisory group and the interviews, employers indicated that they did not focus so much on a particular category of applicant, like youth, but on the kind of job they were seeking to fill. Based on this finding, we recommended that both for our research and for program staff responsible for developing job opportunities for youth, it makes more sense to talk in terms of kinds of jobs than in terms of age. Age may be a category that concerns program administrators and researchers, but jobs was the category that made more sense to employers.

Another example of an occasioned breakdown that became important was employers' reluctance to consider actual dollar costs related to hiring. To them, the red tape of dealing with the government was perceived as a cost not worth the return in tax credits or wage subsidies. There was a general agreement among employers that no sum of money could influence them to hire someone they wouldn't hire anyway. This finding surprised the research sponsor and made it necessary to revise some of the research goals midway through the study.

Significantly for vocational educators, training alone was not a major factor in an employer's decision to hire since employers preferred on-the-job training for the entry-level jobs. On the other hand, an applicant's previous work experience and references from trusted individuals were considered indices of reliability, an important quality of the good worker.

We combined these findings to develop a "marketing tool," or brochure that graphically showed employers how hiring youth could benefit them in terms of their own values and concerns. The brochure presented career education and training programs as offering personnel services that would save employers time and money. The marketing tool was based on our ethnographic understanding of the hiring process—the way in which employers use that process to screen applicants and to maximize their chances of making a good hiring decision. It showed them how they could get the employee they wanted while substituting the efforts of others in recruitment and screening for their own. For example, recruiting by word of mouth, a process many employers saw as slow but more likely than ads to bring in acceptable candidates, was compared in time and money with recruiting from a training program whose director or job developer they trusted. In the marketing tool, financial gains were presented simply as bonuses, since our research indicated employers were not swayed by absolute dollar considerations.

Our selection of the particular theoretical framework of decision making allowed us to portray our research in the proposal in a relatively specific manner, while leaving us the leeway to respond to occasioned breakdowns. Further, we had the ammunition to argue for a refinement of the approach to reflect what we were learning about decision making. Our major findings about criteria used in hiring resulted from the resolution of the core, mandated breakdowns.

SUMMARY

In this chapter, I have sketched a framework for specifying explicit theory in ethnographic evaluation and policy research. I pointed out that, in the interest of defining ethnography for educational research, a generic definition arose that, in itself, is not sufficient to guide ethnographic research. I have intended to show that explicit theory plays a significant role in the ethnographic endeavor and that its specification permits researchers to address the up-front design requirements of typical evaluation and policy research settings. In addition, the specification of explicit theory using the framework suggested here makes ethnography a less mystical process, fostering discourse on the approach, on the analysis, and on the reliability of the research.

NOTES

1. An invited session at the 1983 American Anthropological Association meetings entitled "Ethnography by Any Other Name" included both anthropologists and sociologists in a discussion that attempted to grapple with what ethnography is and in which disciplinary arenas it fits.

2. The application of special, explicit theory to data then generates another level that is content specific—that is, theory about what is happening in a particular situation or cultural setting. Not only does explicit theory guide data collection and analysis, but the data in that setting also serve to test the validity of explicit theory. In this way, it is possible to develop hypotheses about possible new theoretical outlooks even from a

single ethnography, which can be tested or refined when applied to other ethnographic material (Birdwhistell, 1977).

3. Fetterman (1982) describes an effective ethnographic evaluation that was limited in duration. Agar (1980) considers some work of short duration can be ethnographic, though less ethnographic than work of longer duration.

4. Wolcott (1975) and McDermott et al. (1977) argue that sufficient data must be presented. Wolcott cites Kutsche's (1971:957) statement, given below.

> This reviewer takes the old fashioned view that good ethnographic facts clearly and accurately presented are likely to survive the theoretical frame of reference of the man who recorded them.

5. See Dobbert (1978) for a detailed matrix matching education problems/issues and theoretical perspectives.

6. NIE awarded the research contract jointly to two organizations, the Center for Educational Policy and Management at the University of Oregon and the Center For New Schools, a non-profit research and technical assistance group based in Chicago. The Center for New Schools had overall responsibility for carrying out contractual obligations. The research project was called the Documentation and Technical Assistance Project, or DTA, contract #400-75-0018.

7. Regarding boundaries, Erickson (1973) offers a very general guideline consonant with the meta-theory of ethnographic research, saying an ethnographer can describe "any social network forming a corporate entity in which social relationships are regulated by custom" (Erickson 1973:10). Erickson's criterion for what is ethnographcally describable allows one to make group distinctions in the absence of tangible characteristics like a classroom or school.

8. Unique to studying innovation projects ethnographically is that there exists both an ideal culture of the innovation in the change agent's head, and the real culture of the innovation project which is seen in participants' interaction. The success of the change agent's strategy can be measured, in a sense, by how similar these two cultures are. See Simon (1983) for an elaboration of these ideas.

9. These were not exhaustive of all the interactions that occurred over the course of the three-year project life, but they were representative of the range of types of interactions.

REFERENCES CITED

Agar, M.
    1980 The Professional Stranger. New York: Academic Press.
    1982 Toward an Ethnographic Language. American Anthropologist 84:779-795.
Barth, F.
    1969 Ethnic Groups and Boundaries. Boston: Little, Brown.
Bateson, G.
    1972 The Logical Categories of Learning and Communication. *In* Steps to an Ecology of Mind. pp 279-308. New York: Ballantine.
Berreman, G.
    1968 Ethnography: Method and Product. *In* Introduction to Cultural Anthropology: Essays in the Scope and Methods of the Science of Man. J. A. Clifton, ed. pp. 337-373. Boston: Houghton Mifflin.

Birdwhistell, R.
   1977 Some Discussion of Ethnography, Theory, and Method. *In* About Bateson.
        J. Brockman, ed. pp. 103-144. New York: Dutton.
Cassell, J.
   1978 A Fieldwork Manual for Studying Desegregated Schools. Washington,
        DC: National Institute of Education.
Cicourel, A.
   n.d. Three Models of Discourse Analysis: The Role of Social Structure. Manu-
        script, Department of Sociology, University of California, San Diego.
Corsaro, W. A.
   1981 Communicative Processes in Studies of Social Organization: Sociological
        Processes in Discourse Analysis. Text 1:5-63.
Dobbert, M.
   1978 Practical Anthropology: A Procedural Guide to Fieldbased Educational Re-
        search and Evaluation. Manuscript, Minneapolis, University of Minnesota.
Erickson, F.
   1973 What Makes School Ethnography "Ethnographic?" Anthropology and Edu-
        cation Quarterly 4:10-19.
   1975 Gatekeeping and the Melting Pot: Interaction in Counseling Encounters. Har-
        vard Educational Review 45:44-70.
   1976 Gatekeeping Encounters: A Social Selection Process. *In* Anthropology and
        the Public Interest. P. R. Sanday, ed. pp. 111-145. New York: Academic Press.
   1977 Some Approaches to Inquiry in School/Community Ethnography. Anthro-
        pology and Education Quarterly 8:58-69.
Erickson, F., and G. Mohatt
   1982 Cultural Organization of Participation Structures in Two Classrooms of
        Indian Students. *In* Doing the Ethnography of Schooling: Educational Anthro-
        pology in Action. G. Spindler, ed. pp 132-174. New York: Holt, Rinehart &
        Winston.
Everhart, R. B.
   1971 Ethnography and Educational Policy: Love and Marriage or Strange Bedfel-
        lows? Anthropology and Education Quarterly 7:17-25.
Fetterman, D. M.
   1982 Ethnography in Educational Research: The Dynamics of Diffusion. Educa-
        tional Researcher (March):17-29.
Frake, C.
   1969 A Structural Description of Subanum "Religious Behavior." *In* Cognitive An-
        thropology. S. A. Tyler, ed. pp 470-486. New York: Holt, Rinehart & Winston.
Geoghegan, W. H.
   n.d. Decision-making and Residence on Tagtabon Island. Manuscript, Berkeley,
        University of California.
Gittell, M.
   1967 Participants and Participation: A Study of School Policy in New York City.
        New York: Praeger.
Gladwin, C., and H. Gladwin
   n.d. Marketing Decision-Making by Cape Coast Fish Sellers: A Portfolio Model.
        Manuscript, University of California, Irvine.
Glaser, G., and A. Strauss
   1967 The Discovery of Grounded Theory. Chicago: Aldine.

Goodenough, W., ed.
    1964 Explorations in Cultural Anthropology. New York: McGraw-Hill.
Herriot, R.
    1977 Ethnographic Case Studies in Federally Funded Multi-Disciplinary Policy Re-
    search: Some Design and Implementation Issues. Anthropology and Education
    Quarterly 8:106-114.
Howard, A.
1982 Interactional Psychology: Some Implications for Psychological Anthropology.
    American Anthropologist 84:37-57.
Ianni, F.A.J.
    1971 Anthropology and Educational Research: A Report on Federal Agency Pro-
    grams, Policies, and Issues. Anthropology and Educational Quarterly 7:3-11.
Kluckhohn, C.
    1952 Universal Categories of Culture. In Anthropology Today: Selections. Sol Tax,
    ed. pp 304-320. Chicago: University of Chicago Press.
Kutsche, P.
    1971 Review of Tijerina and the Courthouse Raid, La Raza, and Chicano. Amer-
    ican Anthropologist 73:957-58.
McDermott, R.P., K. Gospodinoff, and J. Aron
    1977 Criteria for an Ethnographically Adequate Description of Concerted Activ-
    ities and their Contexts. Paper presented at a Conference on Epistemology for the
    Practicing Behavioral Scientist, Buffalo, SUNY.
McDermott, R. P., and D. Roth
    1978 The Social Organization of Behavior: Interactional Approaches. Annual Re-
    view of Anthropology 7:321-45.
Mulhauser, F.
    1975 Ethnography and Policy Making: The Case of Education. Human Organiza-
    tion 34:311-315.
National Manpower Institute
    1973 Study of Corporate Youth Employment Policies and Practices. Washington,
    DC: Author.
National Urban League
    1980 A National Survey of Employer Attitudes and Practices Toward Youth.
    Washington, DC: Author.
Pelto, P. J.
    1970 Anthropological Research: The Structure of Inquiry. New York: Harper &
    Row.
Philips, S. U.
    1972 Participant Structures and Communicative Competence: Warm Springs
    Children in Community and Classroom. In Functions of Language in the Class-
    room. C. Cazden et al., eds. pp 370-394. New York: Teachers College Press.
Quinn, N.
    1971 Decision-Making Models of Social Structure: A Critical Review. Paper Pre-
    sented at MSSB Advanced Research Seminar in Natural Decision-Making Be-
    havior, Palo Alto, CA.
Rist, R.
    1977 On the Relations Among Educational Paradigms: From Disdain to Detente.
    Anthropology and Education Quarterly 8:42-49.

Sarason, S.
   1971 The Culture of the School and the Problem of Change. Boston: Allyn &
      Bacon.
Simon, E.
   1983 The High Cost of Small Change: An Anthropological Study of Implementing
      a School Innovation Project. Ph.D dissertation, Temple University.
Simon, E., and K. Curtis
   1981a Small Business Hiring Practices and Implications for Employment and
      Training. Final Report for Public/Private Ventures Subcontract 080-33-15-104.
      Philadelphia: Philadelphia Private Industry Council.
   1981b Employers as Gatekeepers: The Social Consequences of Decision-Making in
      Hiring Practices. Paper presented at the meetings of the American Anthropolog-
      ical Association, Los Angeles.
Smith, L., and P. M. Keith
   1971 Anatomy of an Educational Innovation: An Organizational Analysis of an
      Elementary School. New York: John Wiley.
Spindler, G.
   1963 The Role of the School Administrator *In* Education and Culture: Anthropo-
      logical Approaches. G. Spindler, ed. pp 234-258. New York: Holt, Rinehart &
      Winston.
Stepick, A.
   1974 The Rationality of the Urban Poor: Ethnography and Methodology for a
      Oaxacan Value System. Ph.D. dissertation, University of California, Irvine.
Wolcott, H.
   1975 Criteria for an Ethnographic Approach to Research in Schools. Human Or-
      ganization 34:111-127.
   1977 Teachers vs. Technocrats: An Educational Innovation in Anthropological
      Perspective. Eugene: Center for Educational Policy and Management, University
      of Oregon.

4

The Use of Explicit Anthropological Theory in Educational Evaluation

A Case Study

MARY ANNE PITMAN
MARION LUNDY DOBBERT

The data presented in ethnographic evaluations differ from that of traditional evaluations in one significant way; the method by which it is obtained. In the tradition of their science, anthropologist evaluators "go to the field." However, it is possible for qualitative research, like quantitative research, to focus on methods and ignore the context in which those methods were developed and in which they are being employed. Because of this possibility, Hymes (1977) has advised that fieldwork be distinguished from ethnography, that they be viewed as different, nonsynonymous research activities (see also Fetterman 1982; Herriot 1977; and Wolcott 1975, for additional "protective" measures. See especially Simon, this volume, for a critical evaluation of all the above). Hymes's (1977) distinction between fieldwork and ethnography has two components. First, being in the field equipped only with insight and intuition would not be sufficient for ethnography. The ethnographer must also be equipped with substantial knowledge of human systems. Likewise, going to the field to collect information to be used as data in a prestructured model would also not be ethnography, for the insights of ethnographic research must be allowed to generate new or unsuspected configurations (see Pitman 1979, for further explication of this distinction).

The aim of this chapter is to provide an example of an evaluation that followed the canons of "true" ethnography as opposed to popular ethnography or fieldwork. Whereas the latter relies upon observation and interview data to produce a descriptive picture that is then used for evaluation purposes, ethnographic evaluation is founded upon anthropological theory. The authors agree with Ianni (1976) that a single theoretical framework for the application of anthropology to evaluation has not been developed. But we would assert that when anthropologists do evaluation research, they draw on their training and experience to develop theoretical and methodological approaches to specific evaluation problems. They also generate (though they do not always report) the necessary, explicit theoretical frameworks for the particular evaluation.

Using a variety of research techniques, ethnographic evaluation seeks to produce an understanding of social, material, and ideological patterns. Recommending changes in pattern configuration has been the province of the field of applied anthropology for nearly one hundred years (Clifton 1970).[1] The authors believe that "true" ethnography, both basic and applied, including ethnographic evaluation, is explicitly theory-based, meaning that it relies on theory utilization, and that it may contribute to the testing and improvement of theory. Ethnological theory about the structure and function of social groups is critical for evaluation purposes. Such theory has been derived most often from ethnographic study and in turn can be reversed and applied in new settings. A number of evaluative and applied studies have demonstrated this type of theory use: Hendricks (1975) used rites of passage theory in his study of college registration; Kleinfeld's (1979) study of an Eskimo school used linguistic theory; Schofield, in *Black and White in School* (1982), used various theories of prejudice; Robert's (1971) study for project TRUE utilized small group theory, derived originally from the ethnographic study of a workplace, to show teachers how to improve classroom learning.

This chapter reports on an evaluation of a teacher training program in a day care center. The aim is to provide an example of the process of matching theory and method with the research situation. The time alloted for this evaluation was only 10 weeks; but, as will be seen, the use of a team of researchers helped offset that time constraint. Although a traditional (i.e. Malinowskian) approach was obviously not possible, standard, legitimate, rigorous ethnographic methods were used to collect the data. In addition, the analysis and subsequent recommendations specified explicit theories, such as Turner's (1970) interpretation of rites of passage theory, Homan's (1950) small group theory, and Gearing's (1977) theory of transaction. This experience convinced the authors that although there is no single theoretical framework for anthropological evaluation, evaluation based on existing anthropological theory and method is possible, and, further, educational evaluation that is truly ethnographic cannot be conducted without relying on explicit theory. This chapter includes a description of the team process of documentation and analysis, a summary of the study, a summary of the recommendations and of the explicit theory on which they were based, and suggestions for future evaluation research.

THE EVALUATION TEAM

The research team consisted of five field investigators and a field director.[2] Project personnel had varying levels of expertise. Three investigators, including the authors, had had considerable experience in doing fieldwork. The other three were beginners with an interest in ethnographic research and evaluation. Each fieldworker had a strong interest in conducting a demonstration project, that is, an ethnographic evaluation that could be completed within contemporary time and budget constraints while still being scientifically sound and theoretically based. This demonstration project, which was to be conducted gratis, could then serve as a model for other evaluation projects. The members' specific agendas were (1) to test a procedural outline for complete ethnographic evaluations that had been devised by the field director (Dobbert 1978), (2) to identify and refine a manageable team evaluation process (Pitman 1978), and (3) to lobby for the increased use of qualitative methodology within the team members' several professions, that is, home economics education, educational administration, museum education, and social planning in government agencies.

THE CAPRICORN CHILD CARE CENTER (CCCC)

Capricorn, a child care center affiliated with a private urban college, provided year-round day care for children from approximately 80 student, staff, and faculty families in the college community. It was divided into four distinct sections, each section having a lead teacher who was responsible for staffing, coordinating activities, and communicating with parents. In addition to the lead teacher, each section had an assistant teacher who was in charge whenever the lead teacher was absent or occupied, and several part-time staff necessary to meet state and federal requirements for teacher-child ratios.

The lead teachers were answerable to the center's coordinator, who in turn reported directly to the office of the college president, the same office that provided a portion (30%) of the Center's funding, the remainder being provided by parent fees. This governance structure was established by the college's board of trustees, and their original mandate to the center was a significant factor in the initiation of this research.

THE EVALUATION AGREEMENT

The center had been serving as a field placement site for practicum students. Because the number of practicum students to be placed at the center was expected to more than double in the coming year, the staff asked for an investigation of its field placement program. Specifically, they asked for information that would enable them to maximize the role of practicum students in the general functioning of the center and to improve the training program before its expected growth occurred. Since Capricorn's mandate from the board of trustees required that it serve as a research and training resource, they were comfortable with the research team's plan to use the center as the site for a demonstration project. Thus, the research began with clear and specified goals: first, to conduct a demonstration project that would provide the members of the team with an opportunity to advocate the continued application of qualitative research methods and, second, to assess Capricorn's field placement program.

THE DOCUMENTATION PROCESS

In March 1978, the entire team met with Capricorn's coordinator. By the end of that brief introductory meeting, the staff had communicated what their interests were in relation to the study, and the team had explained how it hoped to conduct the research. Several team members drafted an outline of the proposed study which they presented at Capricorn's next weekly staff meeting—the lead teachers' and coordinator's meeting—for information and comments. The outline included the names and titles of the team members, the purpose of the study as the team saw it, a brief description of the methods that would be used, including participant observation, structured interviews and document review, and a time line for reporting both progress and conclusions.

During the following three weeks, team members engaged in three separate activities: initial site visits, literature review, and formal proposal writing. All team members made at least one preliminary visit to the child care center in order to observe, to be observed, and to become familiar with the field site. Previous similar ethnographic studies were reviewed and potentially usable field techniques were surveyed. The use of six specific methodologies was investigated and weighed—participant observation, informant interviews, ethno-science, event and network analysis, analysis of archives and memos, and systematic observation. At the same time, each team member identified and reviewed areas of explicit theory thought to be poten-tially relevant to the issues and problems of a training program at a child care center.

These early activities reflected a commitment to the natural history research process. According to Kimball (1974), the natural history or Darwinian method that is the basis of the analytic paradigm of anthropology is inherently and necessarily theoretical. It relies upon careful, minute and painstaking observation, guided by an informed theoretical/conceptual system that guides data analysis and, in turn, is tested for adequacy through the quality and utility of its performance. Consequently, as the team's initial activities were completed, attention was turned to finding useful theory to guide research. Six explicit theories most likely to provide interpretive power for the study were (1) symbolic interactionism because it looked toward the production of a depth interpretation; (2) cognitive anthropological approaches in-cluding ethnoscience for the comparative world view perspective; (3) rites of passage theory, which was clearly relevant to issues about a student practicum; (4) small group theory, which seemed likely to be productive in analyzing a microsetting such as the center; (5) Gearing's notion of old hands and new hands in transaction; and (6) role theory with its emphasis on rights, duties, and statuses. Although team members surveyed the literature in these areas and presented reports on the potential utility of each approach, they also did not close off the possibility of using additional theories and expected to continue the search for utilitarian theory as fieldwork was carried out.

At a team meeting during the fourth week of the project, members generated an exhaustive list of items thought to be essential as com-ponents of the research design if it was to address the total practicum program. Then, matching previous surveys of theory and research techniques, team members selected six specific techniques designed to produce a broadly based holistic study: A physical pattern study; a census of personnel, of formal roles, and of distribution of them throughout the center; a study of routines and schedules; observation of teachers, staff meetings, and practicum processes; interviews designed to uncover the formal structure of the Center especially as it related to the outside world; and a set of interviews with current and former practicum students recorded in their own words to permit content analysis for emic (internal, local) meanings.

Following that, a full proposal for the study was drafted. It included a statement of objectives, a rationale, and a discussion of the significance of the research. It identified some of the specific information that would be sought concerning four different aspects of the center's program—its physical patterns, formal social structure, ideological patterns, and daily behavior—and laid out the methods that would be used to study them. The proposal concluded with a schedule for data collection and a bibliography of potentially relevent sources regarding both method and theory.

The proposal was then presented to and accepted by the center staff, and data collection began in earnest.

The fieldwork was conducted primarily during the five weeks between April 24 and May 22. During that time, approximately 120 hours per person were spent on data gathering and related field analysis. Each team member was assigned, by a process of consensus, to accomplish one of five different data collection tasks. Several fieldworkers were assigned to document the physical and human settings through observations, informal discussions, and attendance at staff meetings. Another fieldworker was assigned to shadow each of the lead teachers and to note the observable daily patterns, including the kinds of work done, other activities engaged in, interactions with children, staff, and others, and communication processes used. Three members of the team were assigned to contact and interview present and former practicum students. Finally, a single investigator was assigned to contact and interview the center's coordinator and the several academic personnel who were responsible for placing and supervising the practicum students.

The interviews were planned jointly by all of the team members who would be conducting them. Separate sets of questions were developed for each of the three sets of interviews'; that is, practicum students, lead teachers, and academic personnel, but the basic subjects for investigation were held constant.

Following each experience in the field, the fieldworker summarized his or her notes, made pertinent but sparse initial analyses, and appended other comments and theoretical notes that seemed warranted or interesting. These summaries, which were copied and distributed to the full team, played an important role in our final data analysis. One of the team members, for example, was familiar with Herzberg's (1966) Motivation-Hygiene theory and applied it in field analysis. This theory, which describes the basic work needs that affect job satisfaction, later became a key factor in the team's recommendations to Capricorn's staff.

The team held weekly data review and analysis meetings in order to determine which, if any, areas needed further research and how best to accomplish it. Because this initial data analysis revealed antagonisms between practicum students and lead teachers, the team decided to conduct a second set of in-depth interviews with each of the lead teachers, focusing this time on their job responsibilities rather than on the placement program. Team members also decided to have one of their group shadow an assistant teacher as they had the lead teachers and student teachers. It was necessary to find out and document whether or not lead teachers were overworked, as team members suspected they were, thus making supervision of practicum students just one more burden, and to ascertain whether there were other personnel, assistant teachers in particular, who could, if necessary, take on more responsibility.

When the team was satisfied that it had completed enough fieldwork to proceed with a final analysis, members were divided into subteams to comb different sections of the entire body of data for the purpose of identifying and listing central patterns. Patterns were identified separately for each role in the program—lead teachers, practicum students, coordinator and placement personnel—and for each of two major analytical categories. The first involved a social anlaysis of patterns relating to statuses, activities, and values for the whole center. The second was a cognitive analysis of expressed values and belief patterns of all lead teachers, other staff, practicum students, and college staff. For example, in the category "Practicum Students' Beliefs About Expectations," every detail from the raw field notes that was clearly in that category was culled from the data and listed. Similarly, under the category "All Center Activities," the activities were listed, and a count was made of the numbers of times each was performed by any staff member, including practicum students. Tasks were then classified by types (e.g., maintenance, custodial child care, supervision of adults) and the percentage of time spent at each task by each class of staff member was indicated. Once the lists of social and cognitive patterns were complete, and there were approximately fifty

such categories across all roles, topics, and levels, each team memb.
was assigned a number of them to write up in paragraph form.[3] The
field director used the written summaries to construct a descriptive
ethnography, which in turn became the basis for the final phase of our
research, that of evaluation.

Using their knowledge of the full data base in conjunction with the
ethnography, each team member developed independently a list of
recommendations believed to be suggested by the data as it was interpreted in the light of the relevant, explicit anthropological theory that
had been reviewed earlier. These recommendations were presented
and discussed at a lengthy (eight-hour) team meeting from which
members emerged with a complete and uniform set of recommendations for the Capricorn Child Care Center Practicum Program.

SUMMARY OF FINDINGS

Although the specified research task was to document the training
of practicum students, the final report focused on the role of the lead
teachers. Indeed, it was precisely because the research task was to
document the practicum program that the focus finally was trained on
the lead teachers. It became clear to the evaluators that the lead
teachers were the focus of the practicum students' attention, that they
managed the day-to-day functioning of both the child care and practicum programs. These demands on the lead teachers' time were found
to be excessive and ultimately the cause of considerable dissatisfaction
on the part of practicum students. Because the evaluators were following the canons of "true" ethnography, they were able to go where the
data led, that is, to the role of the lead teachers rather than only going
where the research proposal directed them.

Therefore, to understand the function of the Capricorn Child Care
Center's student teaching program, one must understand thoroughly
the role and responsibilities of its lead teachers. For the practicum
students, the role of the lead teacher was critical because (1) the lead
teacher was their role model representing what they were trying to
become; (2) the lead teacher guided and evaluated them; (3) practicum
students were the responsibility of the lead teacher.

Capricorn Child Care Center functioned as a normal day care
center whose college faculty, staff, and student clients paid a weekly
fee adjusted according to income for care that occurred, essentially, at
their own work site. The college's central administration provided an

additional supplement (30% of the total operating budget), and it both provided and absorbed the cost of maintaining the center's building, parking lot, and play yard. Most of the children attended the center full-time, from about 7:30 a.m. to about 5:30 p.m. The children were cared for in separate, permanent, age-based groups, each with its own central suite of rooms or space and its own permanent staff.

The most general pattern anyone entering the center felt was that this was a good place for children: clean, quiet, safe, and interesting, with many adults all seeming to be caring and sensitive to the needs of the children. From the earliest arrival to the last departure, the children were with adults who took good care of their physical, mental, and emotional needs. Our data indicated that for each entering practicum student, the center was like a "foreign" country populated with more than one hundred strangers. First impressions of constant activity lacking reason or order began to dissipate when the students met and observed the lead teacher. However, the students quickly perceived, as we did, that their cooperating teachers would have little time for supervising student teachers.

The most important staff member to the child was the lead teacher. She was the staff person with whom the child had the most contact, who was there daily, and knew the child and parents the best. The lead teacher had contact nearly daily with the parent of each child in her group and even if this contact was very brief, information as to the important things that were going on in the child's life were communicated directly. These most often concerned matters dealing with the health of the child but also covered other aspects of the child's life. Lead teachers were responsible for everything that went on in their area—the people, the program, and equipment. The people included the children, the parents, other teachers and staff, practicum students, volunteers, and research personnel. They held two or three conferences with each child's parents per year. For children who were not working out at the center, lead teachers visited other programs and recommended new placements for that child.

Lead teachers were responsible for the curriculum, including daily scheduling of activities, setting up the room and securing necessary equipment and materials, organizing field trips, and leading activities such as singing. Lead teachers also joined in the routines for giving children care: They gave medication, took children to the toilet, dressed and undressed them, served their lunches or made their bottles, and cleaned up nosebleeds. They also kept developmental records on each child and were expected to deal with emergencies (contact parents, take child to hospital).

Lead teachers were also responsible for purchasing supplies, providing for any extraordinary maintenance of building and grounds including painting and sewing curtains, buying sand for the play yard, and making trips throughout the city to pick up supplies.

Each lead teacher also organized a weekly staff meeting for her own teaching staff, attended the weekly lead teachers' meeting with the coordinator, was on a CCCC parent/staff committee (nutrition, building, research), and served in some capacity on state or local child care policy boards. This is not a complete listing of what lead teachers did, but it does depict the range and quantity of responsibilities that they had even before the student teaching supervision was added.

Ideally, the lead teachers would have liked to spend six hours a day in child care and two hours for planning, meetings, recording, and all other duties. However, the lead teachers felt like they had two full-time jobs—one related to child care and the other administrative. As a result, they did many of their duties in the evenings and during their time off. Meetings, clean-up, and purchasing of materials often were done on evenings and Saturdays. Lead teachers reported feeling that they had so many activities they did not have time to do anything well. It was not unusual for lead teachers to get phone calls when they were at home in the evenings if there were problems in their area at the center. Thus, though they would have liked to spend six hours a day with the children, they were too harried to do so. An analysis of seven actual days indicated that time spent with children ranged from one hour, 20 minutes to six hours with a mean of four hours and 38 minutes per day.

Despite their heavy work loads, the lead teachers looked upon the CCCC as the best possible place to be employed. They felt they had a qualified and responsible staff, good aides, good children, and good child/staff ratios.[4] They liked the pay, the sick leave and vacation benefits, which were better than any other nursery school or day care center.[5] But the main reason they continued to work in child care was that they wanted to work with children at "the most crucial times in their lives" and because they wanted "to make a difference in what's going to happen in the next generation." They liked the responsibilities they had, but, nevertheless, found the total job overwhelming.

Lead teachers identified a few problems at the center including some based upon their cooperation with the College. Each trimester there were new staff, some new children, and sometimes new research teams to work with. The space also was very limited, with no place to talk to children alone or to meet with practicum students or others, or to have staff meetings. The one staff office included a desk for each lead teacher, one phone for use by all staff, and numerous miscellaneous supplies. Therefore, time often was wasted in looking around the neighborhood for a semi-empty cafe. There was no quiet place for teachers to go to work on reports without being interrupted. Often they completed such tasks at home on their own time.

It was this situation that a practicum student entered when setting out to practice teach at the center. When they arrived at the center, each practicum student saw the program from a personal perspective; it was to each something new and none knew what to expect because there had been little contact between current and former practicum students. Some asked: "How is this place organized?" "How do people, including the kids, know where to go and what to do next?" Some practicum students felt confused, isolated, and concerned that they never would learn what was expected. One measure of this feeling was the fact that one former student teacher suggested that staff wear name tags and another that staff size be decreased by hiring only full-time personnel.

As part of their training at the center, the practicum students generally were required to (1) design and direct two activities in major program areas (science, art, music, large and small muscles), (2) do an intense observation of one child, resulting in a parent conference or a summative paper, (3) do some lead teaching, usually two weeks, at the third and at the seventh and eighth weeks of the trimester, (4) take part in the ordinary routine work of diapering, toileting, feeding, and napping children. Some practicum students also were assigned to observe in the programs for the age groups where they were not practicing and were expected to attend staff meetings for their own group. The number of hours required was set up by the credit load for student teaching and most practicum students discussed this with their advisors, negotiating actual work hours with their lead teacher.

Most practicum students evaluated the center and its child care program positively. All former practicum students interviewed felt that the lead teachers were very responsible and related well with children and their needs. They had respect for the total professional competence of most of the lead teachers, but one teacher was judged by two of them as incompetent in the area of handling staff relations. In looking at the whole center, former practicum students said, "I learned to be part of a good child care program. I have some respect for the CCCC." "There is a variety among the children who attend the CCCC. The differences in background are good and help to make the center a . . . 'real situation.'" "I had many new experiences and learned to work without ideal space or equipment." This perceived "reality of the center" matched the practicum students' picture of an ideal program.

Though the students generally viewed the center favorably, their views of the practicum program were more negative. Positive comments focused mainly on the outcomes—most felt they learned much: "I guess I learned about as much as I could have in that amount of time." "I learned a great deal about young children and how to assess their needs and then meet those needs. I also became skilled at helping children express their emotions." "I learned a good deal about how to be a good lead teacher."

A major set of criticisms centered about what the practicum students unanimously felt was a lack of clarity about what was expected of them in terms of their overall performance in the practicum (academic requirements for student teaching seemed clear, however). In regard to their specific responsibilities, some students knew what they were and believed them to have been communicated as clearly as possible. Some of these included being in the job only when the lead teacher was present and planning specified, isolated activities. Others felt that responsibilities could not be specified because the staff cannot work in isolation, but must work as a team.

One practicum student had no clear idea regarding the expectations. Consequently, she spent the first few weeks "mostly finding and feeling my way," and going "where I seemed to be needed." Also, perhaps a minor but sore point, no practicum student had a clear idea about whether or when they were allowed to take breaks.

In describing their ideal practicum programs, most of the interviewees emphasized the need for clarification of expectations: State clearly the center's philosophy of child care, the roles of the staff, the role and expectations for practicum students, and the criteria and process for student evaluation; clarify issues and identify routines related to safety, health, food, naps, toileting, and staff schedules; allow practicum students to observe all areas of the center; give the practicum students a good deal of direction and see that they continue to get information about the center and its expectations as the trimester progresses.

A second major problem area was that of evaluation of the practicum student. Practicum students had a variety of experiences in evaluation during the practicum, but all received a formal oral evaluation from the lead teacher at the end of the practicum. Other evaluation came in the form of informal comments throughout the day, occasional short conferences in the staff office, a half-hour discussion every two weeks, and a daily 15 to 20 minute conference with the lead teacher. A third of the interviewees were relatively satisfied with the evaluation process, although all thought there were problems. About 20% of the practicum students were certain that concerns would be stated; the other 80% were continually unsure about their progress and would have liked more regular, formal or informal, feedback. The seriousness of this uncertainty was underlined by the fact that all the students who received negative evaluations at the end of their practicum had not expected a negative report.

When discussing an ideal training program, the students were unanimous in expressing a desire for more feedback than what they got at the center. They felt that feedback was very important, and should come from the lead teacher to the student often, even though it would mean reducing the workload that lead teachers usually have in day care. All of the students remarked that the lead teachers legitimately lacked the time for regular interaction. Nevertheless, evaluation remained a critical issue, because, as several interviewees noted, practicum students were in a vulnerable position.

A third area of expressed dissatisfaction that was brought up by two-thirds of the practicum students was a feeling of being exploited. They felt that they gave more than was returned to them. Some complained that they had to give up paying jobs to practice teach. At least half felt that student teachers should be paid. This feeling of being exploited was exacerbated by the lack of time the lead teachers had for them and by the less than satisfactory relationships with other staff experienced by half the students.

A fourth problem also stemmed from the general overload of responsibility upon the lead teachers and their consequent inability to communicate with the students. Half the practicum students said that they never got to feel at home or welcome in the center: "Isolation was a problem. The staff was never routinely introduced and I did not know their schedules." Some used phrases such as "low person on the totem pole" and "outsider" to describe their feelings. It should be noted in connection with this point that half the student teachers felt that their lead teacher did not like them.

Practicum students listed a number of other problems they had. Several mentioned conflict with the lead teachers about their philosophies of child care. Some had problems with the definition of their required hours, others felt that lead teachers did not really understand the practicum students' level of competence and/or the amount of work they actually did do. Someone complained about parking facilities. But these and other problems not reviewed here seemed to be personal problems or individual concerns and not general issues or patterns.

The evaluation team concluded, as noted above, that the core of the student teaching program centered around the relationship between each individual practicum student and a given lead teacher. In fact, the lead teachers were the most important persons in the center; it was they who gave the center order and focus and kept it running smoothly.

All the lead teachers valued the student teaching program. They felt that practicum students brought new ways and new ideas to the center, and two lead teachers used the same phrases—it was like a "shot in the arm" and helped to keep them "on their toes." Another benefit of the student teaching program was that practicum students were not counted as part of the ratio and hence became extra help—if they were good. Practicum students also were financially helpful for the center and were good for the center's relations with the college.

When evaluating the student teaching program, the lead teachers agreed with the practicum students that there were problems with communication and evaluation. But because they looked at evaluation from a different perspective, their concerns were not entirely identical to the students.

The lead teachers agreed that it was difficult to find time to meet with students because the children, the program, and parents, and their supervisory responsibilities for their staff took precedence. But the teachers seemed to feel they had done more evaluation than the students indicated receiving. Lead teachers reported that they met with practicum students every day in the youngest children's section, about two days out of every three in the next group, and once a week in the two older groups, with some evaluation taking place at these meetings. After the practicum student planned an activity, the lead teacher may have given an immediate evaluative comment, such as, "That was a good job." After the practicum students had been at the center for three or four weeks, they were given an indication as to how they were doing. This generally was written first and then discussed with the student. Any improvements that were needed were mapped out and after about two weeks another evaluative meeting was held.

Whereas the practicum students were concerned with what they saw as a lack of evaluation, the lead teachers' concerns centered around the nature of those evaluations. They felt a lack of coordination and cooperation with the program placing students with them. They received no evaluation criteria from the programs, which made them feel that their evaluations were very subjective. To help alleviate this problem, lead teachers called in other lead teachers or observers from the placement program if they felt a student was failing. They also kept records documenting the student's areas of incompetence.

The lead teachers did not view the practicum students as exploited, but they did share some basic concerns with the students about how their time should be used. Both felt that students needed time to observe and learn and should not be swallowed up into the daily routine. The lead teachers expressed their concerns mainly with regard to the proposal to begin using practicum students as part of the child-staff ratio in the coming year. All four felt uncomfortable with the idea and gave reasons: (1) It would not give the student time to assimilate before they would have to be responsible. (2) It would make less time available for planning with the student and for evaluation, because two staff members would have to be out of the room and replaced in the ratio. (3) If the student needed a lot of help, there would be less staff to free up the lead teacher to give it. (4) It would be psychologically difficult and unfair to students to permit them to make mistakes when they were actually responsible for the children. (5) During trimester breaks, there would be staffing problems. (6) The short tenure of practicum students was already a difficult enough problem for children to handle with a full permanent staff. (7) Some practicum students were not competent and were not really willing to learn. For instance, one was quoted as saying, "You don't have to explain to me what to do. I already know what I want to do." Or, another said, "Don't tell me what to do. I'll just learn from my mistakes." Sometimes people came in who thought they were experienced, even though their experiences may not have been good ones. Nevertheless, they were not willing to take suggestions.

Whereas practicum students were worrying about conforming to what was expected of them, the leader teachers did not have specific expectations. Rather, they expected good practicum students to be active, observant, and responsive to individual differences. They would have a knowledge of child development and would utilize it to be sensitive to children and their needs, to discern which children may need help. "Good" practicum students would be in tune with what was going on in the room and would discipline appropriately and consistently. "Good" students would be extremely flexible, able to handle frustrations, and would work well with other adults. They would be cooperative, open to suggestions, and have an attitude of responsibility and professional commitment toward their job, which meant, in part, not being a clock watcher and doing some extras.

Interviews conducted with placement personnel indicated that these persons valued the center as a placement for students. They labeled the center "a good option," "a model program," and a "realistic model, with realistic equipment, facilities, and even staff/child ratios." None of them viewed the center as a source of major problems; most felt that the cooperating teachers would see that their students filled the requirements for observation, lead teaching experience, and for hours worked. None felt that student complaints about the center were at a higher level than complaints about other placements.

SUMMARY OF RECOMMENDATIONS

Having completed its descriptive ethnography, the team's next task was to formulate recommendations. The evaluation team's fundamental approach to the formulation of recommendations rested upon the explicit application of relevant theory. The research team did not see itself as merely collectors of descriptive data about a particular social group, that is, as fieldworkers. Rather, they were ethnographers. As such, they could and did utilize their substantial collective knowledge of human systems and apply that knowledge even to this relatively small and focused evaluation effort. This determinedly ethnographic intent already had generated the unexpected focus on lead teachers. But the determination did not stop at this level of theory, the "meta-theory" referred to by Pelto and Pelto (1970) or what Simon (this volume) has termed "generic brand anthropology." Rather, team members returned to the theory review that had been conducted as part of the planning process and identified which of those explicit theories could illuminate and make sense of the now analyzed data.

The eventual formulation of recommendations rested upon applications of Gearing's (1977) theory regarding transactional processes in cultural transmission. In its analysis of relations between practicum students and lead teachers, the team utilized specifically Gearing's notion that maximum transfer of information from old hand to new occurs when maps, agendas, pacing, roles, and general equivalence structures are well matched. Team members further elaborated the concept of "old hand-new hand" transactions by means of Turner's (1970) notion of liminality in rites of passage. His discussion of the area of the margin or *limin* had direct application to this study of practicum students who were no longer students, having finished courses, but who were not yet professionals, since they lacked certification. As Weiss (1971) pointed out, the state of liminality is one fraught with anxiety, and rites of passage are a way of channeling anxiety so that it may be used to enhance performance and thus accomplish the process of change to a new social status. To explore the range of social interaction that may occur during liminality, at least in the CCCC setting, the evaluators utilized Homans's social theory about the processes of small group interaction (1950). They focused here on Homans's hypothesized activity-interaction-sentiment cycle, in which a positive increase in the third term functions to increase positively the other two terms. Of particular interest was the increase, decrease, and influence of positive and negative sentiment in creating good learning environments. Finally, team members utilized Herzberg's ideas to explore this process in some detail for an American occupational setting. Herzberg's research (1966) led him to conclusions similar to Homans's: that positive job satisfaction could not arise unless basic work needs first had been met. These basic needs, according to Herzberg, include factors in the job environment pertaining to policies and administration, supervision, working conditions, interpersonal relations, money, status, and security. Failure to fill these needs creates dissatisfaction that prevents all other positive aspects of a job from delivering psychological satisfaction and motivation. In analyzing lead teacher workloads, the evaluation team felt that this theory supplied critical insight. Finally, recommendations also utilized the general anthropological concepts of world view and roles and statuses.

The recommendations, summarized below, focused on seven problem areas related to the practicum program: (1) initial contact with practicum students, (2) maintenance and improvement of relations with the preschool education faculty, (3) the center's requirements and expectations for practicum students, (4) evaluation and feedback to practicum students (5) creation of a positive experience for the practicum students, (6) provision of adequate time for the lead teachers to work with students, and (7) in-service workshops for lead teachers.

The research team's recommendations were based on their findings that the center had an excellent child care program that in turn could provide a firm foundation for a practicum program. At the time, the practicum program was adequate but needed considerable work before it could become the model program the CCCC desired. The weakness of the program lay not in the center itself, nor in its personnel, but in its organization. Thus, recommendations centered around the improvement of organization and the creation of positive sentiment about and within the teacher training program.

The first set of recommendations addressed the liminal role of practicum students. Relying on Turner's (1970) interpretation of rites of passage theory to illuminate the nature of student anxiety, the research team recommended the establishment of a formal orientation for all practicum students. This would initiate them into the center and channel their anxiety toward their specific upcoming roles and tasks and thus transform it from a free-floating and potentially destructive force into a focused and thus positive force. It also was recommended that students meet formally with individual lead teachers during their first week on the job to contract with them about methods of fulfilling these requirements and expectations. It was our judgment that such formalization could further focus transition anxieties.

Next, it was recommended that the coordinator use the expected enlargement of the student program as a reason for suggesting to the college's pre-school and kindergarten program joint preparation of a handbook for student teachers. This would serve to increase communication with placement offices and thus create a positive image of the CCCC among students. Similarly, relying on Homans's and Herzberg's theories, we recommended that the center take an additional step to create positive student perceptions by distributing a handout that would provide solid information about its policies and philosophies. We determined that specific data about the CCCC's egalitarian distribution of "chores" needed to be presented to help avoid the dissatisfaction created when students felt that they were being used as mere "aides." This, in turn, set off a chain reaction of negativism through the interaction/activity/sentiment cycle. The team further recommended the development of a formal statement of performance expectations as a substitute for the heretofore informal expectations.

Again, informed by rites of passage theory and Gearing's (1977) learning theory, the team recommended that the early week of lead teaching be eliminated to create a gradual increase in responsibility and a sense of accomplishment and progress for students. The team also recommended the addition of a requirement for students—that they be required to attend area staff meetings. Relying on Homans (1950), the full report pointed out the manner in which the engendered increased interaction would lead to greater student and staff satisfaction.

To further promote this gradual progression (Gearing 1977), to pace the transition so that it would build to a climax near the end of the experience (Turner 1970) and to increase student-lead teacher interaction and positive regard (Homans 1950), regular, formal weekly evaluations were recommended with major evaluations, using a standardized form developed or adopted by the CCCC, occurring at the fifth and tenth weeks. Use of such a form was seen as a device for channeling negative evaluation tension for both student and lead teacher.

It was also our judgment that an informal structure complementary to the above recommended formal structures should be created. Specifically, we recommended that each student be given a staff mentor to orient them and provide continued friendship and support. It was recommended that assistant teachers be given this nonteaching, nonevaluative role, thus providing students with a much needed sounding board (Gearing 1977) and center point for interaction (Homans 1950).

Finally, we recommended that the formal and informal structures meet through the vehicle of an exit ceremony in the form of a formal reception at the end of the quarter where official letters of evaluation would be handed out, thus providing students with a sense of climax, closure, and accomplishment.

The second set of recommendations focused on the lead teachers and their role in the center. All the data pointed to the fact that lead teachers were overburdened. Again informed by Homans's theory, coupled with Herzberg's (1966) Motivation-Hygiene theory, the team indicated how this structuring of the workload had led to decreased interaction with practicum students. This, in turn, had increased the negative sentiment in students, a feeling that was communicated to staff and that resulted in an accelerating chain reaction of negativity. In order to reverse this process, it appeared necessary to free up the lead teachers to undertake the increased interaction and activity with practicum students that could lead to positive sentiment. It was recommended, therefore, that lead teachers shift aide schedules slightly to arrange a 45-minute lunch break and that practicum students have their work schedules arranged to fit the lead teacher's convenience.

In addition, the team recommended that a lead teacher station be established in all four classroom areas of the center so that teachers could work at the administrative portions of their jobs without having to give up supervisory responsibility or be replaced in the ratio. Also, it was suggested that some of their administrative tasks be taken over by other personnel.

The final recommendation advised holding in-service workshops for lead teachers on the topic of student supervision. It was the evaluators' conclusion that increased professional development would contribute to building a model program, would help raise center prestige in the eyes of its professional audiences, and would aid in channeling teacher anxiety about evaluation into more positive directions.

CONCLUSION

In this chapter we have sketched the distinguishing characteristics of "true" ethnography versus other kinds of fieldwork. It was pointed out that theory utilization has been characteristic of applied research in anthropology. Rather than abandoning that tradition in ethnographic evaluation research, the authors advocate an even more explicit application of specified theories in the design and conduct of evaluations. An evaluation of a child care center conducted by the authors and their colleagues was described in terms of how the research proceeded so as to be a "true" ethnography. A summary of the findings was presented followed by a summary of the recommendations. The latter emphasized the explicit theories that were used to formulate the recommendations.

It was noted that potentially useful theory was reviewed before the data were collected. This step may be even more necessary in evaluation research conducted under time constraints that are fairly new to anthropological research. Short-term fieldwork may need to depend more on prior theory formulation to get the job done than long-term research, which has the luxury of many months to allow themes and issues to emerge. Nevertheless, our short-term research, which followed the Darwinian method outlined above, had to attend to those issues and themes that *did* emerge during the course of the research: the place of lead teachers in the practicum program and the relevance of motivation theory. However, explicit theory is most crucial to the evaluation process at the stage of formulating recommendations. Recommendations are based not only on the emic concerns, issues, and realities of that particular site, but also are founded on the accumulated wisdom of the science of anthropology. Therefore, theoretical formulations inform the evaluation process at each stage. They are crucial to communication of intent at the initial, the negotiating stages. They become less central acting as a backdrop or a series of check points during data collection. They reemerge and assume a central analytic role at the stage of formulating and especially of offering a rationale for the recommendations made by the evaluator.

Though compromises certainly may be required, as Clinton (1976) has suggested, in order to produce an ethnographic evaluation, that evaluation is not necessarily antithetical to the anthropological tradition of relativism. Though judgments are made and communicated, they are deferred until the ethnography is completed. Holism and relativism continue to direct the research process until the data are in and patterns are analyzed. The data continues to be analyzed for the purpose of identifying the social, material, and ideological patterns that emerge from it.

It is at the point of making recommendations that anthropologist evaluators may have to diverge from the style of traditional anthropology, a style that has been able to assume an anthropologically informed audience. The ethnographic evaluator not only will look to the full body of anthropological theory as well as other social theory in order to formulate an understanding of observed patterns, but, as this chapter has demonstrated, that theory must be made explicit when formulating recommendations. Such explicit use of theory may go far toward demystifying the ethnographic process and outcomes and thus make the work of ethnographic evaluators accessible to educational evaluation colleagues and clients.

NOTES

1. Much of what has been learned has been summed up admirably in the works of Spicer (1959) and Goodenough (1963) and is easily available to anthropologist evaluators.

2. In addition to the authors, the project personnel who participated in the collection, analysis, and presentation of the data upon which this study is based included Gayle Anderson, Joanne Moeller, Steve Sherlock, and Rosemary Smith.

3. This large number of categories reflects the size of the data pool at the end of the data collection period. Pooled, the data collected by all team members was equivalent to the amount that a single ethnographer in an urban setting spending a minimum of twenty hours per week at the field site would have collected after thirty weeks (nearly eight months) of field work. That work would have included formal (and in the case of the lead teachers and coordinator, informant) interviews of at least three hours each with all (12) current and former practicum students, all (4) lead teachers, and all (3) academic and administrative personnel. In addition, it would have been preceded by twelve full-time (40-hour) weeks (three months) of initial site visits, gathering of census and calendar data, literature reviews, and research design.

4. The center's policy was *strictly* to observe the more stringent federal standards regarding child/staff ratios: 4 to 1 for infants, 5 to 1 for toddlers and young preschoolers, and 7 to 1 for four year olds, as compared to the 5 to 1, 7 to 1, and 10 to 1 state standards.

5. Part of the center's mission as a model day care program was to improve the status and pay of its personnel. Thus, the lead teachers were paid professional wages comparable to or greater than their counterparts among the administrative personnel in other units of the college.

REFERENCES CITED

Clifton, J. A., ed.
　1970 Applied Anthropology: Readings in the Uses of the Science of Man. Boston: Houghton Mifflin.
Clinton, C. A.
　1976 On Bargaining with the Devil: Contract Ethnography and Accountability in Fieldwork. Anthropology and Education Quarterly 7:25-28.
Dobbert, M.
　1978 Practical Anthropology: A Procedural Guide to Field-Based Educational Research and Evaluation. Manuscript, Department of Educational Policy and Administration, University of Minnesota.
Everhart, R. B.
　1976 Ethnography and Educational Policy: Love and Marriage or Strange Bedfellows? Anthropology and Education Quarterly 7:17-24.
Fetterman, D. M.
　1982 Ethnography in Educational Research: The Dynamics of Diffusion. Educational Researcher (March):17-29.
Gearing, F., and L. Sangree, eds.
　1977 Toward a General Theory of Cultural Education. The Hague: Mouton.
Goodenough, W.
　1963 Cooperation in Change. New York: Russell Sage.
Hendricks, G.
　1975 College Registration as a Ritual Process. Human Organization 34:173-181.
Herriot, R.
　1977 Ethnographic Case Studies in Federally Funded Multi-Disciplinary Policy

Research: Some Design and Implementation Issues. Anthropology and Education Quarterly 8:106-114.

Herzberg, F.
1966 Work and the Nature of Man. New York: World.

Homans, G. C.
1950 The Human Group. New York: Harcourt, Brace, Jovanovich.

Hymes, D.
1977 Qualitative/Quantitative Research Methodologies in Education: A Linguistic Perspective. Anthropology and Education Quarterly 8:165-176.

Ianni, F.A.J.
1976 Anthropology and Educational Research: A Report on Federal Agency Programs. Anthropology and Education Quarterly 7(3):3-11.

Kimball, S. T., ed.
1974 Culture and the Educative Process: An Anthropological Perspective. New York: Teachers College Press.

Kleinfield, J.
1979 Eskimo School on the Andreafsky. New York: Praeger.

Pelto, P. J., and G. H. Pelto
1970 Anthropological Research: The Structure of Inquiry. New York: Harper & Row.

Pitman, M. A.
1978 Contract Ethnography: A Team Documentation Approach to Educational Evaluation. Paper presented at the American Anthropological Association Annual Meeting, Los Angeles. (ERIC Document ED 175 751)
1979 Fieldwork or Ethnography: A Case Study in Qualitative Research. Kroeber Anthropological Society Papers 59/60:126-132.

Roberts, J. E.
1971 Scene of the Battle. Garden City, NY: Doubleday.

Schofield, J.
1982 Black and White in School. New York: Praeger.

Simon, E.
1983 Theory in Educational Evaluation, Or What Is Wrong with Generic Brand Anthropology. Paper presented at the Eleventh International Conference of Anthropological and Ethnological Sciences, Vancouver, BC.

Spicer, E.
1952 Human Problems in Technological Change. New York: Russell Sage.

Turner, V.
1970 Betwixt and Between: The Liminal Period in Rites of Passage. In Man Makes Sense, E. A. Hammel and W. A. Simmons, eds. Boston: Little, Brown.

Weiss, M. S.
1971 Rebirth in the Airborn. In Conformity and Conflict. J. Spradley and D. McCurdy, eds. Boston: Little, Brown.

Wolcott, H. F.
1975 Criteria for an Ethnographic Approach to Research in Schools. Human Organization 34:111-127.

5

Attrition in Zairian Secondary Schools
Ethnographic Evaluation and
Sociocultural Systems

JOHN D. STUDSTILL

This study seeks to demonstrate the importance of reinvigorating the notion of the cultural system within ethnographic research in industrial cultures. The goal is to point up why ethnographic research in general, and evaluation in particular, should not be defined only in terms of microethnography, of qualitative methods, of participant observation, or of dense description, but also in terms of the concept of the holistic sociocultural system of interrelated parts, that is, the culture concept. Cultural anthropology rarely has separated ethnography from ethnology but generally has sought to develop theories of both culture change and culture stability based on ethnographic typologies and comparisons. This integration is in danger of being lost in much current ethnographic research in education in industrial societies, research in which descriptive, qualitative microethnography and ethnographic evaluation is presented out of the context of holistic sociocultural systems (see Fetterman 1982, Ogbu 1981, for related critiques).

Data for this study were collected in 1972 when the author conducted a 12-month evaluation of ten secondary schools in a medium-sized city in southern Zaire. The applied purpose of the study was to determine the causes and the effects of the extremely high attrition rates that had been reported for Zaire (Studstill 1976a, 1976b). The research was designed as a community-based study that would compare variations in a number of characteristics of the ten different schools in order to note correlations between their various differences and their attrition rates, all within an ethnographic perspective of schools as institutions embedded in a sociocultural matrix. This was not an evaluation study in the restricted sense of an attempt to measure the impact of an educational innovation, but rather in the broader sense of a study designed to inform policy makers and to make suggestions of ways to decrease the high levels of student attrition. In this it was in agreement with a recent effort to redefine evaluation in this broader sense, wherein, according to Comfort (1982:126), one must "assess in a continuing process the changing economic, political, and organizational conditions" within which policies and programs operate.

SETTING OF THE STUDY

The author lived in the rural center, herein called Masomo, a city with a population of some 70,000, for the duration of the research. Close working relations were developed with teachers, students, and school administrators in all ten schools studied. The research was conducted in French. Access to the schools was facilitated by the fact that the author had taught in one of the schools for one year in 1966-1967 and was well known to several of the teachers and directors. There was ready acceptance of the researcher role by all concerned, and the purpose of the research—to investigate the causes of high student attrition—was recognized as a reasonable and useful goal. There was little difficulty in eliciting information about the origins and development of the schools of the three networks in the city—the Catholic, the Protestant, and the official (state-sponsored) systems. As the research progressed, time was made available to administer questionnaires to students during school hours. Frequent invitations were received to visit students and teachers in their homes or in one of the numerous community bars that dot the city.

In Zaire, much leisure time is spent in small bars in animated conversation while a great deal of the locally brewed beer is consumed. In these informal settings, one learns the customs and lifeways of the city, which despite its size had little industry. Rather, it was characterized by many as just a "big village." The major employers were the schools, the brewery, the railroad, and especially the various government bureaucracies centered there. Since the secondary schools of Masomo served a large rural hinterland where only village primary schools existed, many students lived with relatives or friends in the city while attending school. A fortunate minority could afford the cost of the four institutions that accepted boarding students as well as day students.

THEORY AND METHOD

Although a generally inductive stance was adopted in this research, that is, no specific hypotheses were advanced at the outset, an explicit systems-theoretic framework was nonetheless accepted. It was assumed that school systems should be studied within a total sociocultural matrix, wherein values and norms, as well as economic and social organizational factors, must be examined as they relate to student and administrative decisions. It was assumed also that evaluation of attrition rates, particularly in highly selective systems, should not be made by studying only *student* behavior and decisions but also by examining *school* policies of selection and the schools' treatment of students. In other words, a theory of research involving both deductive and inductive aspects was recognized as essential, though specific hypotheses concerning specific causal variables were developed only as the research progressed. The conclusions from this research would appear to substantiate the claim that this is a productive method of applying theory to ethnographic evaluation within a systems-theoretic perspective.

It will be noted that an assumption was made to the effect that attrition is "bad" and should be reduced. Fortunately, the research was not restricted by this assumption, so that the findings reversed this opinion; it became apparent that, paradoxically, high attrition meant more rather than fewer students were being educated and that policy makers would be unable to correct the processes bringing about high attrition without radically transforming the political economy of Zaire. To understand this paradox it is necessary to examine the internal mechanisms of the educational system. This examination, in turn, will serve as a foundation for reflections upon a broader theory of ethnographic evaluation in education.

Dropout studies in U.S. secondary schools served as a point of departure for the research in Masomo. The major research approach to attrition in the United States has been through statistical surveys of the social and psychological characteristics of so-called dropouts. This approach implies voluntary withdrawal from school and focuses attention on the student and his or her problems rather than on the school system, its cultural matrix, and the constraints these may be imposing.

Studies on comparative education take a broader perspective. Certain researchers have emphasized the notion of selectivity. Selectivity is seen as a fundamental diagnostic characteristic that is found in vary-ing degrees in all educational systems (Hopper 1971). This point of view focuses attention on the school system rather than on the in-dividual student, on the institutional structures rather than on in-dividual characteristics. In selective systems students are failed out—they do not withdraw voluntarily. The present study demon-strates that serious research must pay attention to both student and systemic factors in attrition studies.

Recently, a few researchers have begun to develop a more systemic view of the dropout phenomenon in the U.S. (Cope and Hannah 1975, Tinto 1982), but Tinto confirms that "the field of dropout research is in a state of disarray, in large measure because we have been unable to agree about what behaviors constitute an appropriate definition of dropout" (1982:3). In Zaire, the situation has changed little since a UNESCO-funded summary of worldwide research on attrition con-cluded that

> the replies as to causes of wastage reveal a rather serious situation; they
> consist mainly of opinions, impressions, rarely of ascertained facts
> based on scientific research (Brimer and Pauli 1971:111).

Certainly, no coherent policy could emerge from such explanations. Yet attrition appears to be of crucial importance to the functioning of the Zairian educational system. In the 1970s, upward of 90% of seventh-grade students failed to graduate from the twelfth grade and there is no reason to think that the rate has done anything except in-crease since population growth has outstripped the growth of schools in recent years (Hull 1979:142).

For the present study, interviews with teachers, students, and ad-ministrators were conducted in order to get insiders' views of the causes of attrition. At the same time, school statistical reports were collected, historical data on each school were compiled and an attempt was made to create a profile of each school within the total social, cultural, and historical matrix. Student, teacher, and administrator questionnaires were administered. A 10% random sample of students was surveyed. Physical plants were examined as were living arrange-ments in boarding schools. Students were asked to write life histories and other essays. Details of administrative policy concerning admis-sions, selectivity, and community relations were solicited from school directors and were observed directly. No IQ tests were administered by the schools nor the researcher, but standardized achievement test scores were available for the terminal classes of the secondary cycle, since most students sat for the entrance exams to the university system. Adequate statistics for the schools were available to determine the passing and failing rates and also those who would be excluded as opposed to those who would be required to repeat a grade.

THE THREE SCHOOL NETWORKS

Preliminary analysis of the data revealed that although the typical student characteristics associated with success in U.S. schools, namely, intelligence, social class, and motivation, appeared to be important in Zaire also, the failure rates of the different *school systems* varied independently of these factors. It was quickly apparent that radically different admission and selection policies of the several school systems actually were overriding the effects of individual student characteristics, due to the fact that admissions policies and scholastic standards varied greatly from school to school, despite the nominal unity of the national educational system.

As noted above, there are three major networks of schools—the Catholic, the Protestant, and the state-run or Official network. The Catholic, Belgian-imported system is costly (particularly the boarding schools); it is the best-furnished, has the most qualified staff, is recognized widely as having the highest standards of achievement, and attracts the best students. However, it also operates with a policy of high internal selectivity, admitting a fairly large number of students in the lower grades and then weeding them out gradually. The administrators say they believe in giving students a chance to prove themselves and do not like to rely entirely on entrance exams of primary school grades in making their selections for admission.

The Protestant network of schools, British and American in origin, are of medium quality according to general consensus and to research observations. They are well-organized but staffed by many nonnative speakers of French, which is the language of instruction. Though Zairian teachers are replacing this expatriate staff, their schools are not nearly as well equipped, as a rule, as the Catholic sector, and the turnover in foreign staff is greater than among the Catholics due to the Protestants' reliance on family missionary teachers and short-termers, rather than on celibate religious orders as the Catholics do. The Protestant schools are popular and respected though they tend to cater to a more restricted category of students from their own congregations. They are slightly less expensive than the Catholic schools. They are unique in their reliance on entrance exams to preselect a relatively small number of students who are fairly sure to pass in large numbers thereafter. Hence, they have lower attrition rates. It should be noted that both the Protestant and Catholic networks are subsidized by the state, which pays most teacher salaries, and it is thus inaccurate to speak of them as a private sector, although the Protestant network only recently has begun receiving subsidies and always has been somewhat on the fringes of the Belgian-Catholic and now Zairian-Catholic power structure. Also, the parochial systems are mainly boarding schools, whereas the official system is entirely of the day-school type in Masomo.

The Official network is the youngest of the three and dates mainly to the post-Independence period during which the government undertook rapidly to expand education outside the dominance of the churches of the colonial powers whose influence continues to be felt mainly in their control of the principal economic sectors and in their influence in the realm of knowledge, books, and schools. From the beginning, this rapid expansion policy met with little success. Inadequate funding, corruption, and civil war made a shambles of the official sector everywhere except in the major cities near the centers of power. In rural centers such as Masomo, great problems such as waiting months for salaries to arrive from Kinshasa had, by 1972, demoralized administrators and teachers alike. Conditions since that time have gotten even worse according to Hull (1978), difficult as this may seem to believe. Lack of desks, books, and even chalk was already endemic in the early 1970s in this sector. Because they are less expensive day schools and are perceived as a more "public" sector, the official schools, despite their poor quality, come under enormous public pressure for admission of more than the acceptable number of students. They are forced to admit large numbers at the lower levels. They must then fail out the vast majority of students rather rapidly, otherwise they would have no classrooms or teachers at all for the higher grades. These findings are presented in Tables 5.1 and 5.2.

To summarize, Catholic schools have the best-qualified students from the highest socioeconomic status levels; they have medium attrition rates. Understanding variations in attrition rates *within* the Catholic sector itself will require a more fine-grained analysis, which I will provide below. Protestant schools are generally of medium quality and have medium SES students, but they have low attrition. Of-

TABLE 5.1
Characteristics of Masomo Schools, 1971-1972

Network	School	Percentage Failure	Sponsor	Director	Type
Official	Athénée-Cité	52	Zaire	Zairian	Day
Official	Athénée-Base	51	Zaire	Zairian	Day
Official	Athénée-Central	38	Zaire	Belgian	Day
Protestant	Methodist High	35	United States	Zairian	1/6 Board
Catholic	Catholic Girls	30	Belgium	Belgian	1/3 Board
Catholic	Catholic Boys	30	Belgium	Belgian	Day
Catholic	Catholic Tech.	15	Belgium	Belgian	Board
Catholic	Catholic #1	13	Belgium	Belgian	Board
Protestant	English High	10	England	English	Board
Protestant	Adventist High	4	United States	American	Board

TABLE 5.2
Occupation of Fathers of Students in Masomo Schools
1971-1972

Network	Schools	Percentage High SES*	State Exam** 1971	State Exam** 1972
Protestant	English High	50	68	58
Catholic	Catholic Girls	31	–	–
Catholic	Catholic #1	30	29	37
Catholic	Catholic Boys	25	–	–
Official	Athénée-Cité	17	–	–
Protestant	Adventist High	13	–	–
Official	Athénée-Central	13	83	84
Protestant	Methodist	10	–	–
Official	Athénée-Base	7	–	–
Catholic	Catholic Tech	7	–	–

*Percentage of students' fathers who are professionals, managers, or businessmen.
**Percentage of terminal classes failing national achievement exams (only three schools had terminal, twelfth grade, classes).

ficial schools attract poorly prepared students from the lower income families, and, though generally they have the lowest standards of the three networks, they nonetheless have the highest attrition rates of all. In the last case, superficial study might lead one to attribute the high attrition to poor performance of the students, but in the related case of the Catholic sector it becomes obvious that the high internal selectivity policy tends to mask the relatively high level of the students' achievement. The difference in standards is remarked upon by numerous observers who note that many students who fail at the

Catholic schools are admitted to, and are promoted in, the official schools. Thus one must seek further for explanations of attrition that will explain rates in all three sectors.

EXPLAINING ATTRITION RATES

The conclusions thus far, focusing as they do on the policies of admission and selection, do not adequately explain attrition. The more difficult question remains: What are the reasons for the implementation of these various policies of admission and selection? It should be noted that the schools' directors did not explain high or low attrition rates by reference to their schools' policies. Just as most researchers have done, they explained school attrition in terms of student inadequacies—poor preparation, poor performance, poor motivation. Although conscious of the various policies of selection operating, they refused to admit that the setting of passing levels was a purely arbitrary decision. Students, on the other hand, noted that there were not enough classrooms and teachers to accommodate everyone. They did not recognize, however, that attrition rates within secondary school, or within any cycle, depend on the degree of preselection through tests and the degree of internal selection through gradual weeding-out, rather than on the lack of facilities. It was apparent to the researcher, the outsider, that the models of selection that were being implemented were creating particular attrition rates. The insiders' cognitive models were important, but the explanations proffered by both students and administrators were essentially inaccurate and self-serving.

Some of the explanation for the implementation of either the internal selectivity norm or the preselectivity policy has been suggested in the description of the three educational networks. To draw out the causal factors more clearly we may note three types of influence on attrition:

(1) *Cognitive models.* Admissions policies are in the first place largely imported from the country of origin of the schools, namely, Belgium, England, and the United States.

(2) *Social factors.* The admissions policies and ideals can be modified by social pressures in certain cases and under certain conditions, that is, Zairian directors and public-oriented official schools are under enormous sociopolitical demands from parents to admit more students to

schools. Foreign directors and parochial schools are isolated, at least partially, from these pressures.

(3) *Material factors.* A set of economic variables are subsumed under the notion of the supply-demand ratio for schooling—expensive schools are less in demand than inexpensive schools, and boys' schooling is more in demand than girls' schooling. (Of course one might object that these are as much social as they are economic variables, but economic payoffs appear to be at the origin of the various degrees of demand.)

Virtually all observers of education in the Third World, and in Zaire in particular, have emphasized the stupendous expansion of educational aspirations. As Coombs pointed out as early as 1968 (p. 31):

> There are different strategies an educational system can use to deal with the demand-supply gap. It can, at one extreme, throw open its doors, let everyone in who wishes.... At the opposite extreme ... there is the policy whereby everyone (if it can be afforded) is given a chance for primary education, but a severely selective process governs who goes on from there.

At independence in 1960, Zaire had one of the greatest supply-demand gaps in all of Africa. It was one of the more economically developed colonies with one of the lesser developed educational systems beyond the primary level (Young 1965:10, 94). Despite expansion, there is still a very large demand for schooling throughout Zaire relative to the supply, and this creates the overall parameters of the system within which the variations that we have described occur. Figure 5.1 sets forth the various cognitive, social, and material variables that were used to explain the level of attrition rates in various schools. This model, in fact, proved adequate to predict and explain variations in attrition rates that had occurred in several schools between 1968 and 1972 (Table 5.3).

Three schools had changes in directors that would be expected to modify their attrition rates. Adventist High replaced its African director with an American in 1971. The failure rate dropped drastically from 47 to 4% as a change in director's nationality and a change in director's norm of selectivity suggest it should. One official school, Athénée-Central, replaced its Zairian director with a Belgian in 1970 and the failure rate dropped from 51 to 37%, a change to be expected from the decrease in sensitivity to public pressure for high admissions

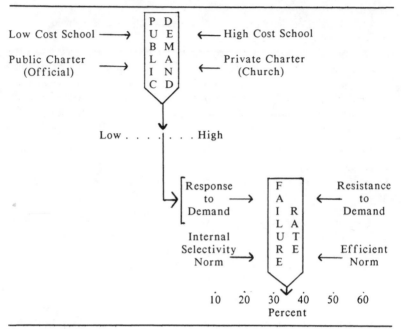

Figure 5.1 Model of Forces Generating Failure-Exclusion Rates

that a foreign director represents. In a third crucial case, the American Methodist school replaced its American director with a Zairian educated in the United States. In his first year, 1968-1969, the attrition rate was only 18%, but subsequently the rate rose and stabilized at around 35%. Interview data indicated that this director was forced to abandon efforts to create a low attrition model through selective admissions because he came into conflict with pastors and church members who favored both expanding enrollments at the lower grades and increasing internal selectivity as opposed to preselectivity.[1]

The conclusions can be summarized as follows: Schools that select students prior to admission through entrance exams (such as the English high school) create low attrition rates but tend to be viewed as elitist in orientation, insulated as they are from extreme public pressures. They tend to give a great deal of education to a few students. On the other hand, schools that admit large numbers of students and then eliminate them gradually through failure give a little education to many students and more advanced training to only a few. This explains, therefore, the original paradox—the schools with the

TABLE 5.3
Failure-Exclusion Rates in Masomo Schools,
Arranged in Descending Order for 1971-1972

Network	School	*1969-1970*	*1970-1971*	*1971-1972*
			Percentage Failure*	
Official	Athénée-Cite	37	46	52
Official	Athénée-Base	44	34	51
Official	Athénée-Central	51	37**	38
Protestant	Methodist High	35	39	35 (18 in 1968-1969)
Catholic	Catholic Boys	32	42	30
Catholic	Catholic Girls	36	38	30
Catholic	Catholic Tech.	26	24	15
Catholic	Catholic #1	20	17	13
Protestant	English High	17	11	10
Protestant	Adventist High	30	47	4***

*Does not include repeaters, transfers, or voluntary withdrawals.
**Belgian director replaced Zairian.
***American director replaced Zairian.

highest attrition rates actually educate the most students. This is a great service to public education in many ways and does not necessarily reduce the quality of the graduates of the system.

As a corollary to this conclusion, we may note that a school with higher average performance may not be producing more high-achieving students, but merely fewer low-achieving students—that is, it simply may be admitting only the cream of the crop.[2]

In Zaire and elsewhere, attempts to create more elitist systems can be masked by government and school officials as attempts to improve quality and increase "excellence." Excellence is thus defined as higher average performance, when in fact the same number of high performers may be produced in a more open and democratic system. What the elitist system achieves is the elimination of more of the lower and average achievers. This is precisely what seems to be taking place in the Zairian education system since Independence. This view is supported by the research of Hull (1979) and Verhaegen (1978). Tables 5.1 and 5.2 show that the two schools whose students did well on the college entrance exam enroll children from professional, managerial, and business-owning families at a relatively much higher rate than other schools. But even these students must still get over the hurdle of the university itself where attrition is also very high.

IMPLICATIONS FOR ETHNOGRAPHIC EVALUATION

The implications of this research can be summarized as follows: (1) qualitative and quantitative research methods are perfectly compatible with, and probably indispensable to each other; (2) insiders' emic views need the corrective lenses of outsiders' more objective observations and controlled comparisons; (3) evaluation must be founded upon adequate theories of sociocultural systems and models that integrate cognitive, social, and material variables; and (4) ethnographic evaluation must not limit itself to microethnography of classrooms, or individual learning transactions if it wishes to understand the full implications of educational policies and processes, but must pay attention to the holistic sociocultural matrix of education and learning.

The time is past when anthropologists and ethnographers need spend time justifying the use of qualitative techniques in educational evaluation (LeCompte and Goetz 1982:387). Nevertheless, some qualitative researchers oppose combining research styles and prefer statistical, densely descriptive, case studies of insiders' beliefs and cultural norms that avoid words like variable and correlation. Bogdan and Biklen (1982), for example, have again questioned the compatibility of qualitative and quantitative methods, arguing that they are based on different assumptions. But there have been at least two types of reaction against this view for some time—one by sociologists such as Rist (1977) and Madey (1982), Webb et al. (1966) Sieber (1973), Cook and Reichardt (1979), and Conner (1981), and the second by anthropologists who have refused to accept microethnography and participant observation as the only acceptable mode of research in our discipline, Pelto (1970), Dobbert (1982), and Ogbu (1974), to name a few.

This evaluation of attrition in secondary schools in Zaire was developed in order to apply the best of ethnographic insights to the description of a total community as a basis for understanding a very specific phenomenon. The research design attempted to avoid what Pelto (1970), Harris (1968) and others have perceived as a weakness in the overly subjective studies of Redfield (1930), Lewis (1960), and Mead (1928). It attempted to develop a more causal model through a comparative method on a small scale.

Systems theory provided a framework for maintaining the holistic concept of culture. But systems theory is hardly a panacea. Kenneth Boulding calls systems theory the "skeleton of science," a phrase that evokes a framework requiring supplementary theory to flesh it out (1968:3). Rapoport (1968:452-58) emphasizes its abstract, mathematical properties, and von Bertalanffy (1972:30) likes to think of it as the overarching theory that includes game theory, cybernetics, network theory, and information theory. Easton says a system is "any set of variables regardless of the degree of interrelationship among them" (1968:430). For Buckley (1967), systems theory helps in the construction of models of sociocultural reality by emphasizing the unique morphogenic and adaptive aspects of sociocultural systems in contrast to more stable mechanical systems.

In this study of attrition, systems theory led to the construction of a model of the school system wherein failure rates were the dependent variable. Through empirical observation and theoretical constructs drawn from game theory and exchange theory it was determined what the crucial cognitive, social, and material variables affecting attrition rates should be. Cognitive models of selection were identified; social status of decision makers and social demands were deemed important, and material factors related to supply and cost of education were integrated into the model.

In the process of elaborating a systems-theoretic model of culture, this research has developed a view of education, enculturation, and learning, that is more than the acquisition of an old culture. From the systems theoretic view, learning also must concern the creative process by which new knowledge is invented for more adequate sociocultural adaptations.

With this view of learning, educational anthropology under the rubric of educational evaluation could begin to play a central role in *proposals for* change, as well as in *studies of* change. A dynamic view of learning as transmission and creativity can be coupled with a systems-theoretic model of culture which includes system-maintaining, system-destroying, and system-elaborating mechanisms. In this light, the attrition rates of Zairian schools are seen as a negative feedback mechanism which serves to satisfy the high educational demands of the lower and middle classes while camouflaging the concentration of power and higher education in the hands of an elite (compare Hull 1979; Nzongolo-Ntalaja 1983).

But systems theory, as Boulding says, is only a skeleton, or meta-theory that must be fleshed out with more specific theoretical propositions concerning the relationships of cognitive, social and material variables. A theory of culture informed by systems theory recognizes structure, function, and process as the three integral and essential aspects of any system, with an added concern for systemic transformation as well. It assumes the importance of a multi-level approach in which small group processes and systems contribute to an understanding of higher levels up to the level of world-system as defined by Wallerstein (1976) and others (Laszlo 1973).

The work of John Ogbu (1974) in educational anthroplogy, which he has termed multilevel, macroethnographic and ecological, is very similar to the method that I have described in the context of the attrition study. As he points out, microethnographic evaluation of the failure of minorities in school can show *how* these students fail. Yet, these studies offer little in the way of explicating the larger forces of discrimination and economic exploitation that are at the heart of *why* they fail (Ogbu 1981:11-12). This observation is somewhat like that of Madey's in reference to experimental-statistical evaluation designs: They may show whether an intervention worked or not, but they often tell little about why it did or did not work (1982:224). Beyond this, attrition research that focuses on the student tends to identify failure exclusively as a student problem, and to ignore the systemic aspects of schooling which may have generated the failure. Such research is another example of blaming the victim and like witchcraft accusations it may mystify the victim by turning scrutiny away from the surrounding social, material, and ideological system. In particular, it may help deflect criticism from those groups that control and benefit most from the system. General theory, therefore, as indicated above, should neglect neither the individual nor the system. Microethnography must complement the study of general sociocultural patterns.

CONCLUSION

In summary and conclusion, this research has attempted to show that what is happening in the schools in Zaire is best understood through analysis of their connections in the total sociocultural matrix. High attrition rates are directly related to the emergence of a new elite (Nzongola-Ntalaja, 1983) as well as to the educational aspirations of the wider population. Although the state schools do serve some of the needs of the children of the middle and lower classes, they are essentially institutions for "cooling out" (Clark 1960) the poor. Both the high attrition and the dual track elite/popular education system are system-maintaining devices that nonetheless reveal the tenuous nature of power in this unstable nation. As one director of an Official school in Masomo put it, "If I abided by the government admissions norms, the people would be up in arms—and the politicians know it." This school had around 80 students in junior high classrooms though the official limit was 40. Zaire appears to be another exemplary case of a Third World nation whose mechanisms for the distribution of advantages to a small elite must inevitably produce continued serious conflict (Lemarchand 1979; Gran 1979).

These conclusions resulted from the combination of microethnographic research in schools and systemic research of general sociocultural patterns. Those who would deny the inextricable connection between these two and instead limit the definition of learning to individualistic, psychological issues, would run the risk of turning anthropologists' attention away from broader policy questions and from large-scale educational transformation. It is to be hoped, therefore, that ethnographic evaluators will contribute not only to microethnography of the classroom and to a more cross-cultural understanding of individual learning processes, but that they will also seek the larger picture and will thus be able to contribute to educational planning for social welfare, and to the implementation of needed change. The function of applied researchers is, therefore, not only to describe and explain but also to evaluate and help transform. It is perhaps presumptuous to think that we will have much effect on the course of policy making and of cultural transformation, but Scriven is to be applauded when he writes "evaluation research must produce as a conclusion exactly the kind of statement that social scientists have for years been taught is illegitimate: a judgment of value, worth, or merit. This is the great scientific and philosophical significance of evaluation research" (1974:4). Systems theory, though it is only a starting point, provides the most adequate meta-theory for these efforts.

NOTES

1. Details of this model of forces generating attrition rates are discussed in more detail in Studstill (1976a, 1976b).

2. This observation offers, therefore, a fundamental objection to the current, widely held belief that certain schools in the United States are of poor quality because average test scores are low on international and interstate comparisons. As some studies reveal, U.S. secondary schools are not necessarily educating fewer high achievers, but are often schooling more average achievers than the more elitist European systems. Two exceptions to this generalization, however, are Sweden and Japan, both of which have

managed to produce virtually universal graduation from secondary school as well as the highest average achievement levels in the world. Their egalitarian policies have obviously not prevented them from achieving excellence as well (Studstill 1984; Wolf 1977).

REFERENCES CITED

Bertalanffy, L. von
   1968 General System Theory—A Critical Review. *In* Modern Systems Research for the Behavioral Scientist. W. Buckley, ed. pp. 11-30. Chicago: Aldine.
   1972 The History and Status of General System Theory. *In* Trends in General Systems Theory. G. J. Klir, ed. pp. 21-41. New York: Wiley-Interscience.
Bogdan, R. C., and S. K. Biklen
   1982 Qualitative Research for Education: An Introduction to Theory and Methods. Boston: Allyn & Bacon.
Boulding, K.
   1968 General Systems Theory—The Skeleton Science. *In* Modern Systems Research for the Behavioral Scientist. W. Buckley, ed. pp. 3-10. Chicago: Aldine.
Brimer, M. A., and L. Pauli
   1971 Wastage in Education—A World Problem. Paris: UNESCO.
Buckley, W.
   1967 Sociology and Modern Systems Theory. Englewood Cliffs, NJ: Prentice-Hall.
Clark, B.
   1960 The "Cooling Out" Function in Higher Education. American Journal of Sociology 65:569-576.
Comfort, L. K.
   1982 Educational Policy and Evaluation: A Context for Change. New York: Pergamon.
Conner, R. F., ed.
   1981 Methodological Advances in Evaluation Research. Beverly Hills, CA: Sage.
Cook, T. C., and C. S. Reichardt, eds.
   1979 Qualitative and Quantitative Methods in Evaluation Research. Beverly Hills, CA: Sage.
Coombs, P. H.
   1968 The World Education Crisis: A System Approach. London: Oxford University Press.
Cope, R., and W. Hannah
   1975 Revolving College Doors: The Causes and Consequences of Dropping Out, Stopping Out, and Transferring. New York: John Wiley.
Dobbert, M. L.
   1982 Ethnographic Research: Theory and Application for Modern Schools and Societies. New York: Praeger.
Easton, D.
   1968 A Systems Analysis of Political Life. *In* Modern Systems Research for the Behavioral Scientist. W. Buckley, ed. pp. 428-436. Chicago: Aldine.
Fetterman, D. M.
   1982 Ethnography in Educational Research: The Dynamics of Diffusion. Educational Researcher 11(3):17-22.

Gran, G.
1979 An Introduction to Zaire's Permanent Development Crisis. *In* Zaire: The Political Economy of Underdevelopment. G. Gran, ed. pp. 1-25. New York: Praeger.

Harris, M.
1968 Rise of Anthropological Theory. New York: Thomas Y. Crowell.

Hopper, E. I., ed.
1971 Readings in the Theory of Educational Systems. London: Hutchinson University Library.

Hull, G.
1979 Education in Zaire: Instrument of Underdevelopment. *In* Zaire: The Political Economy of Underdevelopment. G. Gran, ed. pp. 137-158. New York: Praeger.

Laszlo, E., ed.
1973 The World System. New York: Braziller.

LeCompte, M. D., and J. P. Goetz
1982 Ethnographic Data Collection in Evaluation Research. Educational Evaluation and Policy Analysis 4(3):387-400.

Lemarchand, R.
1979 The Politics of Penury in Rural Zaire: The View from Bandundu. *In* Zaire: The Political Economy of Underdevelopment. G. Gran, ed. pp. 237-260, New York: Praeger.

Lewis, G.
1960 Tepoztlan: Village in Mexico. New York: Holt, Rinehart & Winston.

Madey, D. L.
1982 Some Benefits of Integrating Qualitative and Quantitative Methods in Program Evaluation with Illustrations. Educational Evaluation and Policy Analysis 4(2):223-236.

Mead, M.
1928 Coming of Age in Samoa. New York: William Morrow.

Nzongola-Ntalaja
1983 Class Struggle and National Liberation in Zaire. *In* Proletarianization and Class Struggle in Africa. B. Magubane and Nzongola-Ntalaja, eds. pp. 57-94. San Francisco: Synthesis.

Ogbu, J.
1974 The Next Generation. New York: Academic Press.
1981 School Ethnography: A Multilevel Approach. Anthropology and Education Quarterly 12(1):3-29.

Pelto, P. J.
1970 Anthropological Research: The Structure of Inquiry. New York: Harper and Row.

Rapoport, A.
1968 Systems Analysis: General Systems Theory. *In* Encyclopedia of the Social Sciences. D. L. Sills, ed. pp. 454-458. New York: Free Press.

Redfield, R.
1930 Tepoztlan: A Mexican Village. Chicago: University of Chicago Press.

Rist, R. C.
1977 On the Relations Among Educational Research Paradigms: From Disdain to Detente. Anthropology and Education Quarterly 8(2):42-49.

Scriven, M.
    1974 Evaluation Perspectives and Procedures. *In* Evaluation in Education: Current
        Application. W. J. Popham, ed. pp. 3-93. Berkeley, CA: McCutchan.
Sieber, S. D.
    1973 The Integration of Fieldwork and Survey Methods. American Journal of Soci-
        ology 28(6):1335-1359.
Studstill, J. D.
    1976a Student Attrition in Zaire: The System and the Game in the Secondary
        Schools of Masomo. Ph.D. dissertation, Indiana University.
    1976b Why Students Fail in Masomo. Journal of Research and Development in
        Education 9(4):124-136.
    1984 Educational Funding and Student Achievement in Japan, Sweden, and
        Georgia. Paper read at the Southern Society for Comparative and International
        Education, Georgia State University, Atlanta.
Tinto, V.
    1982 Defining Dropout: A Matter of Perspective. *In* New Directions for Institu-
        tional Research: Studying Student Attrition, No. 36. E. Pascarella, ed. pp. 3-15.
        San Francisco: Jossey-Bass.
Verhaegen, B.
    1978 L'Enseignement Universitaire au Zaire: De Lovanium a L'UNAZA 1958-
        1978. Brussels: Centre d'Etude et de Documentation Africaine.
Wallerstein, I.
    1976 The Three Stages of African Involvement in the World-Economy. *In* The
        Political Economy of Contemporary Africa. P.C.W. Gutkind and I. Wallerstein,
        eds. Beverly Hills, CA: Sage.
Webb, E. J. et al.
    1966 Unobtrusive Measures: Nonreactive Research in the Social Sciences. Chicago:
        Rand McNally.
Wolf, R. M.
    1977 Achievement in America: National Report of the United States for the Inter-
        national Education Achievement Project. New York: Teachers College Press.
Young, C.
    1965 Politics in the Congo. Princeton, NJ: Princeton University Press.

PART III

Practice

6

Combining Ethnographic and Experimental Methods in Educational Evaluation

A Case Study

JOSEPH A. MAXWELL
PHILIP G. BASHOOK
LESLIE J. SANDLOW

There has been a long-standing disagreement over the relative superiority of "quantitative" and "qualitative" research methods for the study of social phenomena; Pelto and Pelto (1978:ix) refer to this as "the central methodological debate of the 1970s." To a large extent this debate has been a confrontation between two schools of social research, each with its own paradigm for the conduct of valid inquiry. On one side are the "hard science" advocates of precisely defined variables, objective methods of data collection, and statistical analysis of results, with the controlled experiment as the ideal of rigorous research design. On the other are the proponents of "naturalistic," "humanistic," or "holistic" investigations, who emphasize inductive and phenomenological approaches and present ethnographic field investigation as a model for research. Each school has tended to portray its own paradigm as an integrated package, forcing a choice between two alternative and incompatible ways of conducting research (Reichardt and Cook 1979:9).

More recently, however, there has been a reaction against this polarization of the issue. Not only have proponents of one paradigm been more willing to recognize the merits of the other, but there have been numerous suggestions for combining the two approaches (e.g., Pelto and Pelto 1978; Campbell 1978; Reichardt and Cook 1979;

AUTHORS' NOTE: This project was supported by the National Fund for Medical Education and the Schering-Plough Foundation (Project SP/H-77).

Meyers 1981). Reichardt and Cook (1979:8) claim that seeing the problem as a choice between conflicting paradigms has obscured the real issues in the debate and created unnecessary schisms. They argue that methods are *not* necessarily linked to paradigms, and that nothing prevents the researcher from "mixing and matching" techniques to achieve the combination most appropriate to a particular research problem and setting. Meyers (1981:152-154, 170) repudiates both the conventional distinctions between qualitative and quantitative methods, and the use of the term "paradigm" to refer to these. He proposes that we speak of qualitative and quantitative *data*, instead of methods, and argues that both can easily be used in the same study.

This deemphasis of the connection between methods and paradigms has been attacked in turn by some proponents of qualitative methods. Ianni and Orr (1979), Rist (1980), and Fetterman (1982) charge that the growing interest in qualitative and ethnographic techniques by researchers who lack sufficient grounding in the conceptual framework and training underlying these techniques, has led to shallow, poorly conducted research that fails to utilize the real strengths of qualitative methods. Britan (1978) and Guba and Lincoln (1981) claim that the presuppositions of qualitative and quantitative methods make them appropriate for different goals and situations, while Smith (1983) sees the two approaches as epistemologically incompatible given our present knowledge.

We take a middle position on this debate, combining arguments from both of these perspectives. We agree with Britan and Fetterman that research methods cannot be used productively without taking account of their theoretical and methodological presuppositions, and that these presuppositions impose certain constraints on the overall research design and the combined use of different methods. However, we disagree with the claim that the presuppositions of all "quantitative" and "qualitative" methods are *necessarily* in conflict. Specifically, we argue that the two methods often considered the most "extreme" examples of quantitative and qualitative research, experimental design and ethnographic investigation, can be productively combined within a single research framework.

We are not referring simply to the parallel or sequential use of quantitative and qualitative investigations of a single social setting or program (e.g., Trend 1979; Ianni and Orr 1979; Green and Wallat 1981; Rodin, Rowitz, and Rydman 1983; Patel and Cranton 1983). Such use has gained widespread acceptance (Conner, Altman, and Jackson 1984; Whyte 1984:129-151), and can be seen as one form of "triangulation" (Webb et al. 1966; Denzin 1978; Jick 1983), in which the results of several different lines of investigation are used to mutually support one another. What we are proposing, in contrast, is an integral joining of two methods, ethnography and experimental design, that have usually been seen as polar opposites.

A similar argument for the compatibility of quantitative and qualitative approaches has been presented by Jacob (1982), whose research involved the ethnographic study of Puerto Rican children's development within the basic framework of a quantitative model. Our approach differs from Jacob's in employing an explicitly experimental design, rather than simply a quantitative one, thus combining ethnographic investigation with experimental controls. (Fetterman [in press] also describes a study combining experimental design with ethnographic investigation, but focuses on the use of ethnography to evaluate the experimental findings and the use of experimental findings to provide insights in ethnography, rather than the use of experimental controls *in* ethnography.)

This joining of the two methods can be conceptualized from the point of view of either the experimentalist or the ethnographer. From the experimentalist's perspective, our proposal resembles a standard experimental design, with an intervention, pre- and postintervention collection of data, and a variety of control conditions. However, the data are collected not by the standard quantitative techniques, but through ethnographic investigation. From the ethnographer's point of view, the design is essentially ethnographic but involves the comparison of the ethnographic results, both over time and between different groups, to assess the impact of a particular intervention.

We demonstrate this proposal with a study of the educational value of physicians' participation in what are called medical care evaluation (MCE) committees. These committees, also known as medical audit or peer review committees, are found in most hospitals; they review patient records against explicit criteria for the treatment of particular disorders in order to identify patterns or instances of inappropriate care and make recommendations for dealing with these problems.

We began our study by conducting an ethnographic investigation of existing MCE committees and systematically comparing the descriptions of these committees to identify the factors that contributed to their educational value. We then designed and implemented an experimental program intended to increase this educational value and continued the ethnographic investigation in order to assess the program's impact on the committees' functioning and on the learning that took place in committee meetings. In addition, we used a number of quantitative techniques to measure the committees' educational value and the effect of the experimental program on the participating physicians. Before presenting this example, however, we will examine the presuppositions of ethnography and experimental design in order to demonstrate that they are not inherently incompatible.

THE PRESUPPOSITIONS OF ETHNOGRAPHIC AND EXPERIMENTAL RESEARCH

The basic presuppositions of ethnographic investigation can be summarized as follows (compare Knapp 1979; Wilson 1977; Smith 1982):

(1) It is based on the relatively intensive and long-term involvement of the investigator in the setting being studied.

(2) It requires a holistic, contextual approach to the setting and to the problems chosen for investigation rather than analytically separating out some aspect of the setting for study without considering its connection to the rest of the sociocultural context.

(3) It describes and analyzes the setting from the participants' point of view rather than from that of an outside observer. It therefore requires an initially exploratory and open-ended approach. Ethnography can go beyond the participants' perspective, but it must begin with and be grounded in this perspective.

This view of ethnography does not prohibit its use for causal explanation. Some practitioners of qualitative research (e.g., Lofland 1971; Geertz 1973) deliberately reject the search for causes, arguing that this is inappropriate for qualitative or ethnographic methods. Instead, they see their goal as the description or interpretation of social phenomena. However, Cook and Campbell (1979:93-94) claim that

careful linguistic analysis of their reports shows that they are rarely successful. Their understandings, insights, meanings, analysis of intentions and the like are strongly colored by causal conclusions even when the terms "effects," "gains," "benefits" and "results" are carefully avoided.

Kidder (1981) likewise states that causal assertions are often incorporated in the conclusions of qualitative studies. She suggests that many qualitative researchers are reluctant to say "this caused that" because their work does not satisfy the assumptions of statistical hypothesis testing in quantitative research, and that they therefore retreat to the "safe" position of claiming that their work is only descriptive. She argues, however, that careful qualitative research contains implicit checks on threats to causal validity and thus allows the researcher legitimately to draw causal conclusions.

This is a position that has recently received considerable support (Light and Pillemer 1982; Runciman 1983; Goetz and LeCompte 1984:220-228; Huberman and Miles 1985). In our opinion, the rejection of causation is neither necessary nor desirable; ethnographic investigation *can* be used to understand causal relationships (Maxwell 1984). In fact, one of the strengths of qualitative methods is that they can directly investigate causal processes that are unavailable to correlational studies or to "black box" experimental designs (Bennis 1968; Britan 1979; Fetterman 1982).

The presuppositions of the experimental method are less easy to define. Both Kaplan (1964:144-170) and Cook and Campbell (1979:2-8) focus on the concept of *control* as the crucial feature of the experiment. Cook and Campbell (1979:7-8) define several different senses of "control," and state that "whatever its manifestation, the major function of control is the same: to rule out threats to valid inference" (1979:8).

In nineteenth-century physical science this was accomplished by actual physical shielding and control of conditions, allowing the manipulation of a single variable and observation of its effects. Subsequently, educational and biological researchers developed methods for the systematic assignment of subjects to treatments and the explicit comparison of these groups of subjects in order to determine the effect of different treatments; this is the origin of the "control group" design (Boring 1954; Campbell 1984). According to Cook and Campbell, "All experiments involve at least a treatment, an outcome measure, units of assignment, and some comparison from which change can be inferred and hopefully attributed to the treatment" (1979:5).

Some writers restrict the term "experiment" to a research design in which units are randomly assigned to "treatment" or "control" groups, and the influences on the groups are identical except for the presence or absence of the "treatment." Others, such as Cook and Campbell (1979:5-6), use the term "experiment" more broadly to refer to a variety of designs that involve the systematic comparison of particular groups or settings with others that are similar in important respects, or with the same group or setting at different times, in order to determine the effect or influence of some event or intervention. Cook and Campbell distinguish several types of experiments, including randomized experiments and a variety of quasi-experiments such as nonequivalent group designs and interrupted time-series designs. We therefore take the basic presupposition of experimental research to be the use of controlled comparison to decide between alternative causal interpretations, rather than the use of randomized assignment.

However, our purpose in this chapter is not to defend a particular definition of the term "experiment." Instead, it is to demonstrate that particular types of controlled comparisons can be combined with ethnographic methods to provide a greater understanding of program settings and processes. We do not see our use of such controls as a radical departure from traditional anthropological methods. The concept of "controlled comparison" has a long and respected history in anthropology (Eggan 1954), and our use of specific comparisons incorporated in the research design is a logical extension of Eggan's use of historical and geographic controls in comparing societies.

We therefore see no inherent incompatibility in the presuppositions of experimental and ethnographic research methods. Ethnographic investigation, employing inductive, holistic and emic categories of analysis, can be conducted within a research framework that involves the systematic comparison of different groups in order to determine the effect of some intervention.

COMBINING EXPERIMENTAL CONTROLS AND ETHNOGRAPHY

The theoretical possibility of combining ethnographic investigation with experimental controls has been suggested by Reichardt and Cook, who propose "using randomized experiments with participant observers as the measuring instruments" (1979:22). Similarly, Campbell (1978:199) has argued that anthropologists studying an experimental program in a school system would be better able to draw causal conclusions if they spent half their time studying another school system without the program or studying the school system prior to the program implementation, adding that "this has apparently not been considered."

More recently, Firestone and Herriot (1984) and Miles and Huberman (1984) have provided extensive discussions of multisite qualitative research, but are concerned almost entirely with using this approach to achieve greater generalizability of results, rather than to increase internal causal validity. On the other hand, Kidder (1981) has claimed that qualitative researchers often *do* utilize quasi-experimental controls to increase internal validity, but do so implicitly, without employing the language of experimentation.

We are aware of only one other study that explicitly used ethnographic methods in combination with experimental controls. This was an evaluation of a computerized medical information system in a hospital ward (Lundsgaarde, Fischer, and Steele 1981). The evaluation employed two comparable medical wards, which were initially studied while both were using a manual medical record system; one of the wards then converted to a computerized record system, while the "control" ward retained the manual system. The researchers employed both ethnographic and quantitative methods to determine what effect the computerized system had on the clinical activities of the ward.

The ethnographic component of the evaluation involved participant observation and informal interviewing, behavioral observations, structured interviews and a questionnaire, and document analysis. Fieldwork was conducted on both wards for eight months. The overall goals of the ethnographic research were to describe the local context within which the computerized system was implemented, to provide a more meaningful interpretation of the quantitative outcome measures, and to document the events surrounding the implementation of the computerized system and the experiences of the health care providers using the system (Lundsgaarde, Fischer, and Steele 1981:1-16).

A CASE STUDY: MEDICAL CARE EVALUATION

Our study likewise involved the use of ethnographic methods within an overall experimental design. The study was concerned with the educational effect on physicians of participation in the MCE committees at Michael Reese Hospital and Medical Center in Chicago. There have been numerous anecdotal accounts of the educational value of serving on MCE committees. However, when we began our investigation, no one had attempted systematically to identify or document this educational effect or to influence the operation of the committees so as to make them more educational. Through a two-year study of these committees at Michael Reese Hospital (Sandlow et al. 1981; Bashook et al. 1982; Maxwell et al. 1984), we sought to determine the committees' influence on physicians' knowledge and performance, to identify the committee characteristics that contributed to this influence, and to design and evaluate a program for improving the educational value of the committees.

The MCE committees at Michael Reese were of two types: (1) criteria development committees, which formulated criteria for the diagnosis and treatment of particular disorders, and (2) audit committees, which reviewed the hospital's overall performance against these criteria, examined individual patient records, and made recommendations for improving the quality of care. Both types of committees were composed mainly of physicians from a single clinical department and were chaired by a physician member. (At the time of the study, a small number of the committees involved physicians from several departments, working on a topic of joint relevance; a few committees also included nurses or other health professionals.) Membership of the committees that we studied ranged from four to eight physicians, with the exception of two committees that had fewer physician members and a majority of nurses.

During the period of the study (1978 to 1980), the committee meetings also involved two members of the hospital MCE staff: a facilitator, usually a physician, who led the meetings and provided information on the MCE procedures, and a program coordinator, who prepared summaries of each meeting, wrote the instructions for the personnel who abstracted the medical records for comparison with the criteria, and handled the administrative tasks of the committee. The committees met either biweekly or monthly; meetings generally lasted for one hour.

The criteria development committees that we studied usually began by developing a list of possible topics for further study. These topics were usually specific diagnoses, but were sometimes particular medical or surgical procedures. The selection of topics was based on the morbidity and mortality associated with the diagnosis or procedure, the possibility for reducing these, and the overall impact on the health care system at Michael Reese Hospital. The topics were then ranked according to their potential for improvement in patient care practices.

Having selected a topic, the committee developed a set of criteria for the care of patients with that diagnosis or undergoing that procedure. These criteria addressed both the processes and outcomes of care. The criteria were defined in explicit terms to allow a non-physician abstractor to determine from the patient's record whether each criterion had been met or not. Once developed, the criteria were tested by means of a trial audit of 25 patient records and revised if necessary.

When the criteria had received final approval, a full audit of patient records was performed (usually the 100 most-recent cases with that diagnosis or procedure), and the results presented to the audit committee. The data were summarized in a tabular form that allowed the committee both to review overall compliance with each criterion and to select particular problematic cases for in-depth review. The latter cases were reviewed by individual physicians, and a summary of each case was normally presented to the whole committee. The committee then discussed the management of the case and decided whether any action was warranted. It also made recommendations for the overall improvement of care, and, if necessary, for changes in the criteria.

The study involved three researchers: an anthropologist (Maxwell); an educator who had been involved in establishing the MCE program at Michael Reese (Bashook); and a physician who had developed the program, was currently responsible for its operation, and chaired one of the committees (Sandlow). The fact that two of the researchers were insiders, known to many of the committee members, greatly facilitated the study. The original research design was developed by two of the investigators (Bashook and Sandlow) with backgrounds in biology and education, and psychology and medicine, respectively, and was explicitly intended as an experiment—or, to use Cook and Campbell's term, a quasi-experiment. It was only with the involvement of the third investigator that ethnographic methods were incorporated into the research design.

The initial stage of the research was primarily ethnographic. One of the authors (Maxwell) acted as a participant observer in 13 committees over a seven-month period; although his role was largely passive, he assisted the MCE staff with some tasks during the meetings. He also audiotaped the meetings, and took written notes on what occurred. The observer was treated for the most part simply as a member of the MCE staff by the committee members. A total of 52 committee meetings were observed during this stage of the research. The goal of this stage was to identify the naturally occurring learning that took place in committee meetings and to determine the factors affecting this learning.

Following each meeting, the audiotape was reviewed by the observer, and an edited transcript prepared, based on the tape and the observation notes. This transcript was indexed for information pertaining to the leader's style and goals, the character of committee interaction, and evidence of learning. A coding system was then developed to identify and categorize "learning opportunities" occurring during committee meetings. These learning opportunities were occasions on which information was presented, or discussion took place, that appeared to be of potentially educational value to participants. The initial categories for coding learning opportunities were primarily "etic" in nature; they distinguished learning opportunities by who initiated them, how this occurred, the type of content presented, their duration, and whether they consisted of a presentation by one person or a discussion.

However, the categories were grounded in the extensive experience of two of the researchers with the MCE committees at Michael Reese and in the interviews with physician committee members described below. In addition, the identification of the learning opportunities was largely based on the observed reactions of the committee members. In many instances, physicians would comment, "This was a very interesting case," or "I don't understand why this was done," or indicate their interest by paying close attention; for other cases, they would comment, "There's nothing to learn from this one," or engage in side conversations during a presentation. The identification of learning opportunities was also validated by having all three investigators listen to selected tapes and independently identify learning opportunities. All of the coding of learning opportunities was done by the observer.

The observer interviewed eight physician members of the committees. These interviews were open-ended, exploring the educational value of MCE committees, their structure and operation, and the physician's attitudes toward MCE. The interviews averaged 30 minutes in length and were audiotaped, transcribed, and analyzed. In addition, information on committee operation and the educational value of the committees was obtained informally from committee members and from the MCE staff, providing a better understanding of the data obtained from observation and interviews.

All but one of the 13 committees could be unambiguously classified as having high or low educational value based on the number and significance of the learning opportunities. Five committees (three criteria development and two audit) were of high educational value, while seven (three criteria development and four audit) were of low educational value. (The thirteenth committee was intermediate in educational value and was not observed often enough to permit a definite classification.) These two groups of committees could be most clearly defined on the basis of two characteristics: the number of potentially educational *discussions* per meeting that focused on the medical problem under consideration and its appropriate management and the total amount of time per meeting spent in learning opportunities related to this problem (Table 6.1). In addition, qualitative differences in the educational value of the two groups of committees were substantial.

The observations, interviews, and data from the MCE staff were then used to develop an ethnographic description, or portrayal, of each committee. These portrayals were analyzed and compared to discover the differences between the committees with high and low educational value, and to determine how these differences affected the educational value of the committees. We found the following contrasts:

(1) Criteria development committees with high educational value dealt primarily with the optimal (rather than the minimally acceptable) management of the medical problem under consideration. This led to an exploration of alternative approaches to the problem and the presentation and justification of committee members' views on these. In contrast, criteria development committees with low educational value tended to focus on the minimal, generally held standards of acceptable care; as a result, most points raised in meetings were ones on which the members already agreed.

(2) In audit committees with high educational value, members reviewed records prior to the meeting and presented them at the meeting as case problems which were then discussed by the committee. In audit committees with low educational value, on the other hand, records were reviewed (often at the meeting itself) primarily to determine whether the criteria were met or not. Cases were rarely discussed by the committee unless there was a question as to whether the patient's treatment was justified.

(3) The attitude and goals of the committee chairperson had an important influence on the educational value of committee meetings. A majority of the committees with high educational value were led by physicians who saw the committees as having an important educational function, as evidenced by their statements and actions. In contrast, none of the leaders of committees with low educational value felt that education was an important function of the committees.

(4) There appeared to be a "critical mass" of physicians required to regularly sustain an educationally valuable interaction. Committee meetings with fewer than four physicians present had significantly (p < .01) fewer learning opportunities than those with four or more

TABLE 6.1

Comparison of Medical Care Evaluation Committees Having
High and Low Educational Value, Michael Reese Hospital

Committees	Number of Committees	Number of Discussions of Problems per Meeting		Minutes Spent in Learning Opportunities per Meeting	
		Mean	Range of Committee Means	Mean	Range of Committee Means
High value	5	3.2	2.0 to 5.0	10.1	4.3 to 18.2
Low value	7	0.3	0.0 to 0.7	0.9	0.0 to 1.8

SOURCE: Sandlow et al. (1981).

physicians. However, high attendance was not in itself sufficient to generate educational interaction.

The identification of these four characteristics as important influences on the educational potential of the committees was not based simply on their correlation with the frequency and significance of learning opportunities. Using the participant-observational data, we were able to demonstrate *how* each characteristic acted to increase this educational potential. This illustrates the point made earlier: that qualitative data can provide direct evidence regarding causal processes that is not available to traditional experimental or correlational designs.

Our original plan for improving the educational value of the committees had been to develop a formal educational structure, with predefined learning objectives and distinct educational activities. However, the ethnographic research revealed two important points about the committees. First, it became clear that the educational strength of the committees lay primarily in the informal, unplanned interaction that occurred during meetings. The most informative exchanges that occurred during committee meetings were often peripheral to the stated topic and would have been largely unpredictable to someone attempting to design the committee's educational "curriculum." It also became clear that most physicians considered the educational value of the committees to be secondary to their functions of criteria development and record review, and would resent any substantial interference with the latter tasks.

We therefore designed a model MCE program that was intended to increase the *informal* discussion among physicians that occurred as part of the criteria development and audit process. This model program has been described in detail elsewhere (Bashook et al. 1982); it was structured to ensure that committee discussion considered the optimal management of particular disorders or the optimal care of individual patients, that committee members prepared draft criteria or reviewed records prior to the meeting, that the committee leaders emphasized educational aspects of the committee's activities, and that a sufficient number of physicians was present to generate an educationally optimal amount of discussion. At the same time, the model program was designed to meet the hospital's needs for effective record review.

We gained permission from three clinical departments in the hospital to institute this program in their MCE committees. Five committees in these departments were already in operation; we established a sixth committee, so that each department had one criteria development and one audit committee. Members of existing committees were reoriented to the model program, and new members were selected by the department head. One of the investigators served as MCE facilitator for each of the committees.

The model program was studied in each of these six committees for a period of 12 to 15 months. We continued the participant observation methods of the previous phase of the research, with one of the investigators attending and audiotaping meetings, preparing an edited transcript, and indexing the transcript for learning opportunities and committee operation. These transcripts were circulated and discussed by all three investigators.

In addition, we attempted to measure the committees' effect on participants' knowledge and performance. To do this, we used multiple-choice knowledge tests and a review of the records of patients treated by physicians participating in the study. We also developed a form of stimulated-recall interview, which we call the "clinical case recall interview," to investigate how physicians participating on the committees changed their management of a particular disorder following committee discussion of the disorder. This involved questioning a physician in detail about how specific patients with particular diagnoses were managed following the committee's discussion of these diagnoses, and whether committee participation had resulted in any changes in the physician's management strategy. Twelve physicians were interviewed in this manner. Finally, we sent questionnaires dealing with their perception of and attitudes toward the committees to all of the participating physicians, and conducted follow-up interviews with a sample of these physicians.

We used several types of quasi-experimental controls in this phase of research. First, we compared the same committees before and after the model program was introduced. Second, we established control groups of physicians who did not serve on the committees, but who participated in the knowledge testing and record review. The members of the control group in each department were approximately equivalent to the experimental subjects in subspecialty training and in type and length of practice. Third, for the knowledge tests and record review, we utilized several "control" topics that were not discussed by the committees, in addition to the topics that the committees dealt with. Fourth, we found that the model program was successfully established in only three of the six committees, as determined by adherence to the four characteristics stated above. This allowed us to compare the "successful" and "unsuccessful" committees and thus to separate the effects of the model program (which was fully realized in only three committees) from the influence of the investigative methods (which were employed in all six committees). The categorization of the committees as "successful" or "unsuccessful" was made before the results of the knowledge tests and performance audit were obtained.

The six experimental committees had a relatively high number of learning opportunities in comparison with the preintervention committees, and there was a statistically significant increase in the number of learning opportunities in three of the four committees for which pre-intervention data exist (Table 6.2). Far more significant than these quantitative differences between committees, however, was the qualitative difference in the educational interchange. In the three "successful" committees (Criteria Development committees A and B and Audit Committee A), there was often a high-level discussion of the issues surrounding a problem or patient. These learning opportunities often were extended discussions, with citation of literature. In Audit Committee B and Criteria Development Committee C, on the other hand, learning opportunities tended to be shorter and lower-level, and in the Audit Committee C they were normally quite brief and of minimal educational significance. The questionnaire showed that all but one member of the "successful" committees saw their participation as "very" or "moderately" educational, while less than half of the members of the "unsuccessful" committees considered their participation to be "very" or "moderately" educational.

TABLE 6.2
Learning Opportunities Occurring During Committee Meetings

	Preintervention		Postintervention		
	Committees with High Educational Value	Committees with Low Educational Value	Dept A***	Dept B***	Dept C
Criteria Development Committees					
Learning opportunities per meeting	5.9	2.2	11.3**	5.8	3.6**
Standard deviation	3.0	2.5	6.4	5.1	2.6
Number of meetings	13	12	9	17	9
Audit Committees					
Learning opportunities per meeting	5.1	1.2	6.9*	5.9*	3.6*
Standard deviation	2.0	1.2	2.1	3.4	2.4
Number of meetings	14	10	15	7	9

SOURCE: Bashook et al. (1982).
*Difference from preintervention value is statistically significant at $p < .05$.
**No preintervention data.
***"Successful" committees.

The physicians we interviewed were divided on what they saw as the major educational impact of the committees. Some members felt that these committees were useful mainly for review and updating. These members tended to emphasize the value of presentations by experts. Other members cited the value of committee meetings in forcing them to reexamine basic definitions and management principles. These physicians usually felt that the most educational aspect of the meetings was the discussion among members; many of them mentioned the importance of learning how others do things, and of being exposed to different points of view. On the whole, the second group of physicians had a higher opinion of the committees' educational value than the first group; they also tended to be older, and were somewhat more likely to be in private practice.

There was a striking difference between physicians in Departments A and B in terms of what they saw as the main educational impact of the committees. Members of the committees in Department A emphasized the educational value of the committee meetings themselves, while members of the committees in Department B tended to see the major influence as being the development and distribution of criteria sets and audit reports, and the sanctions against physicians whose practice did not meet departmental standards. Members of the committees in Department C were intermediate between Departments A and B in this respect.

The results of the quantitative measures of the impact of committee participation (the knowledge tests and the medical record review) were positive but inconclusive. The committees showed an overall gain in knowledge test scores on the experimental topics. For the committees in Department A, which conformed most closely to the model program, this gain was statistically significant ($p < .05$); for the committees in departments B and C, the gain was not statistically significant. The gains by members of the three successful committees were statistically significant by comparison with the gains of their matched controls on the experimental topics, and by comparison with the members' gain on the control topics ($p < .01$). However, the magnitude of the gains was small.

The medical record audit did not reveal any statistically significant changes in the physicians' performance, due primarily to two problems that were not foreseen when the audit was planned. First, following the committee's discussion of the experimental topics, there were usually too few records for each physician to allow meaningful statistical comparison. Second, the audit procedures turned out to be insensitive to the actual changes in performance that occurred, as these changes were revealed by the clinical case recall interviews.

Despite the failure of the record audit to demonstrate changes in behavior, the clinical case recall interviews identified four instances (all from committees in Department A) in which members had made substantial changes in the way they treated patients with particular disorders, and which they unequivocally attributed to the committees' discussion of these disorders. The committees' role in these changes was verified by comparing the physicians' accounts with the meeting transcripts, to confirm that the meetings were a plausible impetus for the reported changes.

These changes were not incremental improvements in performance, the type of change that the medical record review was designed to detect, but were instead shifts in overall management strategy for these disorders. One gastroenterologist said that he had been made more aware of the fact that there's no single recipe for treating patients with gastrointestinal bleeding. Prior to the Criteria Development Committee's discussion of this topic, he had tended to use endoscopy as a routine initial procedure. Now he tends to individualize his management; he described a middle-aged male patient with gastrointestinal bleeding whom he had put at bedrest for several days and then began plans for workup. Previously, he would have used immediate endoscopy without considering the particular factors indicating a different approach for this patient.

Another member of the Criteria Development Committee, a general internist, also changed his management of patients with gastrointestinal bleeding. Prior to the committee's discussion of this topic, he had employed X-rays as his main diagnostic procedure. He now uses endoscopy as his procedure of choice, and when there is no immediate danger, waits 24 to 36 hours after the acute episode before having a gastroenterologist see the patient. Formerly, he would have admitted the patient immediately and sent them for X-rays the next morning; most of the time he would not have used endoscopy even if the source of bleeding was not located. There was no question in his mind that his method of management had changed as a result of his participation in the committee's discussion of the topic.

Two members of the Audit Committee in Department A cited significant changes in their management of diabetics as a result of the committee's discussion of this topic. One, an older physician who maintains a part-time practice, now places much more emphasis on outpatient management of patients with elevated blood sugar; he recently had a patient with a blood sugar of 550 mg/dl whom he successfully treated as an outpatient. He had tended to use outpatient management for less extreme cases before the committee's audit of this topic, but said that he would never have had the nerve to attempt it in this case, or even been sure it was the best approach, without the influence of the committee discussion. He was quite enthusiastic about the success of this approach, and was positive that participation on the committee had provided the impetus for him to change his practice.

Another Audit Committee member, a general internist who had completed his residency a few years earlier, reported a similar shift in his approach to the management of diabetics. He gave as an example an older woman, a newly diagnosed diabetic, whom he had managed as an outpatient despite pressure from her children to have her admitted to the hospital. The management was quite successful; the patient was asymptomatic the whole time and was "thrilled" that she did not have to leave work and go to the hospital. He had no doubt that before the committee's discussion of diabetes, he would have admitted the patient, because he would have lacked the confidence to stand up to the pressure. Now, he feels he has completely changed his practice in this area.

The interviews also showed that the changes were not the result of a simple "updating" of knowledge, as much continuing medical education has assumed, but resulted from a major rethinking of the physician's previous practice. In fact, two physicians emphasized that the committee discussions had *not* provided new medical knowledge but instead had given them the confidence to *apply* knowledge that they already had. This aspect of the committees' educational value was confirmed by the follow-up interviews with other physicians and was an outcome of committee participation that had not been anticipated in designing the quantitative measures of knowledge and performance change.

IMPLICATIONS FOR ETHNOGRAPHIC EVALUATION

The ethnographic component of the study thus turned out to be more productive than the quantitative procedures in terms of understanding the educational processes that occur in MCE committees. There were two main advantages to the ethnographic approach: It allowed us to discover aspects of the committees' educational functioning that we had not anticipated and would have missed had we relied entirely on quantitative methods, and it provided insight into the processes by which the committees influenced physicians' knowledge and performance.

However, the value of the ethnographic research was substantially increased by the experimental controls incorporated in the research design. For the ethnographic portion of the research, these controls were the comparison of the high-value and low-value committees, the comparison of the same committees before and after the model program was introduced, and the comparison of the "successful" and "unsuccessful" committees.

The experimental controls, in combination with the quantitative results, helped us to rule out certain alternative explanations for the results we obtained; these alternative explanations included the possibility that the changes that took place for members of the "successful" committees were due to learning from sources other than committee meetings, or to a "Hawthorne effect" of the research on the committees. The fact that the knowledge gains did not occur in the matched control groups, or for the control topics included in the knowledge tests, and that the major changes took place in the "successful" committees, strengthened our conclusion that the features of the model MCE program had a causal role in the changes in knowledge and performance that we identified.

Our joint use of ethnographic, quantitative, and experimental methods differs from most reported combinations of quantitative/experimental and qualitative/ethnographic methods in which the two types of investigation are conducted separately and their *results* are combined. What we have done is to use ethnographic methods *within* an experimental framework incorporating particular types of controls. These controls were employed with both the quantitative and ethnographic methods, allowing us to address certain validity threats that would have been much more serious in the absence of these controls.

The importance of controls against bias in qualitative research has recently been emphasized by Huberman and Miles (1985), who argue that "clinical judgments ... are consistently less accurate than statistical/actuarial ones," and that "any 'clinical' researcher operating in a natural setting had best be well-armed with the safeguards against bias described in the social judgment literature." We believe that the sorts of experimental controls that we describe can reduce these biases without sacrificing the richness of data and access to participants' meanings provided by ethnographic methods. Experimental controls can also permit the researchers to evaluate competing explanations that may all have some plausibility on ethnographic grounds.

On the other hand, exclusively experimental designs usually treat the setting being studied as a "black box," providing no information about the actual causal processes operating in the setting. Ethnographic investigation can identify these causal processes, increasing the interpretability of experimental outcomes and contributing to the development of a causal model.

Our advocacy of the use of ethnographic investigation in conjunction with an experimental framework is grounded in the concept of causal validity, which is in turn based on the examination of plausible alternative causes ("validity threats") that must be ruled out in order to validate the proposed causal relationship (Cook and Campbell 1979:38; Kidder 1981). This procedure has been labeled "strong inference" by Platt (1964), and has been further elaborated by Scriven (1976) in what he refers to as the "modus operandi" method. In our view, it is this critical examination of alternative hypotheses, and not the use of specific research techniques, that is the essence of scientific research and evaluation.

We have tried to demonstrate, through a description of our study of the educational value of a model medical care evaluation program, that it is both possible and productive to combine ethnographic methods with experimental controls in evaluation research. We have also analyzed the presuppositions of the two approaches, attempting to show that they are not methodologically or philosophically incompatible. If our example and arguments are valid, the joint use of these two methods should produce research and evaluations that have significantly greater validity than those employing either method alone.

REFERENCES CITED

Bashook, P. G., L. J. Sandlow, and J. A. Maxwell
    1982 Increasing the Educational Value of Medical Care Evaluation: A Model Program. Journal of Medical Education 57:701-707.
Bennis, W. G.
    1968 The Case Study. Journal of Applied Behavioral Science 4:227-231.
Boring, E. G.
    1954 The Nature and History of Experimental Control. American Journal of Psychology 57:701-707.
Britan, G. M.
    1978 Experimental and Contextual Models of Program Evaluation. Evaluation and Program Planning 1:229-234.
Campbell, D. T.
    1978 Qualitative Knowing in Action Research. In The Social Contexts of Method. M. Brenner, P. Marsh, and M. Brenner, eds. New York: St. Martin's.
    1979 Degrees of Freedom and the Case Study. In Qualitative and Quantitative Methods in Evaluation. T. D. Cook and C. S. Reichardt, eds. pp. 49-67. Beverly Hills, CA: Sage.
    1984 Can We Be Scientific in Applied Social Science? In Evaluation Studies Review Annual, Vol. 9. R. F. Connor, D. G. Altman, and C. Jackson, eds. pp. 26-48. Beverly Hills, CA: Sage.
Connor, R. F., D. G. Altman, and C. Jackson
    1984 1984: A Brave New World for Evaluation? In Evaluation Studies Review Annual, Vol. 9. R. F. Connor, D. G. Altman, and C. Jackson, eds. Beverly Hills, CA: Sage.
Cook, T. D., and D. T. Campbell
    1979 Quasi-Experimentation: Design and Analysis Issues for Field Settings. Boston: Houghton Mifflin.

Cook, T. D., and C. S. Reichardt, eds.
  1979 Qualitative and Quantitative Methods in Evaluation Research. Beverly Hills,
    CA: Sage.
Denzin, N. K.
  1978 The Research Act. 2nd ed. Chicago: Aldine.
Eggan, F.
  1954 Social Anthropology and the Method of Controlled Comparison. American
    Anthropologist 56:743-763.
Fetterman, D. M.
  1982 Ethnography in Educational Research: The Dynamics of Diffusion. Edu-
    cational Researcher (March): 17-29. Reprinted in Ethnography in Educational
    Evaluation. D. Fetterman, ed. Beverly Hills, CA: Sage.
  in press Ethnographic Educational Evaluation. *In* Toward an Interpretive Ethnog-
    raphy of Education at Home and Abroad, G. D. Spundler, ed. Beverly Hills, CA:
    Sage.
Firestone, W. A., and R. E. Herriott
  1984 Multisite Qualitative Policy Research: Some Design and Implementation Is-
    sues. *In* Ethnography in Educational Evaluation. D. M. Fetterman, ed. Beverly
    Hills, CA: Sage.
Geertz, C.
  1973 The Interpretation of Cultures. New York: Basic Books.
Goetz, J. P. and M. D. Le Compte
  1984 Ethnography and Qualitative Design in Educational Research. New York:
    Academic Press.
Green, J. L., and C. Wallat
  1981 Ethnography and Language in Educational Settings. Norwood, NJ: Ablex.
Guba, E. G., and Y. S. Lincoln
  1981 Effective Evaluation. San Francisco: Jossey-Bass.
Huberman, A. M., and M. B. Miles
  1985 Assessing Local Causality in Qualitative Research. *In* Exploring Clinical
    Methods for Social Research. D. N. Berg and K. K. Smith, eds. Beverly Hills,
    CA: Sage.
Ianni, F.A.J., and M. T. Orr
  1979 Toward a Rapprochement of Quantitative and Qualitative Methodologies. *In*
    Qualitative and Quantitative Methods in Evaluation. T. D. Cook and C. S.
    Reichardt, eds. pp. 87-98. Beverly Hills, CA: Sage.
Jacob, E.
  1982 Combining Ethnographic and Quantitative Approaches: Suggestions and
    Examples From a Study on Puerto Rico. *In* Children In and Out of School:
    Ethnography and Education. P. Gilmore and A. A. Glatthorn, eds. Washington,
    DC: Center for Applied Linguistics.
Jick, T. D.
  1983 Mixing Qualitative and Quantitative Methods: Triangulation in Action. *In*
    Qualitative Methodology. J. Van Maanen, ed. Beverly Hills, CA: Sage.
Kaplan, A.
  1964 The Conduct of Inquiry: Methodology for Behavioral Science. San Francisco:
    Chandler.
Kidder, L. H.
  1981 Qualitative Research and Quasi-Experimental Frameworks. *In* Scientific

Inquiry and the Social Sciences: M. B. Brewer and B. E. Collins, eds. San Francisco: Jossey-Bass.

Knapp, M. S.
1979 Ethnographic Contributions to Evaluation Research: The Experimental Schools Program Evaluation and Some Alternatives. *In* Qualitative and Quantitative Methods in Evaluation. T. D. Cook and C. S. Reichardt, eds. pp. 118-139. Beverly Hills, CA: Sage.

Light, R. J., and D. B. Pillemer
1982 Numbers and Narrative: Combining Their Strengths in Research Reviews. Harvard Educational Review 52:1-26.

Lofland, J.
1971 Analyzing Social Settings: A Guide to Qualitative Observation and Analysis. Belmont, CA: Wadsworth.

Lundsgaarde, H. P., P. J. Fischer, and D. J. Steele
1981 Human Problems in Computerized Medicine. Publications in Anthropology 13. Lawrence: University of Kansas, Department of Anthropology.

Maxwell, J. A.
1984 Using Ethnography to Identify Causes. Paper presented at the Annual Meeting of the American Anthropological Association, Denver.

Maxwell, J. A., L. J. Sandlow, and P. G. Bashook
1984 The Effect of a Model Medical Care Evaluation Program on Physician Knowledge and Performance. Journal of Medical Education 59: 33-38.

Meyers, W. R.
1981 The Evaluation Enterprise. San Francisco: Jossey-Bass.

Miles, M. B., and A. M. Huberman
1984 Qualitative Data Analysis: A Sourcebook of New Methods. Beverly Hills, CA: Sage.

Patel, V. L., and P. A. Cranton
1983 Transfer of Student Learning in Medical Education. Journal of Medical Education 58:126-135.

Pelto, P. J., and G. Pelto
1978 Anthropological Research: The Structure of Inquiry. Cambridge: Cambridge University Press.

Platt, J. R.
1964 Strong Inference. Science 146:347-353.

Reichardt, C. S., and T. D. Cook
1979 Beyond Qualitative Versus Quantitative Methods. *In* Qualitative and Quantitative Methods in Evaluation. T. D. Cook and C. S. Reichardt, eds. pp. 7-32. Beverly Hills, CA: Sage.

Rist, R. C.
1980 Blitzkrieg Ethnography: On the Transformation of a Method into a Movement. Educational Researcher (February):8-10.

Rodin, M. B., L. Rowitz, and R. Rydman
1983 Levels of Analysis and Levels of Need: Cultural Factors and the Assessment of Need for Alcoholism Treatment Services in an Urban Community. Human Organization 41:299-306.

Runciman, W. G.
1983 A Treatise on Social Theory. Vol. 1: The Methodology of Social Theory. Cambridge: Cambridge University Press.

Sandlow, L. J., P. G. Bashook, and J. A. Maxwell
1981 Medical Care Evaluation: An Experience in Continuing Medical Education. Journal of Medical Education 56:581-586.
Scriven, M.
1976 Maximizing the Power of Causal Investigations: The Modus Operandi Method. *In* Evaluation Studies Review Annual, Vol. 1. G. V. Glass, ed. pp. 101-118. Beverly Hills, CA: Sage.
Smith, J. K.
1983 Quantitative Versus Qualitative Research: An Attempt to Clarify the Issue. Educational Researcher (March):6-13.
Smith, L. M.
1982 Ethnography. *In* Encyclopedia of Educational Research. 5th ed. H. Mitzel, ed. pp. 587-592. New York: Macmillan.
Trend, M. G.
1979 On the Reconciliation of Qualitative and Quantitative Analyses: A Case Study. *In* Qualitative and Quantitative Methods in Evaluation. T. D. Cook and C. S. Reichardt, eds. pp. 68-86. Beverly Hills, CA: Sage.
Webb, E. J. et al.
1966 Unobtrusive Measures: Nonreactive Research in the Social Sciences. Chicago: Rand McNally.
Whyte, W. F.
1984 Learning from the Field: A Guide from Experience. Beverly Hills, CA: Sage.
Wilson, W.
1977 The Use of Ethnographic Techniques in Educational Research. Review of Educational Research 47:245-265.

7

Qualitative Methodology in the Evaluation of Early Childhood Bilingual Curriculum Models

RAY A. CHESTERFIELD

R ecently the call for the use of qualitative methods in the evaluation of bilingual education programs has become widespread (Cohen and Bruck 1979; Saravia Shore 1979). Generally two reasons are given in arguing for including a qualitative component in the evaluation of bilingual programs. First, it is felt that given the relative newness of bilingual education as a social intervention, assessment of program impact may be premature. Existing instruments are seen as inappropriate for measurement of language proficiency and achievement in core subject areas (Cohen 1973; Gonzalez 1978). In addition, the use of tests alone is felt to be insufficient to advance understanding of how the variety of programs in different stages of implementation affect children or might be improved. Second, it is argued that even in those cases where the evaluation of impact is not premature, the focus of most evaluations has been too global. That is, they have asked whether a bilingual program worked rather than asking what types of bilingual education work best for which types of students (Cohen and Laosa 1976; Center for Applied Linguistics 1977; Intercultural Development Research Association 1977). This question implies that studies of individual classrooms or students of differing first and second language abilities should be incorporated into evaluation designs if results are to be interpretable (Cummins 1977).

Although the principal focus of evaluations of bilingual programs to date has been on the product of the program (i.e., child outcome measures), most have also collected some data on classroom interaction. Generally, however, the results of such efforts have been of limited utility to decision makers. Those studies providing classroom level data (e.g., American Institutes for Research (AIR) 1977; Illinois State Board of Education 1981) are seen as contributing little to the understanding of the treatment variable as it interacts with individual children, whereas those focusing on individual children (e.g., Bruck and Schultz 1979) are considered too limited in scope to be generalizable.

This chapter discusses the way in which the techniques of naturalistic observation[1] were used to expand the experimental pre- and posttest design of a national evaluation of Spanish-English preschool curriculum models. There were three basic objectives that led to the incorporation of qualitative methodology into the study design. The first was to add to the interpretive power of the results of the statistical analysis. Observational data were to be used to guide the statistical analysis and as an explanatory complement to the test results. The second was to measure the nature and extent of program implementation over time. In measuring implementation, the evaluators hoped to show not only what programmatic aspects worked best for which types of students but also the feasibility of successful implementation of the curriculum models at a variety of sites. The third objective was to secure contextual change over time data. Systematic focused observations of individual children at specific times during the year were to provide a complementary and equally valid form of outcome data.

BACKGROUND

During a three-year period between 1976 and 1979, the Head Start Bureau of the Administration for Children, Youth and Families (ACYF), as part of its Strategy for Spanish-Speaking Children, funded an experimental effort by four institutions to develop distinct bilingual bicultural preschool curriculum models. During the first year of development, each curriculum model was designed in consultation with parents and staff at cooperating Head Start centers. In the second year, a pilot implementation of each model took place at selected Head Start centers. The third year of development was that in which the four curricula were considered fully operational. Thus, this was the year chosen for evaluating the effects of the models at the two sites where each of the developers felt their model to be best implemented. ACYF contracted Júarez and Associates, an independent management consulting firm, to carry out the evaluation. Although data on the effectiveness of the curriculum models were collected in the third year of their implementation, the evaluation contractor carried out activities of instrument selection, development, and piloting concurrently with the curriculum development activities of the four curriculum developers.

The major objective of the study was to measure the change in children as a result of their participation in one of the four curriculum models. This was to be accomplished both through a pre- and posttest experimental design that included testing children in Spanish and English on a number of cognitive domains and by observation of the children's experience in the classroom with the domains tapped by the tests. A second major goal was to secure information that would assist others in learning about the potential of each model for implementation elsewhere. The evaluators were to collect data regarding both the process necessary to implement each model and the procedures needed to maintain each model in optimal operation. Finally, the evaluation was to determine the extent to which the models were greeted favorably by Head Start staff, parents, and lay community members.

It was not the intent of the evaluation, however, to undertake a comparative analysis of the four models but to provide informational pamphlets on the overall evaluation results and on the findings for each model which would allow consumers to choose among the curricula. This desire by ACYF to help Head Start programs wanting to implement bilingual curricula to choose the model or models most appropriate for their circumstances and needs created a particular type of research problem. The evaluation design needed to generate findings that would show the overall effectiveness of the curriculum development project and also describe the variation within and across models in a way that would be useful to local Head Start programs attempting to choose among the models.

To meet these multiple goals an evaluation approach that combined many techniques generally associated with ethnographic research, such as relatively long-term immersion at a site, unstructured interviewing, and written narratives of observations, with psychometric testing and surveying of parents, was developed. In order to examine general trends, however, and to provide a framework for comparing the models, a number of the qualitative data collection and data reduction procedures were standardized, resulting in what has been referred to as "formalized" qualitative research (Firestone and Herriot 1984).

EVALUATION DESIGN

As stated previously, the evaluation included the use of an experimental pre- and posttest design. A total of 442 children at the eight replication sites located in California, New York, Texas, and Wisconsin were assigned to treatment and comparison groups. At the beginning of the treatment (Fall 1979) and at its conclusion (Spring 1980), the children were tested on selected competency measures. These measures were intended to assess change in language acquisition, language comprehension, and concept development in both Spanish and English. In addition, at the beginning and end of the preschool year, parents were administered questionnaires that assessed background characteristics, attitudes, and knowledge with regard to education in general and bilingual education in particular, and attitudes toward education and vocational careers for their children. Similarly, Head Start teachers completed a questionnaire designed to assess previous experience, understanding of the terms "bilingual" and "bicultural" in the context of an early childhood program, attitudes toward children and sensitivity to the special needs of limited English-speaking children.

At four of the eight sites, a full-time participant researcher[2] (PR), who was bilingual and had experience in early childhood education, was present for the entire year. Each of these individuals gathered data by means of ethnographic notes, time and event samples, and implementation forms. Of principal concern was the day-to-day implementation of particular curriculum models and behaviors in naturally occurring classroom contexts. In addition to general observations, the participant researchers collected specific focused information as to the classroom behaviors of a sample of approximately 15 children per site at preselected periods throughout the year.

At each of the remaining four evaluation sites an implementation researcher (IR) collected observational data similar to that being collected by the PRs. The primary focus of their observations was the implementation of a curriculum model in the experimental classrooms at their site. These individuals were on site for only two-week periods at specified times during the year and, therefore, although they made some focused observations of a few children in order to better understand the implementation process, these data were too limited to be analyzed in the same way as the more extensive observations of individual children made by the PRs. The data collected by both PRs and IRs while on site were sent weekly to the central office, where they were monitored by the supervisor/coordinator of fieldwork, who had overall responsibility for the collection of all observational data.

The emphasis of the remainder of this chapter is on the qualitative component of the evaluation. Outcomes of the more traditional forms of evaluation research used in the study are discussed only in regard to the contribution made by the qualitative data to their interpretation. All of the results of the evaluation can be found elsewhere (see Chesterfield et al. 1982).

QUALITATIVE DATA COLLECTION

The potential of qualitative research in education research (Wilson 1977) and in evaluations (Fetterman 1984; Patton, 1980) has been well documented, as have the difficulties in the reduction and analysis of data produced from such research (Miles 1975). We attempted to overcome some of the problems of data reduction and analysis by wedding the observational component of the evaluation to the educational goals of the Head Start Strategy for Spanish-Speaking Children and those of the curricula being evaluated. Each curriculum developer helped to identify behavioral criteria that would reflect the impact of the curriculum on students as well as criteria that would be indicative of the degree of implementation of their model. These were operationally defined and became the focus of the observational component of the study. Thus, we chose to call our observers participant researchers rather than ethnographers as their job was not to define the nature of a particular social reality, but rather to focus on contextually relevant data that explained the presence or absence of outcomes or events expected by the model developers.

Three types of observational data were collected: ethnographic notes on the biophysical and sociocultural milieux in which the preschools were found, focused observations of individual children in the classroom, and data on the implementation process as it occurred over time in each experimental classroom. Ethnographic notes in the form of narrative accounts, logs, inventories, and informal interviews were used to gather data on the general context of the study, such as the language use of the community, and specific events external to the classroom (e.g., administrative changes, inclement weather) that related to the implementation of the curriculum models, as well as to examine the in-classroom behaviors from the perspective of the actors themselves.

In examining the behavior of individual children in the classroom a subsample of the entire experimental sample at each site was used. Several steps were involved in selecting the subsample children. Based on their initial observations of all children in each classroom, participant researchers provided information on those characteristics of the children that seemed indicative of distinct experiences with a given model. Sex, language, preference, verbal ability, and ethnic group were common characteristics identified at all sites; cognitive style and family composition were seen as important at individual sites. This information was used by project staff to stratify and randomly select five children in each of the three classrooms at each participant researcher's site for intensive observation.

The principal data collection technique was that of participant observation in which the participant researchers provided written fieldnotes on the behavior of individual children in the classroom throughout a school year. Focused observations were made of the children at each site three times during the school year—November-December,[3] February-March, and April-May. Children were observed on randomly selected days for specific amounts of time until the total amount of observation time approximated that of a normal preschool day.

Data collection combined the strategies of time and event sampling as specific contexts (mealtime, independent play, large and small group) were randomly sampled and each child was observed for amounts of time proportional to the percentage of time devoted to a particular activity in the school day. For example, if large group activities took place for 30 minutes and small group activities for 50, the researcher would observe a child in those activities for time samples of three and five minutes, respectively, until the daily total was reached. The researcher noted the time at which an observation began and then proceeded to describe the behaviors of the designated child and his or her verbal interactions with others. Note was made by any transitions in activities occurring during the observation period and of the time of such transitions. To prevent observer bias and control for the context of observed behavior, each subset of children from each classroom was randomly assigned to each context sampled.

After each day's observations, the participant researchers rewrote the rough notes taken in the classroom and coded them. For the purposes of the evaluation, all utterances recorded during focused observations were coded for language used by the target child and for behaviors identified as objectives of the curriculum models. These included behaviors related to linguistic (use of plural nouns, future tense, etc.) or functional competence (gives verbal instructions, describes own feelings, etc.), to language comprehension (e.g. recall events from a story), and to concept development (visual discrimination, seriation and sequencing, matching/classification, etc.).

Data on the nature and extent of implementation over time were recorded on a series of implementation forms. These consisted of model-specific checklists, frequency counts, rating scales, and informal interview schedules. Data were collected on the scheduling and organization of activities, the room arrangement, material resources, student and teacher behavior, and the instructional strategies used in the experimental classrooms. The individual items making up each of these categories of implementation was based on the objectives for each curriculum model.

The strategies for completing the various parts of the implementation forms included visual sweeps of the classroom in which counts were made of the elements identified in the curriculum as key features in its operation, and a running log of fieldnotes. A log was kept of the actual time during which activities occurred in an observation period (engaged time) as well as the amount of time spent on transition between each activity. Notes were taken on all events occurring within a time period. To ensure that accurate data were collected a list was made of all individuals in the classroom before observations began. The behavior of each individual for each observation period (e.g., children who were engaged in a particular activity and those who were not) was then described. The note-taking procedures, focused on those situations which were specified by a curriculum model as promoting particular behaviors, allowed for an estimate of the congruency between actual activities and those specified in the curriculum guidelines. The data permitted, for example, estimates of the time spent in a specific area by class members or the percentages of Spanish and English used by teachers. Although the data were summarized in the form of a score, the raw data were available for interpretation of the results. Data were collected for three two-week periods by participant researchers and implementation researchers at each of the eight sites.

QUALITY CONTROL

The difficulty in subjecting multisite data collected through naturalistic observations to the tests of reliability and validity normally associated with psychometric measurement have recently been dealt with at length (see, for example, Smith and Robbins 1984; Huberman and Crandall, 1982). The flexibility in instrumentation and focus, the extended periods on site, and the descriptive nature of the data collected generally result in credibility of the information collected and dependability of the field researchers emerging as the main issues in assuring the quality of qualitative data. The plausibility of information collected was assessed through the triangulation of different data sources such as multiple interviews, documents, ethnographic notes, and focused observations. Observer reactivity was controlled to some extent by assigning all fieldworkers a similar role—that of observer (as opposed to evaluator)—and by setting up an administrative system by which senior staff dealt with all evaluation related issues at each site. In addition, researchers monitored their role management and noted any role changes. Fieldnotes were sent to the evaluation headquarters where they were reviewed by senior staff. Feedback was continuously provided on phenomena noted at one site that should be investigated at the others, on accuracy of coded entries, and on the overall quality of the fieldnotes to all researchers while in the field. Finally a midyear flip-flop observation in which the PR and IR collecting data at each of the sites within a model exchanged sites for a week of observations, was undertaken to provide a multiple perspective on the events taking place at each site.

As one of the concerns of the study was collecting information on change over time, a number of procedures aimed at securing consistent data were also carried out. These included (1) an initial three-week training period in the techniques of naturalistic observations including simulation of fieldwork in local preschool classrooms; (2) additional training sessions prior to each phase of fieldwork; (3) the use of standardized formats for data recording; (4) the development of a field manual to supplement training sessions by providing operational definitions of the phenomena under study, delineating role relationships, and specifying ethical and confidentiality considerations; and (5) the conducting of parallel observations by the coordinator of fieldworkers with each PR and IR.[4]

DATA REDUCTION AND ANALYSIS

Ethnographic notes were analyzed through a series of procedures that we have called a site summary. Using a topical outline developed from the literature on bilingual education and the concerns of the model developers and focusing on aspects of the community (e.g., family structure, ethnicity) and the preschool (e.g., decision-making structure, in-service training) the researchers wrote descriptions of the sites at which they had collected data. These descriptions were of an interpretive nature in that they had as an organizing theme the feasibility of implementing a particular model in other locales. The descriptions, once written, were examined by senior staff and distilled into a set of categories, each containing a list of specific factors which the individual researchers had identified as facilitating or impeding implementation of a model at a given site. The fieldworkers then met with the research coordinator, reviewed the categories, and wrote summary statements on those factors noted by their colleagues but not identified by themselves. This summary information was then displayed to locate patterns within and across models. The types of findings generated from this analysis are that, for example, a single half-day session was the most effective type of daily schedule across all sites. Although all the classroom activities were also carried out in full day programs and by teachers teaching two sessions a day, ancillary activities and paperwork, such as individual assessment of the children, associated with the curricula suffered as a result of time constraints; parent participation in the classroom was adversely affected by distance and lack of transportation to those sites outside the immediate neighborhood of the children attending a particular program.

In order to examine the patterns of individual behavior the focused observations of individual children were quantified. Using the codes, the relative frequency of the use of Spanish and English by subsample children at each observation period was calculated. Similarly, the relative frequency of input received by each child was computed, as were the frequencies with which coded behavior related to the cross-model objectives for language acquisition, language comprehension, and concept development were exhibited. These data were used to interpret the results of the quantitative data and to generate additional hypotheses to be tested quantitatively.

The following example illustrates the principal way in which findings related to the behavior of individual children in the classroom were used to direct the quantitative data analysis. At each of the PR sites analysis of the qualitative data revealed that the experience the Spanish-preferring children had varied depending on the level of linguistic development in English with which they entered preschool.[5] Across all sites the children could be divided into two main groups: those children who began the year with productive ability in English (SP_2) and those with little or no productive ability in English (SP_1).

Tables 7.1 and 7.2 show the pattern of language use at a Los Angeles site and are illustrative of those found at each of the four PR sites. Three of the Spanish-preferring children at this site—Lea,

TABLE 7.1
Percentage of Spanish and English Used by Spanish-Preferring Subsample Children

	Spanish			English			Language Mixing*		
	Time I	Time II	Time III	Time I	Time II	Time III	Time I	Time II	Time III
Spanish Preferring									
Irma	100	93	100	0	3	0	0	4	0
Victoria	100	96	87	0	2	12	0	2	1
Crispine	90	85	56	0	7	42	10	8	2
Lea	44	3	22	53	97	77	3	0	1
Carolina	76	67	42	14	28	57	10	5	1
José	65	60	2	27	27	92	8	13	6

NOTE: Subsample taken at a Los Angeles preschool three times over the school year. Percentage totals may not equal 100 due to rounding.
*Indicates switching of language within a single sentence or phrase (e.g., Me das un *yellow*).

154

TABLE 7.2

Direct Verbal Input by Peers and Teachers to Spanish-Preferring Children

	Irma		Victoria		Crispine		Lea		Carolina		José	
	Spanish	English	Spanish	English	Spanish	English	Spanish	English	Spanish	English	Spanish	English
Time I												
Teacher	100	0	95	5	93	7	0	100	57	43	79	21
Peer	100	0	0	0	0	0	91	9	33	67	63	33
Overall	100	0	95	5	93	7	26	74	50	50	69	31
Time II												
Teacher	92	8	100	0	87	13	0	100	48	52	48	52
Peer	100	0	100	0	93	7	0	100	76	24	58	42
Overall	97	3	100	0	11	89	0	100	57	43	51	49
Time II												
Teacher	63	27	83	17	53	47	13	87	32	68	9	91
Peer	74	26	38	62	33	67	50	50	26	74	40	60
Overall	70	30	72	28	49	51	29	71	29	71	17	83

NOTE: Percentages taken three times over the school year. Percentage totals may not equal 100 due to rounding.

Carolina, and José—were identified as having productive abilities at the beginning of the year. As can be seen, each of these children used English in at least one-fourth of their classroom interactions even early in the year. Similarly, at least a third of the input directed to each child was in English, and in the case of Lea, the vast majority of her interactions were in English. The SP_2 children at all sites had sufficient knowledge of English vocabulary and grammatical structures to understand and answer questions addressed to them, although they usually initiated spontaneous conversation in the first language. By the end of the year the three children at the Los Angeles site and most of the children at all sites[6] had a majority of their classroom interactions in English. They often used English in spontaneous conversations with peers and exhibited the ability to recall past events in their second language and to use English for a variety of functional purposes. English was also the language in which the majority of the individual input directed to them took place. Four of the ten sample children making up this group across all sites, including José at Los Angeles, went from using primarily Spanish in the classroom to using almost exclusively English, thus changing their classroom language preference. All of these children, however, and seven of the eight children who used a majority of English in their classroom interactions at the end of the year, would have continued to be classified as Spanish dominant based solely on their posttest scores.

The 16 Spanish-preferring children who began the year with little or no productive ability in English, as illustrated by Irma, Victoria, and Crispine at Los Angeles, showed a distinct pattern of second language usage and development. The general pattern was that exhibited by Irma and Victoria. At the beginning of the year they rarely, if ever, interacted in English. Use of English was limited almost totally to repetition of isolated lexical items modeled by the teacher in either structured or unstructured second-language sessions. Their limited direct English input was supplied entirely by the teacher at this time and amounted to a very small proportion of their total language input. For the most part, both teachers and peers tended to address them almost entirely in Spanish. Over the course of the preschool year they gradually increased their second language usage in the classroom. Teachers, and to a lesser extent peers, began to interact more frequently with them in English. They had acquired a sufficient lexical and morphological repertoire to respond with single words and short sentences to both teachers and peers in their nonpreferred language.

Most of their spontaneous conversation with both peers and teachers was, however, still in their preferred language.

These findings led to a reanalysis of the test results, which had shown significant differences favoring the Spanish-preferring children over their comparison group counterparts on three of four English language measures when data from all sites were aggregated. When the data from individual sites were analyzed, however, results consistent with the overall findings were found at only one site. The qualitative data on classroom interactions suggested that considering all Spanish-preferring children as a group could be masking the effects of the curricula on children with differing linguistic abilities. Thus, the data were reanalyzed with Spanish-preferring children with productive abilities in their second language and those without considered as separate groups. Findings showed that overall, experimental children with productive abilities outperformed comparison children on the measure of English comprehension whereas the experimental children with no productive abilities did significantly better on measures of English acquisition and concept development. These results were consistent with the findings at each site where such comparisons were possible.[7]

Tables 7.3 and 7.4 typify the experience of most English-preferring children. Despite the fact that dual language development for all children was a stated goal of each of the curriculum models, children in three of the four sites[8] interacted almost entirely in English. Thus, as might be expected, they performed as well as the English-preferring comparison groups on all English measures and were generally unable to respond to tests administered in Spanish. Thus, the qualitative data helped to avoid the evaluation of a nonevent, practice in Spanish for English-preferring children.

The preceding tables present only two examples of the behaviors that were coded and quantified for cross-site comparison. The same procedure was followed for the behaviors within each of the categories of curricula objectives. The focused observations were also used, however, for an in-depth analysis of the experience of individual children in the different social contexts of each curriculum model. The following examples of the experiences of the child whom we have called José during the planning sessions that initiated the preschool day at his Los Angeles preschool, illustrate this level of analysis and demonstrate how interpretations of the general findings were made.

TABLE 7.3
Percentage of Spanish and English Used by English-Preferring Subsample Children

| | Spanish | | | English | | | Language Mixing* | | |
	Time I	Time II	Time III	Time I	Time II	Time III	Time I	Time II	Time III
English Preferring									
Ernesto	0	5	0	100	95	100	0	0	0
Lucia	0	0	0	100	100	100	0	0	0
Candido	0	0	0	100	100	100	0	0	0
Barbara	0	0	0	100	100	100	0	0	0
Danny	0	0	0	100	100	100	0	0	0

NOTE: Subsample taken at a Los Angeles preschool three times during the school year. Percentage totals may not equal 100 due to rounding.
*Indicates switching of languages within a single sentence or phrase (e.g., Me das un *yellow*).

TABLE 7.4
Direct Verbal Input by Peers and Teachers to English-Preferring Children

	Ernesto		Lucia		Candido		Barbara		Danny	
	Spanish	English	Spanish	English	Spanish	English	Spanish	English	Spanish	English
Time I										
Teacher	9	91	0	100	0	100	0	100	0	100
Peer	0	100	0	200	0	100	0	100	25	75
Overall	8	92	0	100	0	100	0	100	3	97
Time II										
Teacher	2	98	0	100	5	95	0	100	0	100
Peer	0	100	0	100	50	50	0	100	0	100
Overall	2	98	0	100	9	91	0	100	0	100
Time III										
Teacher	4	96	0	100	0	100	4	96	0	100
Peer	27	73	0	100	0	100	0	100	0	100
Overall	8	92	0	100	0	100	3	97	0	100

NOTE: Subsample taken at a Los Angeles preschool three times during the school year. Percentage totals may not equal 100 due to rounding.

José, one of the children who showed a great increase in his English usage over the year, was an attractive child with straight black hair and large brown eyes. He was extremely active and often took the lead in organizing games among his peers. Although he was generally well behaved in the classroom, José's eagerness to participate in group situations sometimes caused him to speak out of turn and distract other children. On the pretest he performed better on all Spanish measures but also exhibited some verbal ability and understanding of English. Early in the year his preferred language in the classroom was also Spanish, as noted in a planning activity.

Teacher: What area? . . . ¿Qué area?
José: Area tranquila.
Teacher: ¿Con que vas a jugar?
José: Con esos (points to some balls of string.)
Teacher: What are you going to do?
José: Ponerlos en una cinta.
Teacher: Put them on a string.
José: Con bolitas de contar.
Teacher: Counting balls. . . .Anything else?
José: (Fails to respond to the teacher, but goes to get symbols requested by other children.)

Although the teacher made repeated attempts to elicit responses in English through similarly structured WH questions (e.g., who, what, where, why) and simultaneous translation, José persisted in answering in Spanish. His responses were, however, appropriate to the questions, revealing his comprehension of English. The teacher used this comprehension to provide José with vocabulary through the continued translation of his utterances in Spanish.

By midyear José's productive ability in English has expanded to where he often spontaneously responded with incomplete English utterances, even to questions addressed to him in Spanish by the teacher. He still, however, exhibited a lack of familiarity with basic English vocabulary and tended to language-switch back to Spanish to fill in for unlearned lexical items. The exchange below, recorded during a planning activity in March, shows this behavior.

Teacher: ¿Qué vas a hacer?
José: A house.
Teacher: ¿Qué vas a hacer?
José: Una casa con dos ventanas, *it gonna have five doors,* un techo.
Teacher: How do you say it in English?
José: (No response.)

As the end of the year approached, José demonstrated a greatly improved vocabularly in English as well as an ability to effectively handle a variety of functions. Another planning sequence, from June, typifies José's speech after nine months in the preschool program.

Teacher: What's your plan?
José: Block area.
Teacher: What are you going to do?
José: Make a house, use wooden blocks. (Points to hollow blocks.)
Teacher: What are those?
José: Domino blocks.
Teacher: No, hollow blocks. What are you going to put in your house?
José: Windows, doors, roof, and chimney ... that's all.
Teacher: Do you have a second plan?
José: (Nods his head affirmatively.)
Teacher: What is it?
José: Quiet area. I want little sticks.
Teacher: Show me the ones.
José: (Gets up and points to the box of rods.)

Unlike his performance at the beginning of the school year, José responded effectively in English to a variety of questions, including both WH and yes/no type, all of which were now posed by the teacher in English. He not only replied to the questions but voluntarily expanded his answers and elaborated (e.g., "use wooden blocks" to "make a house" as opposed to simply "make a house"). The dialogue also provides evidence of José's ability to respond to directives in English and to successfully use such lexical items as "window" and "roof," which a few months previously he had not mastered. His progress was also reflected in his test results where, with the exception of the English acquisition measure, he performed better or as well as his English-preferring classmates. As can be seen by the above examples, such abilities were fostered in the planning sessions as teachers consistently provided lacking vocabulary and often ended a session with a directive.

The degree of implementation of the four curriculum models in each of the experimental classrooms was assessed by calculating overall implementation scores and scores for each of the five implementation areas—schedule and organization, physical settings, instructional materials, individual behaviors, and instructional strategies. These scores were determined by weighing each item on the implementation forms in terms of the average of scores assigned to it by participant researcher and implementation researcher working with a particular model. Fieldnotes were then reviewed to explain particular scores or fluctuations in scores over time.

The area of instructional strategies best illustrates the utility of this use of the qualitative data. Although items varied, the lowest implementation scores in this area were consistently found at those sites implementing a language separation approach to language instruction. This approach used in varying ways by two of the curriculum models set aside certain periods of the preschool day for the exclusive use of either English or Spanish. The remaining two models, on the other hand, used an approach that stressed the use of both languages concurrently throughout the day.

When the observations of language lessons were reviewed, it was found that, owing to the linguistic abilities of most of the children in the classroom, the approaches recommending separation of languages could not be implemented. The following excerpt from an implementation researcher's fieldnotes typifies the situations observed in classrooms where the majority of the children had limited abilities in English.

> The Spanish-preferring children are gathered in a circle around the teacher for second language development circle. The teacher holds a picture of a table with food and plates, but lacking a cup, and asks "What is missing?" To cue the children to the proper response, she turns the card over to show a picture of a cup. A chorus of voices chimes "taza" along with one child's response of "cafe." The teacher then attempts to give an additional hint in English: "With what do we drink it? ... What is here?" and points to the cup. When the group persists with "taza," the teacher finally indicates the desired response, "cup," which the children repeat. The teacher then reminds the children of why she insisted on the English word: "This is an English circle. Now I'm going to show you a picture. Who is it? Who is the lady?" She holds up a picture of a woman serving a drink to a little boy and girl. The children, picking up on the vocabulary word "lady," respond in unison, "lady." When the teacher asks, "What are they doing?" Sara answers, "boy," and the group repeats after her. The teacher then turns to another child, "Mason, what are they doing? ¿Que están haciendo?" Mason replies appropriately, "Están tomando Koolaide," to which the teacher replies, "In English, Mason. They are drinking Koolaide." While Mason tries to repeat the English phrase, the children start to stir restlessly. The teacher closes the lesson with a suggestion: "I want you to talk English at home. ... Quiero que practiquen hablar ingles con sus

hermanos." She then addresses a question to Amaranta: "¿Tu mama habla inglés?" When the child nods affirmatively, the teacher advises, "Tienes que hablar con ella." The children listen as the teacher announces the next activity. "This is the end—now we are going to make exercises in a big circle because it's too cold to play outside." They eagerly stand and move to the circle area.

The difficulty of maintaining the use of English-only during second language development time is painfully evident from this example. The teacher persisted in the use of English and adapted her language use to the limited second-language abilities of the children only after repeated questions and reformulations to help the children understand and respond appropriately in English were unsuccessful. Although the children repeated isolated words, the content of the questions were generally beyond their receptive abilities. When the teacher resorted to concurrent translation, an inappropriate technique by model guidelines, the children were able to respond correctly in Spanish but had difficulty producing the same phrase in English even after it was modeled for them.

The second example, taken from the fieldnotes of a participant researcher, illustrates the situation that occurred in classrooms implementing a dual language approach that were made up largely of bilingual children.

The teacher who serves as the Spanish language model sits with the Spanish-preferring children at a table laid out with scissors, paste, and circles of different colored construction paper. She begins the activity by asking the children what they are going to do: "¿Que es lo qué vamos a hacer?" Juanita responds, "light," and her classmate, Wanda, chimes in with the colors, "rojo, verde, y amarillo." When the teacher repeats the question, Juanita repeats her answer, but this time in Spanish. The teacher expands on the youngster's answer, saying "la luz del trafico," Wanda and Juanita then begin to talk to each other. When Wanda asks in English if she has all of her colored circles, Juanita responds, "Yeah, I have." Then, checking her materials more closely, she points to the red circle and says, "My red. You have two red. Ana took my red."

Following model directives, the teacher asked all of her questions in Spanish. As happened frequently in classes containing bilingual children, however, there was a tendency to answer spontaneously in English. Similarly, although the lesson was conducted in Spanish, these Spanish-preferring children would use English in their discourse with one another.

The quantitative analysis supported the implementation findings. It was at those sites using a concurrent language use model, which was consistent with the children's naturally occurring conversation in the classroom, that significant differences favoring the experimental children on the greatest number of test measures were found.

DISCUSSION

This chapter has outlined three ways in which naturalistic observations were used in a national evaluation of bilingual bicultural preschool models. The purpose was not to present the results of that evaluation nor to suggest a methodology for all evaluations of bilingual programs but rather to discuss some of the ways in which observational data were used to address some of the concerns of the funding agency and of bilingual educators in general. Each of the data collection procedures was tied to the objectives of the curriculum models and to the evaluation goals, and thus were considered focused observations rather than an ethnography per se. The questions to be answered through the focused observations as well as the methodology employed were largely determined prior to the hiring of the fieldworkers. Within the context of the evaluation the PRs and IRs were allowed to reformulate certain types of questions and add variables to be investigated. In many instances, however, they were requested to collect data in exactly the same manner at different points in time.[9] Although this may have limited the flexibility of the fieldworkers to explore promising leads not directly related to the research questions, it had the advantage of permitting systematic within-model and cross-model comparisons.

Observations of the individual children in the naturally occurring activities of the classroom furnished descriptive data over time on individuals participating as subjects in the study and permitted a characterization of the treatment as implemented with children of different linguistic abilities in the same classrooms. The analysis of these data led to additional analysis of the test results and thereby to a more precise estimate of treatment effects. Observation of classroom activities identified by the curriculum developers as central to the appropriate functioning of the curricula provided criteria for assessing the extent to which the treatment was implemented as planned and to the classroom characteristics affecting implementation. Similarly, participant observation outside the classrooms was used to gather information on factors beyond the classroom that facilitated or impeded the implementation process.

The study differed from most multisite qualitative evaluations in that one unit of analysis was the individual learner. Although participant researchers were located at sites in California, New York, and Texas, each of which was implementing a distinct curriculum model and had a different ratio of children with varying linguistic abilities, consistent trends in the behaviors of children with similar linguistic characteristics were found. Thus, by selecting a workable subsample of children with different entry-level abilities, it was possible to examine the extent to which the programs yielded a similar set of outcomes or nonoutcomes across similar children. The findings suggest that, at least in evaluations where observations are focused, extensive quality control of qualitative data collection is maintained, and a sufficient variety of cases to determine common patterns are studied, generalizable results can be obtained.

In addition to providing an explanatory complement to the test data, the observations of the individual children were used to provide contextually relevant outcome data. A number of children were shown to use a majority of English in the classroom at the end of the year. On the test data, however, these same children would have been judged as dominant in Spanish despite the fact that they seldom used that language in the classroom.

Finally, the data gathered on program implementation permitted a determination of those common aspects of some curricula (e.g., concurrent language use in language lessons) most likely to be effectively implemented and of the factors inhibiting the effective implementation of others. Thus, the qualitative analysis furnished information on issues of concern to teachers, program staff, and policy planners as well as enabling evaluators to provide a more specific and accurate interpretation of the effect of participation in a given model on individual children.

NOTES

1. The term "naturalistic observation" is used here to refer to a series of logically related behavioral records and other measures gathered in the naturally occurring contexts of the classroom, school, and local community. Throughout the text this term is used synonymously with "qualitative methodology" and "the qualitative component of the evaluation." As will be shown, the approach taken shares a phenomenological

perspective as well as a number of data collection procedures with anthropological ethnography and especially ethnographies of schooling. It differs, however, in that the study lacks the theory based approach and orientation to culture that might characterize an "ethnographic" evaluation.

2. It was originally envisioned that the participant researchers would also be responsible for supervising the standardized testing of children at their site. Owing to both time considerations and anticipated difficulties in role management, this task was assigned to other individuals prior to the beginning of testing. Thus, as their final responsibilities entailed relatively prolonged and intense interaction and involvement with those being studied they were analogous to what is generally called a participant observer in anthropological literature.

3. Owing to a series of fieldtrips and vacations related to the holiday season, the total observation time was somewhat shorter at this observation period than at subsequent ones. Thus, relative frequencies were used throughout the analyses over time.

4. The percentage of interrater agreement between the coordinator and each PR or IR calculated for the approximately 120 items of the implementation forms at two different observation periods was consistently high for both the fall and spring parallel observations. Overall agreement ranged from 81% to 92% at the fall observation and from 82% to 89% in the spring. Similarly, parallel observations of individual children conducted for a total of 90 minutes with each PR over a two day period in the spring yielded a high percentage of agreement (83% to 96%) in the coding of all common observations.

5. The exceptions to these patterns were what might be termed "nontalkers" and "good language learners." The nontalkers were those children who, despite teachers' efforts to draw them out, rarely spoke in the classroom. The good language learners were those children, who despite entering Head Start with little productive ability in their second language, sought out interactions in English. These children by the second observation period were limiting their interactions with peers to English. Together, these two types of children accounted for approximately 15% of the Spanish-preferring sample.

6. The exceptions were the few SP_2 children at the Texas site where Spanish predominated in the classroom. These children followed the same trends as other SP_2 children but the nature of the classroom limited their opportunities for interaction in English.

7. Sample size limited such comparisons to four of the eight sites.

8. The one exception was the Texas site where Spanish predominated in the classroom. At this site, the language use patterns of the three English preferring children in the sample were similar to those of the SP_1 children at all sites.

9. This is not to say that the material for theory building was not gathered. For example, the information is available to investigate the nature of language preference and the usefulness of this construct when compared to that of language dominance. Such an investigation was, however beyond the scope of the evaluation.

REFERENCES CITED

American Institutes for Research
   1977 Evaluation of the Impact of ESEA Title VII Spanish/English Bilingual Education Program. Palo Alto, CA: Author.

Bruck, M., J. Schultz, and F. Rodriguez-Brown
 1979 Assessing Language Use in Bilingual Classrooms: An Ethnographic Analysis. *In* Evaluating Evaluations. A. D. Cohen and M. Bruck, eds. Arlington, VA: Center for Applied Linguistics.
Center for Applied Linguistics
 1977 Response to the AIR Study: Evaluation of the Impact of ESEA Title VII Spanish/English Evaluation Program. Arlington, VA: Author.
Chesterfield, R. et al.
 1982 Final Report: An Evaluation of the Head Start Bilingual Bicultural Curriculum Development Project. Report submitted to the Administration for Children, Youth and Families. Los Angeles: Júarez and Associates.
Cohen, D.
 1973 Politics and Research. *In* School Evaluation: The Politics and Process. E. R. House, ed. Berkeley: McCutchan.
Cohen, A. D. and L. Laosa
 1976 Second Language Instruction: Some Research Considerations. Curriculum Studies, 18: 149-165.
Cohen, A. D., and M. Bruck eds.
 1979 Evaluating Evaluations. Arlington, VA: Center for Applied Linguistics.
Cummins, J.
 1977 Psychological Evidence: *In* Bilingual Education: Current Perspectives. Arlington, VA: Center for Applied Linguistics.
Fetterman, D. M., ed.
 1984 Ethnography in Educational Evaluation. Beverly Hills, CA: Sage.
Firestone, W., and R. Herriot
 1984 Multisite Qualitative Policy Research: Some Design and Implementation Issues. *In* Ethnography in Educational Evaluation. D. M. Fetterman, ed. Beverly Hills, CA: Sage.
Gonzalez, J.
 1978 The Status of Bilingual Education Today: Un Vestazo y un Repaso. Journal of the National Association for Bilingual Education 2:13-20.
Huberman, A. M., and D. Crandall
 1982 Fitting Words to Numbers. American Behavioral Scientist 26:62-83.
Illinois State Board of Education
 1981 The First Annual Program Summary and Evaluation Report of Transitional Bilingual Education Programs in Illinois, 1979-1980. Springfield: Author.
Intercultural Development Research Association
 1977 The AIR Evaluation of the Impact of ESEA Title VII Spanish/English Programs: An IDRA Response. San Antonio, TX: Author.
Miles, M.
 1979 Qualitative Data as an Attractive Nuisance: The Problem of Analysis. Administration Quarterly 24:590-601.
Patton, M.
 1980 Qualitative Evaluation Methods. Beverly Hills, CA: Sage.
Saravia Shore, M.
 1979 An Ethnographic Evaluation/Research Model for Bilingual Programs. *In* Bilingual Education and Public Policy in the United States. R. V. Padilla, ed. pp. 328-348. Ypsilanti: Eastern Michigan University.

Smith, A. G., and A. E. Robbins
    1984 Multimethod Policy Research: A Case Study of Structure and Flexibility.
    In Ethnography in Educational Evaluation. D. M. Fetterman, ed. pp. 115-132.
    Beverly Hills, CA: Sage.
Wilson, S.
    1977 The Use of Ethnographic Techniques in Education Research. Review of Edu-
    cational Research 47:245-265.

PART IV

Politics

8

Use of Ethnographic Techniques for Evaluation in a Large School District

The Vanguard Case

BARBARA G. FERRELL
DONALD W. COMPTON

P rior to the United States Supreme Court decisions in *Brown v. Board of Education,* the Boonetown School District in Texas existed as a dual school system. That is, there were specific schools reserved for Black students and others reserved for White students. Following the *Brown I* and *II* rulings, Brown went through a cycle of desegregation activities similar to those of most southern school systems.

Boonetown began school desegregation in fall 1960 when it implemented a grade-per-year transfer plan. Subsequently, the district has been engaged in other methods to achieve integration such as freedom of choice (1967) and school pairing (1971). None of these methods achieved the desired results.

In 1975, the federal court declared the district out of compliance with federal desegregation policies. In answer to this, the magnet program went into effect, opening with 34 programs. By the 1981-82 school year, 62 programs had been established at all grade levels. These included extended day programs as well as those focused on fine arts and gifted and talented students.

Of the 193,000 students enrolled in the district, a total of 24,000 (12%) were enrolled in magnet schools in 1981-82. The federal court order dealing with magnet schools imposes ethnic quotas of 65% minority (Black and Hispanic), 35% majority (White and Others) students on all magnet programs. The ethnic breakdown of the entire district was 44% Black, 30% Hispanic, 23% White, and 3% Asian.

AUTHORS' NOTE: We would like to acknowledge Dr. Margaret LeCompte, Jyl R. Giles, and Cheryl Stanley for their assistance in designing the evaluation, collecting the data, and editing the chapter.

Vanguard, Boonetown's program for the gifted and talented, was initiated in 1972 on two campuses. In 1975 Vanguard became a part of the district's overall magnet program. Originally offered to students only at the elementary level, it has expanded to include kindergarten through twelfth grade. Currently, there are 11 Vanguard campuses: six elementary programs, three junior high/middle schools, one senior high program, and one offering a Vanguard program at both the elementary and middle school levels. These 11 schools offered a special program to almost 2900 students throughout the district during the 1981-82 school year (see Table 8.1).

Vanguard provides a program of learning for academically able students. The Vanguard philosophy (Boonetown Independent School District 1980:2) states that the program "will develop the student's basic skills, creativity, and intellectual abilities" through a curriculum that is interdisciplinary, individualized and self-paced, stresses self-discipline, and provides the student with the opportunity to explore areas of interest in depth.

Selection for the Vanguard program is based on ranking by race according to court-established ratios. The tools used for identification include (1) a standardized achievement test, (2) additional tests according to grade level, (3) previous academic achievement, (4) other instruments designed to determine the student's level of development in characteristics unique to gifted students, and (5) recommendations from teachers and parents. Students' scores on all these measures are entered into a matrix and a total score is obtained. Students are then rank-ordered by race and accepted in that order until district racial quotas are met.

White students admitted to the program generally are in the eighth or ninth stanines. Minority students, who apply in lower numbers but are admitted in larger numbers, may rank as low as the sixth stanine. Each year a great many more White children apply to the Vanguard program than minority children. This fact presents a problem for Vanguard and has great programmatic impact.

Since the inception of Vanguard, evaluation of the program has consisted of monitoring of program objectives. The monitoring for the past two years has been district-wide. During the 1981-82 school year, nearly a decade after the program's beginning, a more in-depth study was undertaken. This chapter will

(1) present the study design utilized in evaluating the Vanguard program,
(2) discuss some of the findings of the study, and

(3) analyze how pressures from the community and from within the district affected the evaluation design.

A variety of theoretical approaches were reviewed to plan and conduct the study. Stufflebeam and Webster (1980) provide an overview of 13 conceptual frameworks that have been adopted for use in educational evaluation. Of the 13, four models contained elements appropriate for use in the evaluation of the Vanguard program. These included politically oriented studies, questions-oriented studies, objectives-based studies, and accountability studies.

A review of the literature related to ethnographic models also was undertaken. Adopting such a subjective approach would have provided the capacity to incorporate unintended outcomes and other subtle aspects of the educational environment into the study design (Koppelman 1979). Fetterman (1982) has cautioned against educators adopting an ethnographic model without having appropriate training. Nonetheless, although none of the conceptual frameworks reviewed were adequate on their own for the purpose of the Vanguard study, each provided some insight into different aspects of the program. While this study is first and foremost a case study, it can be used as a vehicle to illustrate how ethnographically oriented methods can be used with other techniques.

TABLE 8.1
Vanguard Programs, Grade Levels,
Enrollment, and Ethnic Breakdown,
1981-1982 School Year

Campus	Grade Levels Offered	Enrollment (10/1/81)	Percentage Ethnicity		
			Black	Hispanic	White-Asian-Indian
Elementary I	3-5	138	32	41	27
Elementary II	K-5	149	43	22	35
Elementary III	K-6	181	48	28	24
Elementary IV	K-5	252	27	21	52
Elementary Middle	3-7	257	25	8	67
Elementary VI	1-6	145	37	26	37
Elementary VII	K-5	256	40	11	49
Middle I	7-9	236	29	29	42
Middle II	6-8	300	43	22	35
Middle III	6-8	599	43	16	41
High I	9-12	265	64	7	29
Total	K-12	2778	40	19	41

The conceptual framework adopted for this study was drawn from the social research consultation literature. As is the case with most program evaluation, this study has little to contribute in terms of general theoretical significance. This type of study is of little use other than as providing a factual basis for action. Because of this, the goals of the evaluation and implementation were considered at all stages of the process.

Based on Warren's (1963) conceptual model, evaluation is seen as a political process in which the development of the evaluation design and the construction of the findings is a process of negotiation among the evaluators, administrators and school personnel. This process continues after the study is completed and determines to what extent the recommendations of the study are implemented as well. Warren (1963:68) notes that

> a research project is a social action episode involving task accomplishment (including both the research and its implementation), in which a consultant enters into a relationship with a client system, and of which is set up a study system. Both of these systems undergo planned and unplanned changes as the tasks of research and implementation are attempted.

Warren (1963) also notes that research projects can be seen as social actions that involve people with a variety of motivations and conceptions regarding what the project will accomplish. Their behavior interaction can be analyzed with concepts that have applicability to other forms of social interaction as well. For example, Schein (1969) provides a discussion of the process or collaborative model that could be useful in analyzing the negotiating that takes place when there are differing expectations regarding what the project will accomplish. One way this negotiation process occurred was in the selection of ethnographic techniques for data collection.

Using these techniques for data collection in program evaluation was a new approach to providing information to decision makers in the Boonetown School District. Historically, the evaluation department had relied primarily on product information using data such as standardized test scores and attainment of objectives as measures of educational outcomes. In addition, any evaluation done in magnet schools in Boonetown had to be placed in the context of the history of desegregation in the district and the court-established set of objectives for magnet schools. The legal status of desegregation in the district has had an impact on both the depth and breadth of evaluation studies. Priorities of the court determine evaluation priorities. Ethnographic techniques could have been used as a means to collect data such as availability of transportation and ethnic makeup of the surrounding community. These data could have been of greater use to decision makers in making programmatic changes that would bring the district into compliance with the court order. The real-life constraints of operating in a large district, however, limited the actual use of ethnographic techniques.

While ethnographic techniques and product data potentially provided opportunity for a comprehensive evaluation plan, the political context in which the study was conducted placed constraints on the type and extent of data collected. Although the design and instrumentation for the study were ready in December, data collection did not begin until March when administrative approval was granted.

Competing messages created a variety of problems during execution of the study. Although internal pressure against in-depth evaluation existed because of the court case, the general superintendent also wanted information about how well the Vanguard program was functioning.

Despite the fact that one of the purposes of magnet schools is to integrate the district at both student and staff levels, questions related to whether or not prejudicial attitudes existed and the extent to which integration was taking place were deleted by administration.

Questions dealing with racial conflicts among staff were eliminated because they might have exacerbated problems that were thought to exist in some programs. In piloting an attitude survey, some students complained about questions related to prejudice of teachers toward students. In response to these events, all questions dealing with race were omitted, thus reducing the scope of the study.

In spite of these limitations, negotiations made possible collection of more useful information than would have been the case with an objective-based approach to evaluation. This type of evaluation was somewhat radical by comparison. Even though there was a prevailing political climate emphasizing only achievement test scores as a means to evaluate programs, the Vanguard in-depth study was viewed as a useful tool by decision makers. The proof lies in the fact that numerous requests have been made to do similar studies of other programs in the district.

EVALUATION DESIGN

There were two components to the evaluation of Vanguard during the 1981-82 school year. The first consisted of regular magnet campus monitoring procedures; the second consisted of additional data collection used for a more in-depth study of each Vanguard campus.

Regular monitoring procedures consisted of three site visits, one each in the fall and winter and a visit at the end of the year. The first two visits provided data for process evaluation and the end of the year visit also provided data for assessing the extent to which program objectives were met. During the fall visit a campus action plan consistent with the districtwide Vanguard objectives was developed. In the winter and at the end of the year, the action steps, activities that lead to attainment of objectives, were reviewed. Concrete evidence to document the accomplishment of action steps was presented. Product evaluation took place at the end of the school year and documents the extent to which campus level objectives have been met.

In addition to this routine monitoring, a more in-depth study was undertaken. Each of the Vanguard campuses was visited by the magnet school evaluation team, composed of three or four members. During this visit the principal, Vanguard program coordinator, Vanguard counselor, and some teachers were interviewed. A structured interview schedule was developed for each, and the same questions were asked across roles as well as campuses.

Questions across interview schedules were repeated so that the insights of various roles could be compared. Some questions specific to the individual's role were asked.

The principal's interview schedule consisted of 27 questions and took approximately one hour to complete. A single member of the evaluation team conducted all principal interviews, with 10 of the 11 principals being interviewed.

The coordinator's interview required about one and one-half hours to complete and was made up of 31 questions. The same evaluator interviewed all 11 of the Vanguard coordinators.

Similarly, the Vanguard counselors were interviewed. Their interview schedule consisted of only 10 questions and could be completed in 45 minutes. Nine counselors were interviewed. One school had a vacancy and another counselor was ill on the day of the visit.

Two teachers from each school except one were selected from the *1981-82 Gifted and Talented Staff Directory* using a table of random numbers. Because the Vanguard program at one school is larger, three teachers were interviewed from that school. A total of 23 teachers from a total staff of 120 completed the 29-item, one-hour interview schedule.

The randomly selected teachers represented every grade level from kindergarten to twelfth grade and were representative of subject matter areas. There were three males and 20 females in the group. Nine were Black and 14 were White. Their mean number of years of teaching experience was 11.48, the median was 10. The mean number of years experience in Vanguard was 2.83. Seven of those selected were new to the Vanguard program.

In order to obtain information about the students' perceptions of Vanguard, a technique called a "youth poll" was used.[1] Classes making up the youth poll sample were those classes in session at the time the randomly selected teacher was being interviewed. Thus, the student sample was a sample of convenience. While one member of the evaluation team interviewed the teacher, another conducted the youth poll.

In elementary schools, a series of 11 questions was read aloud to the class as a whole. Students were allowed to respond to the question until they had no more to say before going on to the next question. Student responses were recorded on a portable tape recorder. Students were cautioned not to use their names or the names of other students.

At the secondary level the classes were divided into groups of from four to six students. Each group was given a tape recorder, written directions, and a set of 19 questions. The groups read the questions and tape recorded the responses. Transcripts of the recordings were made and then organized and summarized by theme.

The actual number or percentages of youth who thought one way or another were not tabulated in doing the content analysis of the transcripts. Rather, the attempt was made to enter into the world of youth and to represent and do justice to the meaning of that world. Once the student responses were organized by theme, they were independently reviewed by several researchers. Those comments chosen by all three researchers as best representing the major themes were included in the analysis. Although the students' responses may or may not have served the purpose of answering a particular programmatic question, they did provide depth to the questions asked and provided answers that helped develop research questions for the future.

TABLE 8.2
Ethnic Composition of Responding Parents

Ethnicity	Number	Percentage
Black	212	27
White	418	53
Hispanic	112	14
Asian	27	4
Other	13	2
Total	782	100

A total of 20 classes participated in the youth poll. Eleven were elementary classes; seven were junior high/middle school classes; and two were high school classes. Students represented all grade levels except the primary, kindergarten to second grade, where the technique did not work successfully.

Input from parents also was obtained. A 30-item questionnaire was mailed to the parents of all Vanguard students for whom addresses could be obtained. Of the 2678 surveys mailed, 1020 were returned completed. Another 152 were returned due to insufficient or incorrect addresses, and 20 were returned too late to analyze. The rate of return yielding usable data was 41% of the total number of Vanguard parents.

Although the percentage of return by campus appears to vary a great deal, controlling for the size of student population reveals that the rate of return across campuses is quite similar. Thus, analysis of items based on return should be representative of Vanguard parents as a whole and not be slanted toward the viewpoint of one or two schools.

Tables 8.2 and 8.3 show the racial and economic breakdowns of responding parents. It should be noted that the percentage of White parents returning the questionnaire is higher than their proportion in either the Vanguard program or the district. Parent responses, therefore, will be somewhat biased toward White parents.

FINDINGS

Overall, the Vanguard program was functioning according to design and was satisfactory to most participants. Students, parents, and Vanguard staff were, in general, very positive in their attitudes and opinions about the program. They felt that the program offered a

TABLE 8.3
Annual Family Income of Responding Parents

Income	Number	Percentage
Less than $10,000	29	3.5
$10,001–20,000	122	14.9
$20,001–30,000	118	14.4
$30,001–40,000	119	14.5
$40,001–50,000	104	12.7
Over $50,000	171	20.9
No response	155	19.1
Total	818	100.0

viable alternative to regular instruction and provided a good education for its students.

Some areas in need of improvement were found, however. There were three areas of major concern: quality of Vanguard teachers, lack of a clearly specified and articulated Vanguard curriculum, and variation in the ability levels of students in the program.

VANGUARD TEACHERS

As one parent commented, "The teacher makes it or breaks it," and the reaction to teachers of those interested in Vanguard seems to be bittersweet, at once both the best and the worst part of the program. Boonetown employed 152 full-time and part-time teachers to work with Vanguard students; the teachers varied in their expertise and training for working with gifted children. There is no special certification for teaching gifted/talented students in the state; all that is legally required is a valid teaching certificate.

Of the 23 teachers interviewed, only two had sought a position in gifted education. Fourteen were approached by their building principals to fill a vacancy in Vanguard. Of the seven remaining teachers interviewed, all but two were referred to the program by someone knowing of the vacancy; they had been unaware of Vanguard prior to referral. Few of the teachers interviewed had any background or training in gifted education prior to coming to the program. Two of them had experience in teaching gifted or accelerated students; a few have had some coursework in gifted/talented education; one is completing a master's in the field, but most have only the knowledge gained by attending district in-services since coming to the program.

What, then, differentiated Vanguard teachers from teachers in the regular program? One principal believed there was no difference. Other principals differentiated them in terms of their knowledge of and ability to relate to gifted children, stating that Vanguard teachers were, if not gifted themselves, at least alert, willing, and able to learn. The principals saw the teachers as specialists and able to provide a more flexible learning environment.

Vanguard coordinators frequently mentioned that teachers in the program needed a high energy level and good organizational skills. These were necessary to keep up with the students and to provide an individualized learning environment. They also needed the skill and the willingness to work with parents.

The Vanguard teachers interviewed looked at themselves in a more practical light when compared to teachers in a regular program. They felt they worked harder than other teachers and felt this was necessary in order to keep up with the students.

Although they have extra planning time, Vanguard teachers feel they use it. As one teacher said, "You don't see us in the teacher's lounge." This was substantiated by the principals who reported that many Vanguard teachers came early and stayed late at school as well as used their planning periods. They gave more individual attention to their students and were aware of the needs of the gifted, primarily because of in-services that they attended.

There were a number of things that Vanguard teachers stated they were expected to do in addition to regular teaching duties. Most common of the responses were attending in-services and workshops, sometimes on weekends and in the evening, writing curricula, taking extended field trips, writing learning units, supervising student projects, and working more closely with parents.

In order to determine how well the teachers were perceived as doing those things described by principals, coordinators, and teachers themselves, both parents and students were asked about teachers. Parents were asked how satisfied they were with the teachers working with their children. Of the parents responding to this question, 81% indicated that they were "satisfied" (43%) or "very satisfied" (38%) with their child's teachers. Only 4% of the parents said they were "very dissatisfied" with the teachers. White parents were more likely to show dissatisfaction than any other group, accounting for 70% of those who were "very dissatisfied." Parents with annual family incomes over $50,000 were also more likely to be dissatisfied.

The most common reason for dissatisfaction was the lack of ability to work with gifted/talented children. Parents clearly felt that the Vanguard program should be staffed with teachers who have knowledge and expertise in working with gifted children. Parents felt that first year teachers and teachers with negative attitudes definitely did not belong in Vanguard.

When asked to judge what proportion of the teachers were competent, almost 80% of the parents responded with "most" or "all." Less than 1% felt "none" were and 3% felt "few" were competent. While ethnicity did not appear to be a factor in judging teacher competence, income was a slight one, with teachers more likely to be judged incompetent by higher income parents.

Teachers perceived as incompetent by parents were judged highly incompetent. Parents also highly praised the teachers and considered them to be the best part of the Vanguard program. When asked what was good about the program, teachers were the most frequently cited. When asked what was bad, teachers again came up most frequently. Parents commented that teachers in Vanguard were much superior to those in the regular program.

Students were asked what kind of teachers they had expected before coming to the Vanguard program and how Vanguard teachers differed from those in the regular program. Students had expected teachers in Vanguard to be strict, structured, and unbending, "mean," as one student put it. Instead, Vanguard students indicated that they found a close, caring atmosphere and teachers who differed from others by their true desire to help. These feelings were captured by student comments such as: "I think we're more on a friend-to-friend relationship." "They care about students and students about them." "It's not like they just want to get the paycheck. They want to teach." According to students, there seemed to be more willingness on the part of the teachers to continue to work with students until they understood.

Students also were critical of the teachers and demanded quality from them. Students at the secondary level indicated that they wanted teachers who were qualified to teach gifted students, who were gifted themselves. One student said, "Some of the teachers don't have that much Vanguard ability. I think to teach in the Vanguard program you've got to be Vanguard ability yourself."

There was no districtwide selection process for Vanguard teachers, nor was there a deselection procedure for teachers hired into the program who do not work well with gifted children. Poor teachers or teachers who, while not bad teachers, are unable to work with Vanguard students remain in the program. The present practice of transferring teachers who are already in the building into the Vanguard program cuts down the potential pool of teachers who might be qualified to teach in the program. One parent wanted to know, "Why are teachers not selected as carefully as students for the Vanguard program?"

The coordinators indicated that Vanguard teachers "burn out" rapidly. After two or three years in the program they frequently go on to other areas. They must attend 18 hours of in-service for the program in addition to all other required in-services on their own time. They must write learning units and assist students with projects. Their teaching is individualized. However, unlike teachers in other specialty areas, Vanguard teachers are not eligible for any extra stipends. One parent, who indicated that she was not a teacher, said, "I think that teachers teaching in our Vanguard programs should be well paid in order to keep them in the educational system."

Regular teachers envied the Vanguard teachers' extra planning time. Teachers described conflicts that appear to be quite subtle. As one teacher put it, "It's not like war—but you can feel the tension." "Some of the Vanguard teachers don't even go in the lounge anymore—they don't want to put up with the comments."

Vanguard teachers, then, had little background in the education of gifted and talented students before coming to teach there. Indeed, most did not seek out teaching opportunities with the gifted. They were characterized as gifted, alert, energetic, skillful, competent, and liked by students.

CURRICULUM

The curriculum for the Vanguard program in Boonetown was based upon district curriculum guides. The curriculum for a gifted program should, however, in some way be differentiated for these students if the program is to be justified. The *Vanguard Teacher's Handbook* outlines how curriculum is differentiated (Boonetown Independent School District 1980:10). It is individualized; addresses higher levels of thinking, creative problem solving, and decision making; and allows students to participate in real-life learning.

Individuals involved in Vanguard were asked what made Vanguard different from the regular program. Principals and coordinators outlined its uniqueness in terms of students and individualized instruction. Principals stated that because the students who come to the program have a higher level of skill and motivation, the teachers can work with them to plan activities that would be best for them.

Students were a homogenous, higher ability group and teachers' styles were more individualized. Coordinators also mentioned the lower pupil teacher ratio and availability of materials as unique to the program.

Because most of the students already have acquired the basic skills, teachers stated they could provide enrichment that challenges the students to use their ability. They also mentioned that the environment was less structured and that they were trying to develop creativity, higher level thinking processes, and research skills in their students. A closer relationship with students was also mentioned.

Students listed as special all the types of things they were able to do in Vanguard. The list included such things as field trips, foreign language classes, computers, projects, clubs, and the ability to move at their own pace. Students seemed to recognize the existence of the differentiated individualized curriculum and to cite it as a special feature of the program. Teachers also were frequently cited as more helpful. "At the other school, they'd just tell you what to do and you do it. Here they explain to you and they help you." "At the other school, if you didn't understand it, it was just tough luck."

One of the most common criticisms of the Vanguard curriculum has been that it is not providing students with the basic skills they need. However, fully half of the parents indicated that they felt the school was doing a "very good" job of providing basic skills. Negative responses followed the same patterns as previous items with regard to race and income.

When asked how the classes in Vanguard are differentiated for gifted and talented students, coordinators indicated that the classes are individualized and self-paced. They emphasize thinking and process skills, and they provide both enrichment and acceleration. They also added that students learn research skills by doing individual projects. Teachers' answers to the same question emphasized individualization, acceleration, and projects.

In comparison to their old schools, students indicated that Vanguard was "more complicated," "more of a challenge," or "not boring." One or two felt Vanguard was easier. Those who had been in major works classes for the academically able felt that Vanguard was really not very different in difficulty but was more enjoyable and less structured. A few students thought it was easier than major works. Vanguard also was seen to be more challenging and intellectually exciting than the regular program.

Parents were asked if they felt the Vanguard program was rigorous enough. In all cases the majority of parents answered "yes." The tendency to respond positively went up somewhat in the middle schools. At nine of the 11 schools, some parents thought the program was too rigorous.

These data tend to indicate that there may be two types of students in the Vanguard program. Some come from schools where the campus-level program is quite rigorous; these students do not find much difference between the program offered at Vanguard and that of their home school. Other students find Vanguard to be very challenging and exciting and much more rigorous than their home schools.

The lack of a Vanguard curriculum was a source of frustration for teachers. Teachers felt that district curriculum guidelines did not fit students in Vanguard and said that they were given little guidance from the Vanguard office. They must write their own curricula in the form of learning units, a time-consuming task. Parents expressed the same frustration. When they asked for program goals, objectives, or guidelines, none were available.

One part of the Vanguard curriculum that did differentiate it from regular instruction was its emphasis on the development of research skills by students. Each year students in Vanguard work on a project. As the student proceeds through the grades, the project becomes more sophisticated. When the topics students use for projects were examined across the Vanguard program, an increasing degree of complexity and utilization of research skills could indeed be seen. Students in kindergarten and first grades chose topics such as "cats," "America," or "volcanoes." Students in the middle/junior high school program had their topics specified to a greater extent, for example, "Clothing in Argentina." High school topics were even more specific and expressed a great deal of creativity, such as a documentary film on a local news personality, a survey of Vanguard students' opinions on Vanguard, or a comparison of clothing styles across two decades.

Projects frequently were a cause of complaint. Although students did not complain about projects, parents, particularly at the elementary level, indicated that they were forced to help students with projects and in some cases felt that projects were the work of the parents only. Parents also felt that teachers often did not give students enough direction on how to do the projects.

The problem with the Vanguard curriculum, then, was more a lack of one. Teachers, parents and students all expressed a need for an articulated Vanguard curriculum that could be disseminated to those involved in the program.

STUDENTS

When asked to characterize the students in the Vanguard program, adjectives and phrases such as intellectual ability, emotional stability, maturity, creativity, task-orientation, adaptability, energy, and organization were used. The Vanguard student was seen by principals, coordinators, counselors, and teachers as the kind of child who succeeds in a school setting.

In the youth poll, Vanguard students were asked to describe how they view themselves and to identify issues and problems that may be important to them.

Students indicated that they came to the Vanguard program after realizing it would afford them more educational opportunities. Many students chose to attend a Vanguard school as a way to avoid attending a home school that they perceived as dangerous, overcrowded, or academically substandard. Vanguard students saw themselves as relatively "straight," and the presence of other Vanguard students helped insulate from certain unwanted types of peer pressure. "They (regular students) ask, 'Why do Vanguards dress that way?' 'Why don't you smoke?' 'Why not drink?'"

Vanguard students felt that attendance in the program would provide them with a better education, which in turn would provide opportunities for college scholarships and better jobs in the future. Students mentioned that their old schools were too easy and that they wanted a greater challenge.

These students reported that there is a general climate of anti-intellectualism in Boonetown from which they suffer, and the result was that they tended to downplay their own ability. While they asserted that they were no different from other students, they did feel that they were more ambitious and more motivated to succeed than the regular students. "Vanguard students are more alert, and they want something. They apply themselves, whereas the regular students might not give a damn." "We like to stay in school and all of that stuff, not skip school and smoke dope. And they (other students) say there is something wrong with you." "If you want to be smart, you can be smart. If you want to do no work at all, you can be out of the Vanguard program and be dumb. It's your decision." They felt there were many more students in Boonetown who were qualified to be in Vanguard but who chose not to be because they did not want to work as hard as Vanguard students do and they did not care about their futures.

Students at all levels of the program described a pattern of resentment and conflict directed against Vanguard students by regular students. While it was not always overt, and despite the fact that contact between Vanguard students and non-Vanguard was minimal, it was expressed both within and outside of school. Throughout the program there was teasing and harassment from other students because of the academic talent of Vanguard students. While incidences of physical attack were rare, students expressed a general fear of "regulars," especially at the middle school level. Comments that expressed these feelings were: "Vanguard is mostly scared of regular." "You see, they treat us like we're real creepy." "They mess with you. They don't think you can really take care of yourself."

Students indicated that this was a part of being in the Vanguard program that you had to live with. "This girl—when she got in Vanguard, but she got right back out because the regular students teased her. She couldn't take the pressure." "Well, I've been in the advanced program since kindergarten and I've learned to live with it."

Many students felt that the bad feelings between regular students and Vanguard were fueled by the fact that some Vanguard students felt superior. Some of them felt the teachers in the program reinforced those feelings. "They make us feel like outsiders and that we don't belong with them (other students)." Parents also mentioned this attitude of superiority on the part of Vanguard teachers and students.

Principals, coordinators, and teachers reported conflicts between Vanguard students and regular students and Vanguard teachers and regular teachers. However, unlike the student interviews, the adult interviews for the most part did not emphasize conflict. Almost all the principals said that there were no major conflicts between Vanguard and regular students or Vanguard and regular teachers. Conflicts that were reported were said to be based upon feelings of jealousy on the part of those in the regular program. Students reported that Vanguard students had advantages such as more field trips. One source of conflict lies in the fact that Vanguard students dominate school honors and many of the leadership roles. At each school a long list of Vanguard honors and achievements was obtained, including awards at many district competitions. Some principals indicated that they minimized this problem by giving separate awards for Vanguard and the regular program.

Vanguard students expressed a few frustrations at being in the program although, overall, students were happy and felt Vanguard was an excellent program. One frustration was with the pressure from parents and teachers. Students felt too much was expected of them and that some of the teachers just gave them materials without any help or supporting structure. While they appreciated the independence, they wanted their teachers to teach them. One student said, "They think we're just a bunch of Albert Einsteins, and we're just kids."

Pressure from parents also was described. Students stated that they felt under pressure to be superior not only in academics but in other aspects of their lives. "She expects me to make all As and every time I make one B she gets on my back." "She thinks I'm not trying hard enough and she won't let me do anything at home. All I do at home is homework."

The quantity of homework was another student complaint. Students felt the amount of homework they were given was excessive. Homework interfered with social life and after-school activities. Homework combined with long bus rides took up a great deal of their free time. Many parents expressed the same concern.

Maintaining social life with both Vanguard peers and home school friends was a problem. Because Vanguard peers live all over the city, socialization with them was a problem. Attending a Vanguard school removed them from the day-to-day contact with neighborhood friends and friendships broke down. Elementary school students seemed to have fewer problems maintaining friendships than did students in the upper grades.

Vanguard students themselves, however, really stuck together. They were a very close, multiracial group. Being in the presence of the bright, highly motivated Vanguard peer group was given as a strong point of the program by most of the students and many of the parents.

Across all grade levels Vanguard students suggested that they would like a separate, all-Vanguard school, not one that was housed on a campus with regular students. Such a school would enable them to have their own afterschool activities and alleviate conflict and hostility among Vanguard and non-Vanguard students.

As part of Boonetown's magnet program, one of Vanguard's primary objectives is to provide quality integrated education for its students. By participating in Vanguard, students became part of a racially mixed setting. For some of them, Vanguard was their first experience with children and teachers of other races.

A number of questions were asked that were designed to determine the extent to which integration was being promoted in the Vanguard program aside from the physical mixing of students in the classes. Most characteristic of the responses to these questions was a lack of response. All those interviewed indicated that students in the Vanguard program were truly "colorblind" with regard to other students in the program. Students stated that their relationships in Vanguard were formed on an individual basis rather than upon race.

Students did not mention racial bias or conflict among Vanguard students. They reported that they attended each other's birthday parties, spent the night at each others' houses, talked to each other on the telephone, and, in general, got together as much as time and distance permitted.

An important issue in determining the quality of the Vanguard program was the achievement of its students. Students entering the program generally had high achievement scores as measured by the Iowa Tests of Basic Skills (ITBS).

In the initial screening of potential students for the Vanguard program, ITBS scores are used. Students who have received a percentile rank of 85 or greater on either the reading comprehension subtest or the math composite are solicited by letter as potential applicants for the Vanguard program. Any of these students who wish to apply to the program are then further evaluated using a number of criteria that vary according to grade level.

Students whose ITBS scores are lower than the seventy-fifth percentile on either of the two composite scores ordinarily are not to be admitted to the program. However, ITBS scores are used as but one indicator of suitability for Vanguard and are entered into a matrix with other data for selection into the program. The matrix is so designed that no one single indicator, such as ITBS scores, would prevent a child from being accepted into the program if the other indicators were high enough. Thus, some children are enrolled in Vanguard with ITBS scores below the seventy-fifth percentile.

As one of the districtwide Vanguard objectives, schools are asked each year to compare the percentage of students scoring at or above the

TABLE 8.4

Percentage of Students with Both Reading Comprehension
and Math Composite Scores at or Above
Seventy-Fifth Percentile by Ethnicity

Grade	Black	Hispanic	White-Asian-Indian
1	46.3	59.4	76.2
2	55.4	47.1	87.0
3	39.1	42.4	83.1
4	32.0	45.2	82.6
5	64.0	66.7	85.8
6	37.2	33.3	79.3
7	31.4	40.4	72.5
8	35.4	33.3	73.1
9	32.8	45.0	63.3
10	25.0	25.0	75.0
11	23.8	50.0	76.5
12	30.0	60.0	87.5

85th percentile in either Reading Comprehension or Math Composite
with the last year's percentage. The percentage each year should be the
same as or higher than the last year's scores, but not lower. While this
maintenance objective appears to be a reasonable way to assess overall
achievement, there are some statistical problems involved in evaluating
Vanguard achievement in this way.

First, Vanguard students do not represent a normal distribution with
regard to achievement. They cluster at one extreme of the distribution of
ITBS scores. Missing just one question may cause students who scored
very high one year to slip back a little or appear to "regress" the next
year.

Second, each year it becomes harder and harder to meet the objective of obtaining higher ITBS scores because it is self-inflating. If a
school's scores are higher this year than last, then next year it must obtain even higher scores.

When scores are examined by ethnicity, evidence of variation in
ability levels in the program is found (Table 8.4). The percentage of
White-Indian-Asian students who had scored above the seventy-fifth
percentile on both was about 75%. For Black and Hispanic students,
however, fewer students scored above the seventy-fifth percentile.

The percentage of students who did not score at or above the
seventy-fifth percentile on both subtests remained fairly stable across
grade levels for White-Asian-Indian students but tended to increase at
the upper grades for Blacks. There did not appear to be a pattern for

Hispanics. This discrepancy in achievement test scores may be in part attributed to lower test scores on standardized achievement tests by minorities and the fact that fewer minorities apply to the Vanguard program.

In summary, Vanguard students viewed themselves as different but the extent of these differences was in the level to which they were willing to work to achieve. This difference sometimes caused difficulty for the Vanguard child, particularly in relating to those not in the program. Vanguard students were happy and saw the program as a positive influence. In spite of the fact that Vanguard students were selected using a standard criterion, they were a heterogeneous group.

RECOMMENDATIONS AND CONCLUSIONS

Based on the findings of the Vanguard evaluation study a number of recommendations were made to the district's administration and the Board of Education.

With regard to teachers, recommendations were geared toward ensuring that Vanguard teachers would have the characteristics needed to work with gifted children. First, the development of a districtwide job description for Vanguard teachers was recommended. This would enable the establishment of a screening procedure for applicants for the program. Second, the development of a procedure to evaluate teachers that was specific to teachers of the gifted/talented was recommended. This would enable teachers who had been inappropriately placed to be removed from the program and placed in classrooms that better fit their talents.

With regard to curriculum, the recommendations were related to specifying the ways in which the Vanguard curriculum differs from the basic Boonetown curriculum. The development of a curricular framework with a scope and sequence of learning that would assure consistency across schools was suggested. Written guidelines for projects were also recommended.

Recommendations also were made regarding the quality of students in the Vanguard program. In order to seek greater numbers of qualified minorities it was suggested that Vanguard personnel look for better ways to identify gifted minority children. Students who demonstrate that they are not capable of the level of work in the program should be removed from the program.

Although Warren (1963:91) sees the research process as a social action episode, he states, "Its findings may not themselves become implemented in action." This was indeed the case with the Vanguard study. Some of the recommendations that were made were implemented, at least in part. Some were not.

The implementation of recommendations also became subject to negotiation in the evaluation process. The difference lies in the fact that these negotiations take place among administrators at varying levels within the district and were out of the domain of the evaluators. From the evaluators' perspective, however, the fact that these issues were brought up for discussion at all is of benefit, even if implementation is not achieved.

NOTE

1. The "youth poll" technique was developed at the Center for Youth Development and Research, University of Minnesota (Hedin et al. 1978).

REFERENCES CITED

Boonetown School District
    1980 Vanguard Teacher's Handbook. Houston: Author.
Fetterman, D. M.
    1982 Ethnography in Educational Research: The Dynamics of Diffusion. Educational Researcher 11: 17-29.
Hedin, D., H. Wolfe, and J. Arneson
    1978 Minnesota Youth Poll #4: Youth Views on Money and Success. St. Paul: University of Minnesota.
Koppleman, K. L.
    1979 The Explication Model: An Anthropological Approach to Program Evaluation. Educational Evaluation and Policy Analysis 1:59-64.
Schein, E. H.
    1969 Process Consultation: Its Role in Organization Development. Reading, MA: Addison-Wesley.
Stufflebeam, D. L. and W. J. Webster
    1980 An Analysis of Alternative Approaches to Evaluation. Educational Evaluation and Policy Analysis 2:3-20.
Warren, R. L.
    1963 Social Research Consultation. New York: Russell Sage.

9

"Posin' to Be Chosen"
An Ethnographic Study of In-School Truancy

RICHARD A. MAROTTO

T o be sure "y'all ain't gonna be readin' 'bout no 'jive-ass, ain't wit it' *Archie* comic book story wif Mr. Weatherbee, Miss Grundy, Jughead, Reggie and Moose; y'all better check dis here shit out!''

What Squirrel, a lower class Black streetcorner adolescent, is referring to in his Black peer vocabulary is a picture of Verland High in Buffalo, New York, as an organization composed of two competing rule systems—a formal system within the school, and an informal system brought in from the ghetto streetcorner. To say that the sytems had difficulty integrating and therefore could not coexist would be an understatement. One system would or had to prevail.[1]

As this chapter will demonstrate, the school's system prevails. The purpose of this chapter is to delineate for the reader the "insider's view," the emic perspective on the school's formal system and the school's response to the informal system in the form of disproportionate minority suspensions. In Ericksonian (1984) terms, disproportionate minority suspensions represented the idea base that guided the entire study.

The majority of the ethnographic data is drawn from interviews with and observations of ten lower class Black male teenagers (dubbed the Boulevard Brothers by the researcher) who are enrolled in Verland High[2] and use a corridor intersection (dubbed the Boulevard) as a base of operations. They range in age from sixteen to eighteen. Six are sophomores; three are juniors, and one is a senior.

The time period of the actual study included the two semesters of a full school year and some "extracurricular" hours of the day and night. In brief, I attended "Verland" High School daily, associated myself with a group of Black male teenagers, attended some classes, ate in the cafeteria, "hung out" in the halls, and participated in their informal corridor activity. After becoming accepted as an attached member, I joined their out-of-school social life for the purpose of comparing what they did in school with what they did out of school.[3]

The findings from the investigation are reported in chronological order as they occurred within four classes of persons and events: (1) the group, (2) the routine, (3) the behavior repertoire—the group vis-á-vis the group, and (4) the effects of the group's routine and behavior repertoire on school personnel.

The first thing that became evident to the ethnographer was that the group here called the Boulevard Brothers had a long history. Not only did six of the members grow up in the same ghetto neighborhood, but they also went to elementary and junior high school together. Thus, six members of the group had been best friends since the first grade. Two others became "tight" with these six in junior high school, while two others got to be "runnin' buddies" with all eight shortly after entering high school. In sum, eight of the ten males had been together for at least seven or eight years and had built up a network of interactions and understandings.

The first Boulevard Brother I met was "Squirrel," reported by some students, teachers, and one of the assistant principals to be one of the "coolest and smoothest con artists" in the school. According to his account, Squirrel "did time" at a detention center for committing armed robbery. Other members of the group mentioned this also, admitting that it enhanced Squirrel's reputation.

A second member of the group was "Lil," Squirrel's "runnin' buddy," regarded by both teachers and administrators as the "worst offender" when it came to violating school rules and policies. Three other members of the group were "Bobby," "Theo," and "Butterfly." Bobby talked with a slight speech impediment, was ribbed about it occasionally, and always had a rejoinder. Theo was known for his constant imitation of a disc jockey, his quick wit, and his masterful delivery of barbs or "ribs." Butterfly was noted for carrying around his brief case and being "laid to the maximum [dressed to kill] mostly e'ryday."

Another member of the Boulevard gang was "Crip," a very close friend of Butterfly. Since Crip's father was a minister, the rest of the Brothers would chide him about his behavior by saying jokingly, "You sure you the son of a preacher man? You likes to stay higher-'n a maw-fucker!" The other four members that hung around with the group were "Smokey" and "Rat," who were both small in physical stature in comparison to the rest of the group, and "Reefer Man" and "Milo." "Reefer Man" was one of those who seemed to frequently appear on the daily "Do Not Admit to Class" list, a list that was reserved for those individuals who allegedly breached the standard operating procedures of the school. "Milo" was the first Boulevard Brother to be encouraged by the administration to drop out of Verland because of his deportment. Milo's disruptive behavior and lack of interest in school was documented and measured by the number of teacher complaints filed for class cutting, hall walking, and insubordination (see Marotto 1977:474-553 for details).

Three characteristics of the Boulevard Brothers were essential in the functioning of their group. First, Squirrel was the acknowledged leader of the Brothers. His leadership stemmed from the reputation his stint at the reform or "industry" school brought, his cost and style of clothing, his "stable" of "slims," and his display of verbal expertise when around the administrators, teachers, and other Brothers. Second, none of the Boulevard Brothers participated in the school-sponsored extracurricular activities like athletics, clubs and yearbook or newspaper publication staffs. Third, most of the Brothers had very poor grades and a discipline folder full of "blue slips" (i.e., complaint slips) cataloging their offenses or violations of school rules or acceptable classroom behavior. For example, I recall several teachers saying, "Boy you sure picked the right ones to study," or, "It didn't take you long to latch on to some of our finest (ahem) students. . . . "

These salient characteristics can be illustrated by examining the behavior of Squirrel and the Boulevard Brothers. They all preferred peer-involvement to academic activities. They also deliberately chose to cut classes and to scoff at Verland's rules by "runnin' some shit up under" (conning, deceiving, beguiling, manipulating, goading)[4] their teachers. The Brothers' establishment of and participation in this anomalous "in-school truancy" routine eventually shaped the social and ideological configuration of the school itself. By the time this study was conducted, one of the school's implicit functions was to provide a proving ground for streetcorner or ghetto-specific talents.

The Brothers' informal in-school truancy routine and concomitant display of "streetcorner gamin'-ship"[5] was carried on in such a bold and defiant way that it was perceived by school personnel as a disruptive force interfering with the formal school processes. It was a phenomenon that was referred to as "class-cutting" and "hall wandering" by Verland's teachers and administrators.

The staff, understandably, demanded only that the group respect the organization's rules and regulations. Instead, what the teachers witnessed daily was what Bobby described: "Dey (Brothers) don't 'suspect' (respect) da school as school no mo'. Dey just 'suspect' it as a place to go, 'n get you a girl 'n get high. Talk to 'em (girls) 'n have fun! School ain't nuthin' now but a joke. Now e'rybody just come in, 'grub down' (eat), get high, roam da halls 'n have fun!''

While the size of the group was small, their impact was great. Blacks comprised 33% of Verland's total enrollment. The Brothers were only a very small percentage of that figure. Yet they managed to create a great deal of disruption within the organization. While the group's in-school truancy routine and attendant streetcorner behaviors preserved the group's informal structure and gained for them and their ghetto streetcorner-oriented peers a recognition or status denied by Verland's formal organization, it also closed off their access to formal learning and its accompanying advantages. Simply but pathetically, they win the status conferred by their peers, but lose out on the formal instruction articulated by their teachers—they "lose by winning."[6]

The remainder of this discussion will address (1) what the impetus behind the "lose by winning" syndrome is, and (2) what can be done to abate its self-regenerating and destructive character.

The causes of this phenomenon will be presented from an emic perspective with one of the most recurring phrases or expressions used in their "jive lexicon" as the theme, that is, *"He be cuttin' classes, stayin' in the cafeteria, 'n hangin' in the halls 'posin' to be chosen' to show 'what he is about,' 'n it's all 'bout bein' a 'real live nigga.'"*[7] The goal of this portion of the presentation is to provide a view of streetcorner gamin'-ship as seen through lower class black male adolescent eyes and interpreted according to ghetto streetcorner norms.

"CUTTIN' CLASSES, STAYIN' IN THE CAFETERIA, 'N HANGIN' IN THE HALLS"

The two main meeting places of the group were the cafeteria, where the first two tables near the serving rails were unofficially reserved for the Boulevard Brothers, and the hallway intersection in the new wing of the building, where the assistant principal's office was no more than ten yards away. The Brothers were frequently joined by the "Straddlers" (a group of other Blacks that frequently interacted with the Brothers) and other acquaintances when meeting at these places.

Approximately one-third of the group's time, or two hours of the school day, was spent dodging or occasionally verbally confronting the assigned assistant principal and the teachers supervising the cafeteria during three scheduled lunch periods. The Brothers found the cafeteria relatively free of constraints or interference. They knew that the teachers were less strict in the cafeteria. They also knew that the teachers had to follow the formal rules and schedule of Verland. Since teachers only supervised one lunch period, the Brothers reasoned that their chances of getting caught for "stayin in the caf'" for more than one lunch period were slim. So, on a daily basis, they simply exploited the formal system to their advantage.

Another third of the school day was spent "hangin' aroun'" the Boulevard:

> I am convinced that another main gathering point for the Brothers is the intersection of the hallways near the art room and the girls' gymnasium. Before and after lunch periods, between classes, and throughout the day one can find the Brothers and others assembled at this intersection as if it were a streetcorner. Hence, I dubbed this intersection the "Boulevard" and the Brothers were delighted.

> All kinds of activities go on here. Today there were at least twenty students at or close to the intersection. Smokey and Lil' were smoking openly. Squirrel was "kickin'" at two "slims." Raymond was sparring with Kirk. All of this transpires despite the fact that the assistant principal's office is on the Boulevard, approximately ten yards from the intersection [fieldnote].[8]

Lil' explained that, "It's a meetin' place, a spot where you can't get caught. Ain't got no kinda interference down dere."

Butterfly added, "Dey be dere 'cause not too many teachers down dere. Can't get busted down dere. Too many things dey can do, so many ways you can go when you be down dere, bes' thang's to ac' like you be waitin' on da assistan' principal!"

Bobby stressed the following, "Ain't no classrooms down dere, place to run. Don't be too many people down dere, jus' old teachers, that if dey say somethin', tell 'em, 'Go on! Get out my face, kiss ma ass, maw-fucka! or some shit like dat"! Dey take advantage 'cause dey get their way down dere."

Theo summed up the Boulevard's attraction by explaining that, "Dere so many of 'em (Brothers), dey (school staff) can't write up a thousand blue slips (complaint forms) at once! So dey (school staff)

Figure 9.1 "Strut in Yo' Butt": Hallwalkin' wif Style

just look, and tell you to move on ... dey just walk by like dey never even, you know, like dey never saw nuthin', you know. Dey won't say nuthin' to nobody, dey figure you'll get out of trouble anyway. In their situation, you know, what can dey do?''

Thus, meeting in the cafeteria and at the Boulevard was accomplished by deliberately and intentionally flouting the school's rules and regulations. The Brothers would cut their morning classes, hang around the halls without a pass, usually go to all three lunch periods, and finally return to the Boulevard or roam the halls. Of course, there were times when some of the Brothers were not with the majority of the group, but they always met with the group again—in the cafeteria or on the Boulevard.

Some group members' comments about why they chose to cut classes indicated that enjoyment and satisfaction were attained by "hanging out" at the Boulevard instead of going to classes. For example, Crip related that, "Dey want to be out dere (Boulevard) to see da action. Dey know somebody gonna be dere. Whatever is doin', like a fight jump off or somethin', dey'll see it. Dere be a lotta action dere e'ryday!'' Rat simply stated, "Dey jus' like to skip jus' to have fun. Dey want to learn, but dey tired of workin', dey want to dance and play!''

Other members, Squirrel, Reefer Man, Bobby, Butterfly, and a Straddler's explanations pointed out that lack of teacher concern, the absence of adequate hallway and cafeteria security, and the ineffective sanctions (suspension and parent conferences) employed to deter class cutting encouraged and reinforced their pattern of activity.

For example, Squirrel suggested that, "You know, dey supposed to be in dey class, you know, and dey *not,* you know. It's causin' trouble. . . . You know I just can't speak for all da other peoples (group members), right. But, I go down dere (Boulevard), because like, I'm not worried about too many people sayin' nuthin' to me, right, down dere, you know.''

Reefer Man noted: "How can you break it up (the in-school truancy pattern) when you don't have but th'ee (3) principals and two security guards.''

Bobby gave this account, "Most of da teachers in da school, you know, dey won't tell you to get in da class. Dey just want to keep you quiet. Since you skippin' dey just don't care. Dey just say, 'Let 'em go and skip. He da one be missin' out on da education.' ''

A Straddler's explanation, although similar to Bobby's, had some qualifications, "Some teachers don't care; some teachers do care. Some teachers care, but, you know, they won't say nuthin' 'cause they know that it's a typical thing (class cutting pattern). Some people (teachers) just do it (reprimand) because somebody (administrator) might be standin' there or somethin'. . . . Mr. G., shit, the famous thing he relate back to, 'Kids nowadays were never like the kids back then, 'cause kids back then, hell, they, they just went to their class. They did't fool around out in the hallways and blah-blah-blah.' He talkin' them! Damn! There wasn't that many *Blacks* goin' here then!"

Lastly, Butterfly had this to say about the groups' pattern of activity, "It gives da school a bad reputation. . . . A million students walkin' da hall, you know. Dey (generalized others) feel, 'Hey you don't learn nuthin' in that school.' But, da school teachers all right, jus' da students don't even want to go to school. . . . Teachers doin', I feel dat dey doin' dey best, 'cause da students dat come to class, dey teachin' dem. Da ones dat's in da hall, dey (teachers) can't, dey can't tell 'em to come to class if dey don't really want to come. So, I jus' let dem be, you know, let da hall security take care of 'em. See, and den, when it come da exam time, couple years later, you see da same faces and you know right den. Dey (teachers) say, 'Now look, if you'd a paid attention da firs' time, you'd a been outa here!'"

"'POSIN' TO BE CHOSEN' TO SHOW 'WHAT HE IS ABOUT'"

The conversation and activity at the lunch tables and on the Boulevard which are described in these next three sections are the key to understanding the group's in-school truancy pattern. Lunch table conversation and activity were always the same. It revolved around what the Brothers did as a group—the parties they attended, the dance hall and discos they went to, the times they drank, smoked marijuana, and used drugs, or went downtown to the Mainplace Mall to closely scrutinize girls after school, and it revolved around the following topics: cologne, clothes, live concerts and Black performers, record albums, girls, gambling, money, movies, reefer, sports, and fooling around in school.

Noticeably absent from their conversations were books, teachers, papers, assignments, homework, report cards, or anything academic. That the group never discussed anything academic was initially surprising, it became clear through interview data that this was their way of maintaining the cohesion of the group in school. For example, Butterfly said other people thought, "Hey, you don't learn nuthin' in dat school. But da school teachers all right, jus' da students (Brothers) don't even wan to go to school." And Theo observed that "dey (Brothers) want an education. Dey don't talk about it, dey keep it to dey self. Dey get da education their way." Apparently the Brothers had "idealistic" sentiments regarding academic education or schooling, but group norms did not sanction their expression.

What I observed daily was the Brothers acting out their street corner lifestyle within a class-cutting routine that they established in the mainstream context of Verland High.[9] Because Verland High was a mainstream context, one (i.e., teachers) naturally would expect mainstream-oriented modes of action to prevail. This expectation did not hold true for the Brothers, whose prevalent modes of action were those one would find on a ghetto streetcorner.

Since, "posin'. . . to show what he is about" was associated with the ability to contend with both words and deeds, the important components of the Brothers' streetcorner lifestyle had to be displayed in school. Thus, the Brothers converted Verland High's corridors into an annex of their streetcorner environment—a proving ground for the exhibition, practice, and refinement of their ghetto-specific behaviors, talents, or lifestyle.

A Boulevard Brother's (a Straddler's too) expressions of style are played primarily to other Black males—it is with them that one establishes one's reputation and displays one's machismo—not to school personnel (i.e., expressions of style are played primarily on school personnel). Establishing "what he is about," therefore, involved a great deal of competition. This competitive spirit or quest for status and prestige was found in the recurring and varied expressions used by the Boulevard Brothers to describe and explain their life style or gamin'-ship routines to me as it unfolded within the school: "Fancy, tell what he is about, style, impress, showboatin', hip, you be noticed, status, prestige, sign of coolness, get attention ('props'), you get known, be recognized, profilin', all 'bout bein' seen, show you popular."

The primary group is the major source for maintaining sufficient potency in the competitive situation. According to Coleman (1962), either the student is sustained in school by a primary group or he or she seeks substitutes in the form of high grades or achievement in ex-

Figure 9.2 "Posin' to Be Chosen"

tracurricular activities. The former was the case for the Boulevard Brothers.

"'N IT'S ALL 'BOUT BEIN' A 'REAL LIVE NIGGA'"

To summarize the "lose by winning" syndrome, it is apparent that the Boulevard Brothers dominant orientation to action within Verland High was toward the performance of those "street" roles[10] that gained prestige. Their goal was to achieve a position of positively valued rank—"to be chosen" by their peers. That is, a Brother would much rather be labeled a "real live nigga" (hip, cool, with it) as opposed to a "stiff nigga," (out of it). The drive was toward differentiation—being a trend setter or developing a style worthy of emulation—with recognition of status and away from anonymity.

The Brothers' discussions explained that they ignored the school's rules and regulations regarding hall wandering, class cutting and hall passes in order to hang out with their "runnin' buddies" (friends). To not have friends was to have no one to be with in the hallways and classrooms, no one to walk with in the corridors, no one to eat with, no one to "rib" on (mock, taunt with words), and above all, no one to impress.

One just did not "hang" with anyone, or go to class with anyone, or eat with anyone. He talked to, "strutted" (roamed hallways, corridors) with, ate with, and spent as much time as possible with his "runnin' buddies," the "real live niggas," and paid little attention to those who were not in his group.

In fact, the arrival and presence of some of the Straddlers and other acquaintances on the Boulevard or in the cafeteria was flattering to the Brothers because it assured them that "dey was 'real live niggas.'" As Squirrel put it, "dey jus' followers and jus' wanna be aroun'. You know, the type of peoples that learn the 'game' [gamin'-ship behaviors], so dat dey 'can be down' [with it]!"

The Brothers rated each other by using the central prestige values of ghetto-specific masculinity or a street-corner lifestyle: dress, demeanor, verbal expertise, fighting skills, and so on. In short, each brother's behavior in any specific situation involved a calculation of its effect on his position within the group. Or as Roger Abrahams has (1972:35) suggested:

> Reputation must be maintained, and this too is evaluated according to the number of friends one has, and who they are. One develops these relationships primarily by appearing to be *with it* ("real live") in an age-mate group, and this means maintaining oneself with *style*.

School personnel, however, viewed the Brothers as engaging in deviant and disruptive behavior. Whereas, prestige was conferred on a Brother by the group, notoriety was bestowed on Brothers by the staff. Notoriety was acquired by the Brothers because they were viewed as chronic class cutters, habitual hall wanderers, and constant connivers. That is, not "real live niggas," but "real live pains-in-the-ass."

'N dere ya go! How us maw-fuckas (Brothers) be "losin' by winning"—I tol' ya it wa'nt no maw-fuckin' *Archie* comic book story!

"FREEZIN' THE BROTHERS' SHIT"

I have described the "lose by winning" syndrome in three separate sections above—cuttin', posin', bein' real live—to facilitate an emically oriented understanding. But in actuality it occurs as an almost imperceptible and continuous event, a constant in the lives of the staff. This final section of the chapter addresses solutions and what can be done to abate the syndrome. The self-regenerating pattern continued in part because of two of the three responses that Verland teachers made to the Brothers' gamin'-ship and class cutting. The two most common responses, while understandable, were maladaptive. From the Brothers' perspective, they clearly indicated that their "shit runnin'" was "workin'."

The first type of response is represented in that majority of Verland teachers who are frustrated, threatened, and angry: "There are more damn kids in the hall than are in classes." "We're getting too lax on discipline. Who is running the school? Us or the kids!" "Who can conduct classes with all those 'friggin'' kids in the halls?" "We have to keep track of the repeaters and get them the hell out of this building!" Hence, they became more rigid or custodial in their "dealings" with the Brothers. Their solution to the syndrome was to suspend, fail, and expel the Brothers. However, this type of dependence on Verland's system of pupil control was perceived by the Brothers as one-upmanship or a heightening of the "game." "SHI---IT!" say the Brothers, "Dose maw-fuckas [teachers] think dat dere ole system gonna put us in check, huh, we got news for dem! Us 'real live niggas' gonna 'game' our way aroun' dat 'shit' [suspension, expulsion, failing grades] too! We gonna jus' have to 'run some better shit' up under dem."

With a majority of teachers perceiving the group's streetcorner gamin'-ship as threatening to the teachers' own social position in Verland, and the Brothers' need to assert themselves—while perceiving Verland's formal system as a challenge or something to "beat" or "brink"—one sees in terms of a functional explanation how the "lose by winning" cycle derives its inertia.

Figure 9.3 "Runnin' Some Shit," "Bein' Real Alive . . ."

The second type of response is represented in the Verland teachers who are also frustrated and threatened but appear to be apathetic: "Who wants to put up with the flippant attitude and 'bullshit' antics when you confront those kids in the hall or wherever!" "How the hell can I teach, if I have to drag the students in the classroom from the halls, ask them to move along, or police the halls?" "Who is going to look after my classroom and the kids that are waiting to be instructed!" "There's a security guard to sweep the halls, teacher aides posted in the corridors on every floor, and besides, the responsibility for the entire building belongs to the administration!" Thus, they become more lax or flexible in their "encounters" with (actually, avoidance of) the Brothers. Their solution is to adopt the coping technique of neglect. The gist of their position is that the classroom is the teacher's domain; beyond it is a no man's land. Creatively ignoring the Brothers preserved these teachers' self-respect. They avoided being insulted, ridiculed, denigrated, or humiliated for interfering with the group's pattern of activity.

The Brothers perceived these teachers' policy of salutary neglect as an indication of their "gamin'" expertise. They viewed the time consumed "posin' to be chosen" as if it was won by successfully plying their verbal talents and dramaturgical poses on this segment of Verland's staff. "Dem maw-fuckas [seemingly apathetic teachers] won't even look at you!" "Dey some stiff-ass sissies!" "Dey scared as a maw-fucka to say anythin' to ya! Afraid you might 'charge 'em up' [make someone kowtow]!"

With these teachers perceiving the Brothers' behavior as out of their realm of discipline, and the Brothers perceiving the teachers' coping policy of neglect as Brother-induced fear or apathy, there exists another regenerative impetus for the "lose by winning" syndrome.

What are Verland—and, perhaps other urban—teachers to do? The emic perspective is clear, and citing the Brothers' remarks will help us answer this all-important question: "He/she [teacher] will put yo' ass in check fast, if you fuck wif 'em!" "Dat maw-fucka [teacher] don't 'play' [take any guff, horseplay]!" "You [a Brother] gots ta 'freeze' yo 'shit' [act appropriately or as expected] when you aroun' dat maw-fucka [teacher]!" "Don't nobody fuck wif 'my man' [teacher] right dere, 'cause he be down wif da movements' [knowledgeable about street culture]!"

From the brothers' perspective, then, the solution for teachers is to know and understand the hows and why of streetcorner gamin'-ship, that is, to get a diploma in street knowledge. This is sound and "expert" advice—"right outa da moufs of da Brothers." This advice had been heeded by the third and smallest group of Verland's teachers. This handful of teachers (they drew the above "freezin'" remarks made by the group) possessed "with-it-ness," nipping problems before they could escalate into disruption, aware of what was happening at all times and likely to detect or diagnose inappropriate behavior (i.e., streetcorner gamin'-ship) early and accurately. If there were more than a handful of such culturally knowledgeable teachers at Verland, they may have effectively throttled the syndrome's inertia.

In addition to and in support of the Brothers' suggestion, I would add some final suggestions of my own. As long as we ignore or censor discussion and evaluation of "gamin'-ship" in our educational systems—because skin color is compounding the issue[11]—we will protect and perpetuate its destructive influence in our urban secondary schools. The syndrome described in this chapter is really the "testing games" and other street behavior of the tough, lower class Black adolescent males. These streetcorner testing games are manifestations of survival and coping techniques and norms that are well-established features of the Brothers' streetcorner culture. Obviously, this streetcorner gamin'-ship is quite different from the marginally tolerable and less disruptive games played in schools by other youngsters called "student brinkmanship"—student behavior that publicly gulls the system without substantial risk (Willower 1975). That is, many acts of student brinkmanship like the "contagious hyena laugh," the "exaggerated posture of the tin soldier," and "mock reinforcement of teacher commands" (Licata 1981) are perceived as genuinely funny: a la *Archie* comic books. On the other hand, streetcorner gamin'-ship, when evinced in the mainstream context of school, is usually irksome, fearsome, intolerable, and even terrifying to those who do not understand its purposes.

These games by their nature are manipulative, and the purpose of these particular manipulations is to play upon teachers' fear, ignorance, or apathy so as to shift the balance of power in the school into certain students' favor. However, there is not one of these games that adults have not used on other adults in any other institutional settings, for example, Eric Berne's *Games People Play* (1964) and *Games Mother Never Taught You* (Harragan 1977). American business life assumes diagnosis of each other's and even one's own games playing behavior, either for understanding or to gain the upper hand or both. If others see the necessity for sharpening their perceptions and understanding in their fields of endeavor, then as urban educators and researchers we need to sharpen our understanding in our field of endeavor, and if that field of endeavor includes lower class Black adolescent males, then it behooves us to get our diploma in street knowledge.

Like "my man" Theo tells it, "If you be 'hip to da program,' den I couldn't fuck wif you 'cause you'd 'freeze my shit.'"

A second response requires one to go beyond just knowing how to stop deviant behavior. The Brothers (and other streetcorner youngsters) have to be made aware of their culpability and the need to change their dysfunctional behavior patterns in school. They have to learn, understand, and accept the principle that in an interdependent mainstream society, everyone has "to do what they're supposed to do." Someone (and I'm afraid the onus, once again, falls on the teachers) has to articulate and demonstrate to the Brothers through the use of affective (domain-oriented) materials and techniques what is appropriate and responsible behavior in "this" situation (school) versus "that" situation (street).

More specifically, students of the street have to learn that (1) engaging in streetcorner behavior in order to impress one's peers is not appropriate or acceptable in every context; and (2) relying on or using racism, insensitive teachers, the school system, disproportionate minority suspension statistics, irrevelant curricula, environmental deprivation, and other complaints ad infinitum on which to blame their deviant antics is *not* facing the "cold-blooded" fact that they are responsible for their actions.

In other words, the Brothers have to get the message to face reality. "Dat Damn! Dey gots ta be like a chameleon: changin' der 'style' to blend wif da environment."

To sum up the way the Brothers might "kick it":

Dey need to get "der ass" a diploma in mainstream knowledge. 'Cause if dey was real "real live niggas" dey'd be "down wif da movements" in da street 'n da mainstream! Shi-it! A real "real live nigga" is a cultural straddler; he cool 'n hip in bof [both] worl's. 'N dat, my man, is whutcha call "bein' all the way live"!!

NOTES

1. Since discussing schools as social systems is beyond the scope of this chapter, "formal system" as used in the text refers to the (1) rules and regulations enumerated in Verland's student handbook, *School Policies,* (2) norms in the teacher subculture that sustain the maintenance of social distance between teachers and students, (3) organizational routines that promote universal treatment and processing of clients (Licata 1981);

and (4) the system of rewards, punishments, and grading established in particular classrooms. Note 5 contains a clarification of what elements make up the informal system brought in from the ghetto streetcorner.

2. Out of courtesy, and out of respect for the privacy of the individuals involved, I have employed pseudonyms for the individuals, groups, people, and locations mentioned in the article, except in those instances where concealment was unnecessary or futile or would excessively obscure the narrative.

3. See Appendix A in Marotto (1977: 344-381). It explains more fully the researcher's preparation for the study, selection of the school and students, acceptance of me by the Black male teenagers, and the problems associated with the research role.

4. Any words that have been borrowed from the Brothers' Black idiom and that may need clarification will be placed in quotation marks and paranthetically defined the first time they appear in the text. Subsequently, they will be enclosed with quotation marks only and will not be paranthetically defined unless it is deemed appropriate and necessary.

Moreover, it should be noted that use of words—an emic vocabulary—is often at the root of discipline problems when different cultures interact (Philips 1972, Wax & Dumont 1964). For example, a Brother from the street culture may use a word that to him is a meaningless and perhaps an unconscious interjection or superlative. A teacher from another culture may perceive the use of that word as defiance/insubordination or gross misconduct and the teacher in turn takes threatening action. Thus, conversations turn into threatening situations because of a normative clash.

5. I have coined the term "streetcorner gamin'-ship" for several reasons: (1) It was a recurring theme in the Brothers' description and explanations for why they chose to do what they did; (2) to conjure up a vivid picture and understanding of the behavior; (3) to facilitate comparing and contrasting it with research done on the more familiar kind of deviant school behavior—that is, brinkmanship.

Streetcorner gamin'-ship is expressed by and related to (1) mode of dress, (2) significant nonverbal kinesic features such as greeting, parting, walking, and standing, and (3) physicalness, acting aggressive, and toughness or ability to command respect.

Other aspects of streetcorner gamin'-ship are demonstrated through such verbal games or speech events as (4) "working game" or "putting someone on"; (5) "shuckin' and jivin'"; (6) "woofin'"; (7) "ribbin'"; (8) "signifying"; and (9) "playing the dozens." These speech events or verbal games are usually conducted in a nonstandard dialect and (10) vocabulary referred to as argot, Black English Vernacular, ghettoese, cant, slang, or jive lexicon. All of these verbal encounters usually involve audience participation and reaction.

Two other expressions—streetcorner behavior/lifestyle and ghetto-specific masculinity—were first used by Foster (1974) and Hannerz (1969), respectively.

The definition of lower-class Black male behaviors comes not only from Foster (1974) and Hannerz (1969), but also from a synthesis of interpretations in the works of Abrahams (1962, 1970a, 1970b, 1972), Kochman (1969, 1972), Labov (1972), and Liebow (1967).

6. Other evidence suggests that in-school truancy is a widespread disciplinary phenomenon. Breinin (1981) noted the prevalence of an in-school truancy pattern at a high school located in the same city. A third high school made headlines in the local newspaper because of in-school truancy reports. Ernst (1981) quoted a school board member as saying: "A computer study should be conducted to see which teachers' classes students

were cutting most often. That," he said, "would determine which teachers are teaching and what teachers are drawing paychecks." There was no mention of the part students play in the class cutting.

In-school truancy has been documented in Detroit as well, "nearly 30% of the students in Detroit High Schools will be absent from class on an average day, disrupting or destroying effective instruction" (Teachman 1979:203).

7. Regarding terminology, I share the feelings of the Black youngsters I associated with at Verland High School and many other Blacks that the label "nigger" has unfortunate or unfavorable historical connotations. Therefore, whenever possible the term "Black" is employed throughout; the major exception is when my respondents did not use the word "nigger" in a perjorative sense but in an approbatory manner. Thus, I recorded what they said when using their label of "nigger" (pronounced "nigga") and what they felt it connoted.

8. It was through use of "paper data"—suspension slips, discipline folders. teacher evaluation sheets, and report cards—that I further corroborated what I had observed, experienced, and was told by the Brothers in their lexicon. In general, evaluators can be convinced of a conclusion's validity if they not only have many items of evidence, but many kinds of evidence as well.

9. Lifestyle in this case is defined as "to a great extent an orientation toward participation in a certain social context in which given modes of action tend to prevail" (Hannerz 1969:35).

10. See Nadel (1957:33), who stresses the importance of role labels or role names ("real live nigga," "stiff nigga," "poop butt," "plastic pimp"): "It will often be the names current in a society for different classes or types of persons which first suggest to us the existence of the respective roles."

11. See Foster (1974), especially pages 34 and 43.

REFERENCES CITED

Abrahams, R. D.
    1962 Playing the Dozens. Journal of American Folklore 75:209-220.
    1970a Deep Down in the Jungle. Englewood Cliffs, NJ: Prentice-Hall.
    1970b Positively Black. Englewood Cliffs, NJ: Prentice-Hall.
    1972 "Talking My Talk": Black English and Social Segmentation in Black Communities. Florida FL Reporter 10(1&2):29-38, 58.
Berne, E.
    1964 Games People Play. New York: Ballentine.
Breinin, C.
    1981 Too Many Suspensions? Why Not "Magnetize" Instead? BTF Provocator (January):11. Buffalo, NY: Teachers' Union Publication.
Coleman, J. S.
    1962 The Adolescent Society. New York: Free Press.
Erickson, F.
    1984 What Makes School Ethnography Ethnographic? Anthropology and Education Quarterly 15:51-69.

Ernst, D.
1981 Tension, Truancy Reported Plaguing Kensington High. Buffalo Evening News, April 9 (II):22.
Foster, H. L.
1974 Ribbin', Jivin', and Playing the Dozens: The Unrecognized Dilemma of Inner City Schools. Cambridge, MA: Ballinger.
Hannerz, U.
1969 Soulside. New York: Columbia University Press.
Harragan, B. L.
1977 Games Mother Never Taught You: Corporate Gamesmanship for Women. New York: Rawson Associates.
Kochman, T.
1969 Rappin' in the Black Ghetto. Trans-Action (February):26-34.
1972 Rappin' and Stylin' Out. Chicago: University of Chicago Press.
Labov, W.
1972 Language in the Inner City. Philadelphia: University of Pennsylvania Press.
Licata, J. W.
1981 Student Brinkmanship and School Structure. American Educator 5 (Spring):26-29.
Liebow, E.
1969 Tally's Corner: A Study of Negro Streetcorner Men. Boston: Little, Brown.
Marotto, R. A.
1977 "Posin' to be Chosen": An Ethnographic Study of Ten Lower Class Black Male Adolescents in an Urban High School. Ph.D. dissertation, Faculty of Educational Studies, SUNY at Buffalo. (Dissertation Abstracts International 1978 39: 1234-a. University Microfilms 7814236)
Nadel, S. F.
1957 The Theory of Social Structure. New York: Free Press.
Philips, S. U.
1972 Participation Structures and Communicative Competence: Warm Springs Children in Community and Classroom. In Functions of Language in the Classroom. C. B. Cazden, V. P. John, and D. Hymes, eds. pp. 370-394. New York: Teachers College Press.
Teachman, G. W.
1979 In-School Truancy in Urban Schools: The Problem and a Solution. Phi Delta Kappan 61(3):203-205.
Wax, M. L., R. Wax, and R. Dumont
1964 Formal Education in an American Indian Community. Kalamazoo, MI: Society for the Study of Social Problems.
Willower, D. J.
1975 Some Comments on Inquiries on Schools and Pupil Control. Teachers College Record 77(2):219-230.

PART V

Conclusion

10

The Evolution of a Discipline

DAVID M. FETTERMAN

J ust as an ethnographic evaluator progresses through a life cycle,[1] a discipline evolves through various stages. An editor attempts to reflect the emergent nature of this evolutionary process by selecting the work of scholars that best exemplifies a current theme or—as in Berlioz's Symphonie Fantastique—an idée fixe that recurs throughout the symphony. The editor also has a role in shaping a field by the selection, adaptation, organization, and presentation of mental images and collective impressions. This collection crystallizes one stage—in all its theoretical, methodological, and political dimensions—in the evolution of ethnographic evaluation.

Refinement in approach and style is part of the maturing process in art and science. The explicit use of anthropological theory, building on a meta-theory and personal theory, represents such a refinement in ethnographic evaluation (see Simon this volume, Chapter 3). The use of explicit anthropological theory represents a clear improvement in the quality of this disciplinary endeavor (see Pitman and Dobbert this volume, Chapter 4). It will help focus inquiry, ideally making the ethnographic evaluators' job easier and more intelligible. This refinement, however, occurs within a historical context. Ethnographic evaluators have attempted to introduce explicit anthropological theory into evaluation for some time. In the late 1970s and early 1980s, efforts to introduce symbolic anthropology, ethnoscience, and even structural-functionalism fell on deaf ears.[2] Educational evaluators were concerned with basic questions about the validity, reliability, and applicability of the ethnographic evaluation. Methodology was the tangible link between data collection, analysis, and report findings. Ethnographic evaluators focused on methods to explain their craft in an overtly hostile and resistant environment. Evaluators needed to know the answers to some basic questions before allowing substantial culture contact. Many of these questions were answered or became moot as a result of ethnographic evaluators' solid contributions to real world problems. Ethnographers and educational evaluators have grown increasingly sophisticated over the years. The time is ripe for the introduction of explicit anthropological theory.

At the same time explicit anthropological theory is not a panacea. Many ethnographic evaluators have done excellent work without the use of explicit anthropological theory, just as some of the best ethnographies have been written by individuals who are not ethnographers. There are also many caveats to be considered. Explicit anthropological theory can impose blinders like those placed on carriage horses to direct their steps along well-worn roads—compelling researchers to force square data into round theories. New paths often require new theories and approaches (from different disciplines). When the data do not fit the theory, the researcher must look for a new theory. In addition, researchers must be on guard when adopting a theoretical framework. Although theory can be instructive it can also serve ideological purposes—closing the evaluator's eyes to the larger sociopolitical picture before us. This is true whether we adopt a micro (Erickson and Mohatt 1982; Shultz and Florio 1979) or world systems approach (Boulding 1985; Studstill this volume, Chapter 5; Wallerstein 1985; Laszlo 1973). Moreover, the recent interest in explicit anthropological theory reflects an academic (basic research) orientation that may conflict sharply with practice—particularly in a contract and policy research environment in which the problem and research design is often specified in advance. In addition, psychology and psychological theory rather than anthropology form the dominant disciplinary base (or bias) in educational evaluation. Thus this refinement in ethnographic evaluation may require, as easily as represent, a sociocultural change in educational evaluation. These caveats are not meant to discourage ethnographic evaluators from using and making explicit the anthropological theories used in the field.[3] They do, however, remind us that flexibility and adaptation, rather than a rigid adherence to disciplinary dogma, are required in interdisciplinary settings. More fundamentally, these caveats remind us that academics and practitioners must use their cultural knowledge to work together.

One of the most important attributes of a successful ethnographer is his or her ability to use a cultural perspective—in the artistic and literary Geertzian tradition—to decipher reality. The gem cutter's precision is important, but this artist's most important gift is his or her artistic ability to see the inner beauty of a diamond in the rough and to make its beauty known to the world. Similarly, the theory and methods that shape the behavior of an ethnographer only represent half the picture. The other half involves the ethnographer's ability to use theories and methods as tools to engage in a creative process, to see what others do not see, and to communicate this vision. At the same time, if ethnography is to continue to function as a science and work within a scientific environment, we must make clear what we do and how we do it. This is true whether we are using theories that reflect our ideational cognitive bias—for example, Goodenough, Frake, Levi-Strauss, and others—or whether we are using any one of the multitude of materialist theoretical approaches ranging from Barth to the neohistorical materialists. Making explicit the anthropological theories we apply during various stages of our studies can help us to build upon past work and to communicate more clearly our purpose and method.

The ultimate test of our abilities as ethnographic evaluators, however, is found in practice. While the overall strength of practice is in theory, the actual muscle behind data collection and analysis is in method. The interdisciplinary context of ethnographic evaluation provides opportunities for new and mutually reinforcing combinations of methods. This is an example of what it means to be at the cutting edge of research. The combination of contrasting methods will stimulate some and infuriate others. There are real paradigmatic differences behind most ethnographic and psychometric methods. However, this does not make them incompatible in practice. Ethnographic techniques can be used to establish causal inferences. Researchers who understand the varying philosophical differences that underly their methods will be able to successfully combine contrasting approaches in a mutually beneficial and productive manner. The researcher who haphazardly combines methods from different research traditions will flounder, at best, and produce misleading and distorted work at worst.

There is no one right way to conduct an ethnographic educational evaluation. The evaluator can come closer or move farther from an ideal. An ethnographic evaluator who grounds his or her research questions and variables in field experience, and aims at the deep rather than the surface structure of communication and behavior, will be able to provide a richer picture and more accurate appraisal of the sociocultural system under study. There are many ethnographic evaluations, however, that lack the time or resources to emulate fully the emergent nature of either in-depth ethnographic evaluations or full-blown ethnographies. In large-scale multisite studies, comparability and generalizability are critical. These studies often require a reduced flexibility in the field and an emphasis on pre-established questions for cross site comparisons. Firestone and Herriot (1984) refer to this process as formalization. Smith and Robbins (1984) discuss this process in terms of structure and flexibility. These evaluations typically take the model or program and evaluation goals as given, and use a priori guiding questions throughout the study to determine the impact of the educational innovation. Flexibility is embedded in varying degrees in these studies. Properly classifying or labelling efforts is critical. Multisite studies typically involve the application of ethnographic techniques, rather than the application of ethnography to evaluation. When there is reasonable assurance about the validity of the variables identified for observation and appraisal, this method, although not ideal, is completely appropriate. The risk in this methodological adaptation is that the research may systematically measure the wrong thing. If reasonable assurances can be made regarding the items selected for observation, then comparability and the potential for generalizability can be greatly enhanced by adopting this approach (see Chesterfield this volume, Chapter 7).

Most of us have learned that we do not know everything. Often we do not even know the right questions to ask. Researchers who find themselves faced with a mountain of seemingly insurmountable tasks to be completed on time and within budget have learned to be practical rather than elitist or dogmatic in their use of research tools. Ethnographic methods, whether they are used as an integral or accompanying component of a traditional evaluation, can immeasurably improve the quality of the endeavor. Contextual features can strengthen or question statistical patterns, correlations, and outcomes (Ferrell and Compton this volume, Chapter 8; Fetterman 1982). Ethnographic approaches can provide more precise estimates of treatments and more accurate definitions and explanations of treatments (Fetterman 1981; Chesterfield this volume, Chapter 7; Maxwell et al. this volume, Chapter 6). At the same time, evaluators who use ethnographic techniques must be willing to accept the fact that contrasting methods can generate contrasting and conflicting findings. Hard work, creativity, and some serendipity provide insights into these conflicting findings. The same amount of effort, however, can result only in conflicting findings and a budget in overdraft. The probabilities of finding an explanation or an insight can be improved by the use of guiding theories, seasoned ethnographic evaluators, and meticulous planning and budgeting. But there are no guarantees in research.

The process of selecting a theory and method does not occur in a vacuum. There are a number of real-life political considerations on the local, state, federal, and international levels. Educational evaluation is a highly political environment (Acland 1979; Elisburg 1977; Coward 1976; Cronbach et al. 1980). There are vested interests lurking behind every corner. Most interests, however, are boldly proclaimed. Turf and territoriality are real concerns. Sensitivity to protocol can help keep important channels of communication open. Similarly, insensitivity can erect obstacles throughout the study (see Fetterman 1985).

People have a great deal at stake in educational programs. Reputations, money, empires, and power are factors in the game. Every consideration can be politicized. Knowledge of political morality and an ability to work with and shape the political environment is as important to a successful evaluation as the selection of theoretical and methodological tools.

Research is not above politics, it is a part of politics. The selection of a theory and a method is a political act. Minimally, a statement is made about the evaluators' or sponsors' attitude toward the program. Moreover, choosing between static or homeostatic models reinforces the status quo. From a pragmatic point of view homeostatic models typically focus on deviations rather than adaptations (Fetterman 1981). Dynamic revolutionary theories calling for radical transformation are geared toward replacing rather than reforming the existing system. Exemplary reforms are summarily dismissed or viewed as negative because they inhibit required polarization posited in the theoretical design. Viewing the program as a symbolic manifestation of social and cultural change can be illuminating. Program participants, however, can be lost in the shuffle. When programs are seen only as total abstractions, human beings are forgotten.

The ethnographic evaluator, like all evaluators, is an actor in a political theater. The ethnographic evaluator must be sensitive to the political nature of evaluation research from research design to recommendations. Negotiated settlements occur in all stages of the research enterprise from the initial selection of an evaluation approach to the last line of your research report. In some cases political forces militate for or against specific research designs. Some program managers fear the precision of an experimental design or do not trust an experimental design to be sensitive enough to detect changes in or an impact on their program. Some disseminators who fear too close an examination or too much exposure particulary in politically sensitive settings can severely circumscribe ethnographic endeavors (Ferrell and Compton this volume, Chapter 8). These concerns are understandable given the potential power of evaluation recommendations. They can determine the fate of a program and of the people in them. At the same time, evaluators (including ethnographic evaluators) who think they are all-powerful or all-knowing, or that their recommendations are gospel are fooling themselves. Recommendations that do not make sense or are politically insensitive or unpopular simply sit on a shelf and gather dust. Ethnographic evaluators like all evaluators must recognize that they are only cogs in the larger system of policy decision making. The real test of ethnographic evaluators or any evaluators is how well they deal with existing constraints. At the same time, the entrepreneur considers politically difficult situations opportunities and carves out new areas to adapt his or her craft.

Politics exists on all levels. An understanding of the politics of every day life in the classroom and in the school is just as important as an understanding of the shifting allegiances of federal sponsors. Competing rules, informal social structures (in some cases borrowed from street culture), and various reinforcing patterns dominate school culture. Communicating maladaptive patterns of behavior and adaptive solutions to teachers and students requires an adept politician—and a cultural straddler (Marotto this volume, Chapter 9).

Ethnographic evaluators can increase the impact of their work if they present their work in a clear, relevant, and workable fashion. The use of explicit theory and rigorous methodology, and a mature understanding of the researcher's role in the shifting political currents allows the ethnograpic evaluator to present the best package of programmatic and policy findings and suggestions. As a result, the ethnographic evaluator becomes a more effective change agent. The cultural knowledge shared in this collection has proved effective in getting people to listen and to act on local, state, national, and international levels—moving us all beyond the status quo.

NOTES

1. See Fetterman (in press), for a detailed discussion of the ethnographic evaluator's life cycle.

2. See Fetterman (1980:46) for a symbolic manifestation of the attitude toward introducing the role of theory in educational evaluation at this time. Discussion of this topic was relegated to a footnote. The author may not have appreciated the editorial adjustment at the time, but it should be acknowledged that the editor accurately perceived the needs and interests of the audience during this period.

3. These caveats have also been presented to provide some context to the phenomenon and to describe part of the academic acceptance and routinization of this innovation called ethnographic evaluation.

REFERENCES CITED

Acland, H.
   1979 Are Randomized Experiments the Cadillacs of Design? Policy Analysis 5:233-241.
Boulding, K. E.
   1985 The World as a Total System. Beverly Hills, CA: Sage.
Coward, R.
   1976 The Involvement of Anthropologists in Contract Evaluation: The Federal Perspective. Anthropology and Education Quarterly 7:12-16.
Cronbach, L. et al.
   1980 Toward Reform of Program Evaluation: Aims, Methods, and Institutional Arrangements. San Francisco: Jossey-Bass.
Elisburg, D.
   1977 A Congressional View of Program Evaluation. In A Symposium on the Use of Evaluations by Federal Agencies, Vol. 1. E. Chelimsky, ed. pp. 67-70. McLean, VA: Mitre Corporation.
Erickson, F., and G. Mohatt
   1982 Cultural Organization or Participation Structures in Two Classrooms of Indian Students. In Doing the Ethnography of Schooling: Educational Anthropology in Action. G. Spindler, ed. pp. 132-174. New York: Holt, Rinehart & Winston.
Fetterman, D. M.
   1980 Ethnographic Techniques in Educational Evaluation: An Illustration. Journal of Thought 15(3):31-48.
   1981 Blaming the Victim: The Problem of Evaluation Design and Federal Involvement, and Reinforcing World Views in Education. Human Organization 40(1):67-77.
   1982 Ibsen's Baths: Reactivity and Insensitivity (A Misapplication of the Treatment-Control Design in a National Evaluation). Educational Evaluation and Policy Analysis 4(3):261-279.
   1985 Focusing on a Cross-Cultural Lens in Evaluation. Evaluation Research Society Newsletter 9(2):1-5.
   in press The Ethnographic Evaluator. In Applied Anthropology in America. E. Eddy and W. Partridge, eds. New York: Columbia University Press.
Firestone, W. A., and R. E. Herriott
   1984 Multisite Qualitative Policy Research: Some Design and Implementation Issues. In Ethnography in Educational Evaluation. D. M. Fetterman, ed. pp. 63-88. Beverly Hills, CA: Sage.

Laszlo, E., ed.
   1973 The World System. New York: Braziller.
Shultz, J., and S. Florio
   1979 Stop and Freeze: The Negotiation of Social and Physical Space in a Kinder-
   garten/First Grade Classroom. Anthropology and Education Quarterly 10(3):
   166-181.
Smith, A. G., and A. E. Robbins
   1984 Multimethod Policy Research: A Case Study of Structure and Flexibility. *In*
   Ethnography in Educational Evaluation. D. M. Fetterman, ed. pp. 115-132.
   Beverly Hills, CA: Sage.
Wallerstein, I.
   1985 The Three Stages of African Involvement in the World-Economy. *In* The
   Political Economy of Contemporary Africa. P.C.W. Gutkind and I. Wallerstein,
   eds. pp. 30-57. Beverly Hills, CA: Sage.

Name Index

Abert, J. B., 29
Abrahams, R. D., 203, 209
Abt. C. C., 29
Acland, H., 30, 44, 219
Administration for Children, Youth, and Families, 146
Agar, M., 52-54, 57-63, 74
Altman, D. G., 123
American Institutes for Research, 145
Amsbury, C., 18
Anderson, G., 99
Aristotle, 24
Aron, J., 57, 74

Bailey, F., 31
Baker, K., 28, 44
Barnhardt, R., 18
Barth, F., 31, 51, 217
Bashook, P. G., 16, 121, 127, 129, 133
Bateson, G., 66
Bee, R. L., 31
Bennis, W. G., 125
Berlioz, H., 215
Berne, E., 207
Berreman, G., 60
Bertalanffy, L., 113
Biderman, A. D., 29
Biklen, S. K., 112
Birdwhistell, R., 60, 74
Bishop, R. J., 18
Bogdan, R. C., 112
Boring, E. G., 125
Boulding, K. E., 112, 113, 216
Breinin, C., 209
Brimer, M. A., 104
Britan, G. M., 122, 125
Bruck, M., 145
Buckley, W., 113

Campbell, D. T., 27, 32, 122, 124-126, 129, 139
Cassell, J., 57
Cazden, C. B., 13, 18
Center for Applied Linguistics, 145
Chandler, J. M., 18
Chesterfield, R. A., 16, 44, 149, 218
Cicourel, A., 66
Clark, B., 114
Clifton, J. A., 79
Clinton, C. A., 25, 98
Cohen, A. D., 145
Cohen, D. K., 31, 44
Coleman, J. S., 201
Comfort, L. K., 102
Compton, D. W., 17, 44, 171, 218, 220
Conner, R. F., 112, 123
Cook, T. C., 16, 33, 112, 121, 122, 124-126, 129, 139
Coombs, P. H., 109
Cope, R., 104
Corsaro, W., 66
Coward, R., 30, 31, 44, 219
Crandall, D., 151
Cranton, P. A., 123
Cronbach, L. J., 21, 28, 29, 30, 31, 44, 219
Cummins, J., 145
Curtis, K., 72

Darwin, C., 97
Denzin, N. K., 123
Dobbert, M. L., 15, 16, 44, 74, 78, 80, 112, 215
Dumont, R., 209

Easton, D., 113
Eddy, E. M., 21, 22
Eggan, F., 126

223

Subject Index

About the Contributors

PHILIP G. BASHOOK is Director of the Educational Development Unit at Michael Reese Hospital and Medical Center. He helped develop the Medical Care Evaluation program at the hospital and has designed, conducted, and published evaluation research in medical education.

RAY A. CHESTERFIELD is a Senior Associate for Juarez and Associates. He has directed a number of research studies and evaluations, including a national evaluation of bilingual, bicultural Head Start curriculum models. Dr. Chesterfield also serves as a visiting professor at the Universidade Federal do Sergipe in Brazil. His research focuses on formal and informal education. He has published articles in several professional journals, ranging from *Anthropos* to *The Bilingual Review*.

DONALD W. COMPTON is Director of the Texas Education Agency's Division of Program Evaluation. Formerly, he was a program evaluator for the Houston School District's Department of Planning, Research, and Evaluation.

MARION LUNDY DOBBERT is Associate Professor of Anthropology and Education in the Social and Philosophical Foundations of Education program at the University of Minnesota. Her research has focused on cultural transmission, ethnographic research methodology, dimensional analysis, and cultural futures. She is the author of *Ethnographic Research: Theory and Application for Modern Schools and Societies.*

BARBARA G. FERRELL is Assistant Professor at Texas Woman's University. Her primary areas of specialization include statistics, evaluation, and learning theory. Formerly, she was a research assistant for the Houston Independent School District's Department of Planning, Research, and Evaluation.

DAVID M. FETTERMAN, the senior editor of this volume, is a member of Stanford University's administration and conducts qualitative formative evaluations and audits of the management process in university departments, the hospital, and the linear accelerator center. He is also Assistant Professor in the School of Education. Formerly, he was senior associate and project director at RMC Research Corporation, where he conducted national and state-level ethnographic evaluations. Fetterman is cochairperson of the Council on Anthropology and Education's Ethnographic Approaches to Evaluation in Education committee. In addition, he also served the council as the first contributing editor for the *Anthropology Newsletter.* He has published works in both educational and anthropological journals, and was recently awarded the Praxis Publication Award from the Washington Association of Professional Anthropologists and the President's Award from the Evaluation Research Society for his work in ethnographic educational evaluation. Fetterman is the editor of *Ethnography in Educational Evaluation* (Sage, 1984). He is also the author of *A Beacon of Excellence: Reevaluating Gifted and Talented Education Programs.*

JOSEPH A. MAXWELL is Assistant Professor in the Graduate School of Education at Harvard University. He was formerly a research associate in the Educational Department Unit at Michael Reese Hospital and Medical Center. He has designed, conducted, and published evaluation research in medical education.

RICHARD A. MAROTTO is Assistant Principal at Burgard Vocational High School. He is currently human relations consultant. He was formerly a member of the Board of Education in the Buffalo Public School system. His research interests include racial and ethnic relations, group dynamics, organizational behavior, delinquency, and deviance.

MARY ANNE PITMAN, the coeditor of this book, is Assistant Professor in the Department of Foundations of Education at Youngstown State University. Her current research addresses cultural learning of home schoolers in rural community settings in the northeastern United States. She has served as program chair for the Minnesota Association of Professional Anthropologists, and is currently cochairperson of the Council on Anthropology and Education's Ethnographic Approaches to Evaluation in Education committee. She has published articles on multidisciplinary team and contract research and on cultural learning theory.

LESLIE J. SANDLOW is Vice President for Professional Affairs at Michael Reese Hospital and Medical Center in Chicago. Sandlow, a physician, was responsible for the operation of the Educational Development Unit. He also helped develop the Medical Care Evaluation program at the hospital. He has designed, conducted, and published evaluation research in medical education.

ELAINE L. SIMON is Assistant Professor in the Urban Studies Program at Temple University. Her areas of specialization are education and employment, policy research, and organizational change. She previously conducted research at the Center for New Schools and the Philadelphia Private Industry Council. She is the current Council on Anthropology and Education's contributing editor for the *Anthropology Newsletter*. Simon recently completed her term as cochairperson of the council's Ethnographic Approaches to Evaluation in Education committee, and is currently helping to organize the Philadelphia Association of Practicing Anthropologists.

JOHN D. STUDSTILL is Project Director in the Center for Public and Urban Research at Georgia State University. He conducts research and training projects for teachers in the field of migrant education. Studstill has taught overseas, at the Johns Hopkins University, the University of Maryland, and Georgia State University, and has conducted research in Zaire among the Luba of Shaba. His research interests include educational development, dropout prevention, and ethnographic methods. He is the author of *Les dessens d'arc-en-ciel: epopée et pensée chez les Luba du Zaire.*